To *GENIO C. SCOTT*, who, as an ardent Sportsman and accomplished Writer, has done much towards fostering a love for Field-Sports in this country, this humble attempt to instruct and assist the aspiring youth to become a Crack Shot is *INSCRIBED*, as a slight token of the appreciation entertained for his kindness, and the estimation he is held in as a Gentleman and a Sportsman by the Author.

THE

CRACK SHOT;

OR,

YOUNG RIFLEMAN'S COMPLETE GUIDE:

BEING

A TREATISE ON THE USE OF THE RIFLE,

WITH RUDIMENTARY AND FINISHING LESSONS;
INCLUDING A FULL DESCRIPTION OF THE LATEST IMPROVED BREECH-LOADING
WEAPONS, ILLUSTRATED WITH NUMEROUS ENGRAVINGS; RULES AND
REGULATIONS FOR TARGET PRACTICE; DIRECTIONS FOR
HUNTING GAME FOUND IN THE UNITED STATES
AND BRITISH PROVINCES, ETC., ETC.

BY

EDWARD C. BARBER.

Skyhorse Publishing

First Published in 1873
First Skyhorse Publishing edition 2015

Skyhorse Publishing books may be purchased in bulk at special discounts for sales promotion, corporate gifts, fund-raising, or educational purposes. Special editions can also be created to specifications. For details, contact the Special Sales Department, Skyhorse Publishing, 307 West 36th Street, 11th Floor, New York, NY 10018 or info@skyhorsepublishing.com.

Skyhorse® and Skyhorse Publishing® are registered trademarks of Skyhorse Publishing, Inc.®, a Delaware corporation.

Visit our website at www.skyhorsepublishing.com.

10 9 8 7 6 5 4 3 2 1

Library of Congress Cataloging-in-Publication Data is available on file.

Cover design by Owen Corrigan
Cover photo credit: Thinkstock

Print ISBN: 978-1-63220-270-3
Ebook ISBN: 978-1-63220-784-5

Printed in the United States of America.

TO THE READER.

I HAVE been induced to prepare the following pages from a conviction that a work of this kind was needed. No work has been published since the recent great improvements in breech-loading arms; and moreover, though the books of Cleveland, Chapman, Wilcox, and others are standard works, containing a vast deal of useful and valuable information, yet it has been felt that they are too purely scientific to meet the desired end. At the suggestion of a sporting friend of "credit and renown," I undertook the preparation of a work designed to aid and instruct "the young idea how to shoot." I have acquitted myself to the best of my humble ability, and trust that it may prove useful and interesting to those for whose use it was specially prepared—the young riflemen of America. I do not claim any great originality, nor do I profess to have propounded any peculiar theories; my object being to compile, in brief and readable style, the views and opinions of those who, from time to time, have written upon this subject. I must acknowledge my indebtedness to the authors above mentioned; to Col. Boucher, Capt. Hans Busk, whose works should have a more extended circulation on this side of the Atlantic ; the Text-Book for Schools of Musketry, and that prince of sportsmen and writers, the accomplished and lamented Frank Forrester, besides others of less note, whom I believe have received due credit for any thing I may have quoted.

To the friends who have kindly assisted me, by advice or counsel, I beg to acknowledge my sincerest thanks, more especially to Genio C. Scott, Esq., who by his friendly interest has encouraged me in prosecuting my work.

I also desire to acknowledge the assistance rendered me by practical rifle-makers and others connected directly or indirectly with the trade, who have extended me every courtesy.

I am also requested by the publishers to express their acknowledgments to Messrs. Brown, Coombs & Co., of the "American Artisan," New York, for favors received. These gentlemen (who have devoted a good deal of space in their valuable journal to the subject of fire-arms) very kindly permitted them to take casts from a number of their drawings and engravings, thereby greatly facilitating the publication of the work.

EDWARD C. BARBER.

TABLE OF CONTENTS.

INTRODUCTION.

CHAPTER I.

THE GENERAL PRINCIPLES OF FIRING AND MOTION OF PROJECTILES.

CHAPTER II.

ON RIFLES AND RIFLING.

CHAPTER V.

THE RIFLE AND HOW TO CHOOSE IT.

CHAPTER VI.

THE RIFLE AND HOW TO USE IT.

CHAPTER VII.

PRACTICAL APPLICATION OF THE FOREGOING.

CHAPTER VIII.

THE BISON.

CHAPTER IX.

THE MOOSE.

CHAPTER X.

THE CARIBOU.

CHAPTER XI.

DEER.

CHAPTER XII.

THE HOUND.

CHAPTER XIII.

TURKEY SHOOTING.

APPENDIX.

INTRODUCTION.

"Shooting is, therefore, as I have said, with one arm or other, the head and front of all American field sports . . . . . ; while every animal which we follow for the excitement of the pursuit, or for the sake of its flesh on the table, from the gigantic moose and formidable grizzly bear to the crouching hare; from the heaven-soaring swan or hawnking wild goose to the "twiddling" snipe, is brought to bag by means of *the rifle*, or the fowling-piece; and to his thorough acquaintance and masterly perform-ance, with one or both of these, in his own line, the rank of the sportsman must be mainly attributed, and his claim to pre-emi-nence ascribed."—FRANK FORRESTER.

THE writings of the above-quoted, popular and accom-plished author have exerted a marked influence on the youth of this country; so much so, indeed, that from utter indifference they have been roused to take the greatest inter-est in the chase. The result of this is, that to be accounted a "crack shot" has now become the ambition of a consider-able proportion of our youth, and it will be my endeavor in the following pages to aid and assist in furthering so lauda-ble a desire by a few plain and simple directions, by following which a young man can not fail of becoming a fair shot: after which it depends on nature and himself whether he is ever to attain the coveted distinction of being counted a "crack shot;" for it must be remembered, that like the poet, so with the marksman, "*nascitur, non fit.*"

From the earliest ages, every effort has been made to produce and excel in the use of some death-dealing instrument; and it is a curious and interesting study to trace the gradual development of the idea from the rude sling of the ancients down to our own time, when we have the most beautiful and effective weapons; and though great strides have been made during the past few years, we have not by any means yet reached perfection, as is evidenced by the constant study that is given to perfecting the fire-arms at present in use. It will be sufficient for our purpose to commence with the cross-bow, which appears to have been in general use in England about the year 1100, during the reign of Henry I.; as I think that it is the first weapon which was used with a barrel for guiding or conducting the missile. We find that the stock was hollowed out to receive a tube, which threw stone or metal bullets, and consequently received the name of the pebble-bow, or "arc-a-buse;" *i.e.*, a bow which conducts or directs. The same name (harquebus) was given to one of the early fire-arms.

The invention, or, more properly speaking, the introduction into England, of gunpowder in or about 1346, necessitated the use of some weapon by which it could be utilized; and we read of hand-guns being used at the siege of Arras in 1414, and again at the siege of Lucca in 1430; but they do not appear to have come into general use until 1446. It is claimed by Spanish historians that to Spain belongs the honor of having been the first power to arm the foot-soldier with hand-guns. Various kinds of rude implements were used by different nations during the next 150 years; and the strongest proof of their inefficiency is that the cross-bow was able successfully to contend against them. It was not until 1596 that Elizabeth, by a proclamation, directed that the bows should be changed for muskets. That this was not looked upon as likely to improve the power or prestige of England, is evident from the writings of Michael Montaigne, one of the most remarkable men of the time, who says: "Except the noise in our ears, to which we will be henceforth accustomed, I think that it is an arm of very little effect, and I hope that we shall one day give up its use." Could his spirit re-visit this terrestrial sphere and see the general use this much-despised weapon has come into, and the marvelous accuracy with which the "hunters of Kentucky" and others can draw a bead, he would find that there was little likelihood of its use being given up. Fire-arms were gradually improved through many gradations down to the present time, when we have an arm of great merit, and of which I will proceed to speak, commencing "*de novo*" for the instruction of the novice, and later on, trust that the more experienced may find something worthy of commendation.

Every art of amusement has its own set rules to be known and observed. Even in the acquisition of pleasure, we are so constituted that we must pass through the gradation of regular instruction. Mind must be thrown into every thing before permanent delight can be realized and enjoyed. The art of shooting has, therefore, its maxims and code of rules to be learned and fixed into the judgment and understanding. No man can be a shooting sportsman without obtaining a knowledge of these, either by personal experience or regular tuition, or, more properly and most generally, from both. In accordance with this view of the subject to be treated of, I shall attempt to elucidate its various departments, and in so doing shall endeavor to treat the several points with all possible clearness and brevity, and to impart to the young and aspiring sportsman such a bird's-eye view of the chief things he has to learn and attend to, as will greatly facilitate his acquisition of the whole art of shooting game of every kind.

THE CRACK SHOT.

CHAPTER I.

THE general principles of firing are deduced from
the relation of positions existing between three
imaginary lines named *the line of fire, or projection;
the line of metal, or aim; and the line of the flight of
of the bullet, or trajectory.* Though there is a great
difference between them, they are frequently confounded one with the other, and the greater the
range, the greater the difference.

By the *line of fire*, or *projection*, is meant the axis
of the barrel indefinitely prolonged. It is the primary direction of the center of the bullet; a
direction which this center would not cease to follow
if the bullet were subject to the propelling force of
the powder alone.

The *line of metal*, or *aim*, is a straight line passing along the centre of the back sight, and the top of the front one, to the object aimed at. The line thus obtained is called the *artificial*, in opposition to the natural line, which passes through the highest points on the breech and muzzle of the barrel, and which is also called the natural point-blank range. The line of metal forms, with the line of fire, an angle more or less obtuse, which is called the angle of intersection. In order that the aim should be good, it is requisite that the two points determining the line of metal, and the object aimed at, should be in the same right line.

The *trajectory*, or *line of flight of the bullet*, is the curve described by the bullet in the air, in its course from the barrel to the object aimed at. As long as the bullet is within the barrel, the trajectory is identical with the line of fire; but as soon as it has cleared the muzzle, the trajectory diverges from the line of fire, and this divergence becomes greater the further the bullet is from the rifle. By raising the slide of the back sight, the muzzle of the rifle is elevated, the trajectory of the bullet is raised, and the range increased. By lowering the slide of the back sight, the muzzle is depressed, the trajectory is lowered, and the range of the bullet decreased. The line of fire, with a properly fitting bullet, is constantly above the

FIG. 1.

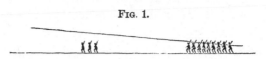

Fig. 1 is a representation of a detachment, the leading part of which is marching uninjured under fire, which, owing to the elevation of the trajectory, is taking effect further in the rear.

FIG. 2.

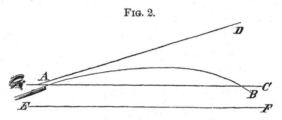

Fig. 2. The line AD indicates the axis of the rifle ; AC the line of sight ; and AB the trajectory or path described by the bullet. EF is a horizontal line, on which the shooter is supposed to be standing.

trajectory, and is a tangent to the latter toward the muzzle.

The *line of fire*, or *projection* and the *line of metal*, or *aim*, will be easily understood on reference to the diagrams ; but the *trajectory*, or *line of flight* of the bullet, will require further explanation, in order that the *course* of the bullet being drawn downward may be clearly understood ; and by what *forces* it is urged from its first direction, the *the line of fire* or *projection*. It will therefore be necesary to explain a few

2

terms used to designate these forces, in order to the proper comprehension of what is to follow.

Inertia—A property of matter by which it can not, of itself, put itself in motion, or, if in motion, has no power within itself to alter the direction or magnitude of its motion.   A body can not produce action on itself.

Velocity—The degree of swiftness with which a body moves over a certain space in a certain time. When a body passes through equal spaces in equal times, its velocity is said to be *uniform ;* when through unequal spaces in equal times, it is *variable ;* when through greater spaces in each equal successive portion of time, it is *accelerated ;* and when through a less space in each equal successive portion of time, it is *retarded*.   Accelerated and retarded velocities may be uniform or variable.

Initial Velocity—The velocity at the instant of the departure of the bullet from the muzzle.   The initial velocity of the bullet fired from the Enfield rifle is twelve hundred sixty-five and one-tenth feet per second.

Final Velocity—The velocity of the bullet at the end of any given range.

Terminal Velocity—The velocity attainable by falling bodies, which they can not exceed on account of the resistance of the air becoming equal to the force of gravity. From this point, if the air were equally dense, the body would fall at a uniform rate. The terminal velocity of a spherical musket ball is said to be two hundred and thirteen feet per second.

Relative Velocity is that which has respect to the velocity of another body.

Velocity of Rotation (initial).—This depends upon the initial velocity and the inclination of the grooves or twist. In order to find the initial velocity of rotation of a bullet, divide the initial velocity in feet by the number of feet in which one complete turn is made by the bullet ; thus, the initial velocity of the Enfield rifle being twelve hundred sixty-five and one-tenth feet per second, and the turn one in six and a half feet, the initial velocity of rotation of the bullet, fired from the Enfield, is one hundred ninety-four and six-tenths revolutions per second. The greater the initial velocity, the greater the initial velocity of rotation from the same rifle, and *vice versa ;* therefore, projectiles fired from two rifles similar in all respects, with the exception of their spirality, may be impelled with the same initial velocity of rotation, the initial velocity of the rifle with the greatest spiral being reduced; so that

$$\frac{\text{in. vel.}}{\text{L for 1 rot.}} = \frac{\text{in. vel.}}{\text{l for 1 rot.}}, \text{ or } \frac{1200}{6} = \frac{1000}{5}$$

Friction is a retarding force, arising from the parts of one body rubbing against the parts of another. A bullet is more or less retarded in its velocity by friction; in the first place, by its friction on the sides of the barrel, and in the next place by the friction of the air, independent of its opposing force. This effect is produced by inequalities of surface, as in every case there is, to a lesser or greater degree, a roughness or unevenness of the surface, arising from a difference in form, and other causes; and therefore, when two bodies come together, the prominent parts of the one rub against the other, so that the *progressive* motion of the bullet is retarded, and often driven out of the straight line.

In the barrel the friction of the bullet will be greatly diminished by lubricating the rubbing surfaces with a greasy substance, for it acts as a polish by filling up the cavities of the rubbing surface, and thus makes the one slide more easily over the other. In the air, the friction, and any tendency to be forced aside, will be greatly diminished by having the surface of the bullet made as smooth and perfect as possible; for an elongated rifle bullet does not *roll* like a spherical ball projected from a smooth bore, but *slides* through the air with a spiral motion, dragged, as it were, by the force of its own momentum.

Gravity is the term used for denoting the tendency

to fall to the earth, or rather toward its center. *Attraction* is also used in the same sense; bodies falling in a straight line have their motion accelerated as they descend. A bullet in its flight partakes of both *falling* and *progressive* motion.

The *force of gravity* is the tendency of every thing to fall in a straight line toward the center of the earth. In vacuo, every thing falls to the earth at the same rate, but not so in nature. Things lighter than air, in consequence of the pressure of the atmosphere, ascend until they reach the strata of air of the same density as themselves; things heavier than the air descend at rates in proportion to their surfaces and densities; this is caused by the air's resistance. In vacuo, every thing falls about sixteen feet in the first second, and it has been found by experiment that the fall increases according to the square of the time the body is exposed to the influence of gravitation. Gravity is thus an increasing force, and at the end of the second second will have caused the body to have fallen four spaces of sixteen feet, or sixty-four feet, and so on. A uniformly accelerating force is measured by twice the space described from rest in one second. In dropping a bullet from a considerable height, we find that during the first second of descent it acquires a velocity of thirty-two feet per second. Its velocity at the commencement was nothing, for it began to

move from a state of rest; at every one of the instants
into which we may conceive a second of time to be
divided, it acquired more and more velocity, until it
attained the final velocity of thirty-two feet in a
second.   All these acquisitions of speed are equal in
equal times, because the force of gravity is constant,
and therefore exerts equal influences in equal times.
Had the bullet descended during the whole second at
the final velocity of thirty-two feet per second, it
would have passed through thirty-two feet of space.
Had it retained its initial velocity, which was nothing,
it would have descended through no feet; but as the
velocity began with nothing and ended with thirty-
two, its average throughout the second was sixteen
feet per second, and therefore the bullet descends in
the first second through sixteen feet.   During the
second second, the bullet starting with a velocity of
thirty-two, acquires an additional velocity of thirty-
two, and therefore ends with a velocity of sixty-four
feet a second, the average being forty-eight feet per
second, and therefore the descent is forty-eight feet
in height; adding this to the space descended during
the first second, sixteen feet, we find that in the first
two seconds the total descent is sixty-four feet, and
so on.   The velocities acquired in descending are in
exact proportion to the times of descent, and the
spaces descended are proportional to the squares of

the times, and therefore to the squares of the velocities. The resistance of the air materially retards velocities; if it did not, every rain-drop, descending, as it does, from a height of several hundred feet, would strike with a force as great as a rifle bullet.

Resistance.—In treating of the motion of projectiles, this refers to common air. The air is an elastic fluid which surrounds the earth to a height of forty-five miles; the nearer the earth the greater the pressure of air from the attraction of gravity and the superincumbent strata; so that at the sea level, the barometer standing at thirty inches, the pressure of the atmosphere is fourteen and three-quarters pounds on the square inch. Now, the bullet in its course displaces the air, and this it can not do without its flight being affected. The resistance varies with the velocity in the same body; the greater the velocity the greater the resistance. A body moving with an increased velocity encounters an increased number of particles and impresses upon them an increased amount of force; from this cause the resistance will be as the square of the velocities.

THEORY OF THE MOTION OF PROJECTILES.

In early times various ideas prevailed as to the path described by a projectile in its flight:

1st. That it went straight, and then fell perpendicularly.

2d. That it went straight for some distance, then in a curve, and then fell perpendicularly.

3d. That its flight was curved throughout, but according to Tartaglid, in the sixteenth century, so slightly that he compared it to the surface of the sea.

4th. That it described a parabola, as asserted by Galileo in the seventeenth century, except insomuch as it might be diverted from that course by the resistance of the atmosphere. A parabola is the section of a cone cut by a plane parallel to one of its sides.

It remained for Robins, in 1742, to point out the actual path of the bullet, for he demonstrated the effect of the resistance of the air, which he stated to be as the squares of the velocities up to twelve hundred feet a second, and this ratio to be trebled after that velocity, in consequence of the vacuum in rear of the projectile. Air rushes into a vacuum at the rate of thirteen hundred and forty-four feet in a second.

Dr. Hutton, toward the end of the last century, came to the conclusion that the resistance was in a

somewhat higher ratio than the square of the velocities (V^2) up to fifteen hundred or sixteen hundred
feet a second, and that then it gradually decreased,
but was never below that ratio.

The force of gravity having been explained, also
the resistance of the air, we will now proceed to consider these forces as affecting the path of the bullet,
which, at the instant of starting from its position next
the charge, is under the influence of three forces; viz.,
the exploded gunpowder, the force of gravity, and the
resistance of the air.

We will commence by considering the effect of the
first two forces. The bullet, although under the in-

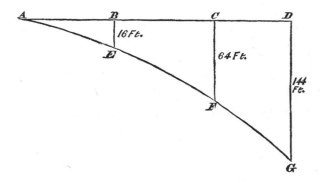

fluence of gravity from its starting point, can not commence to fall until it loses the support of the barrel
and emerges from it. The bullet, from the impressed

force of gunpowder, will travel forward equal spaces in equal times; thus, in the first second from A to B, in the second from B to C, and in the third from C to D; but, in obedience to the law of gravity, it will fall in the first second sixteen feet, BE; at the end of the second second it will have fallen sixty-four feet, CF; and at the end of the third second one hundred and forty-four feet, DG; being at the end of these seconds at the points E, F, G, respectively. Now this is the parabolic curve, which is not generally approached by projectiles, except when moving with very small velocities. The existence of the force of gravity is the sole cause of the course of the bullet being in a curved line, and of the necessity of giving elevation to all arms, varying in an increased ratio according to distance, if this force acted on the bullet in vacuo; but acting as it does in conjunction with the resistance of the air, which greatly increases the curve, the ratio of the elevation necessary is greatly augmented.

The general form of the trajectory, under the forces of gunpowder and gravity, being established, we come to the conclusion that if a rifle is laid so as to have its axis horizontal, the bullet that is projected from it will reach the ground in one second if sixteen feet above it; in two seconds if sixty-four feet, and so on, no matter what the charge of powder, or what the velocity with which the bullet is projected; consequently, if several rifles were laid with their axes in the same horizontal plane, the bullets projected from them at the same instant would reach the ground at the same moment, irrespective of their velocities or height above the ground.

The other force to be considered is the resistance of the air. As previously laid down, the bullet can not proceed through the air without being impelled in its flight. Robins remarks "that he found that when a twenty-four pound shot was impelled by its usual charge of powder, the opposition of the air was equivalent to at least four hundred pounds' weight, which retarded the motion of the bullet so powerfully that it did not range one-fifth part of what it would have done if the resistance of the air had been prevented." It has been found by experiments that the greatest range of the common musket, with spherical bullet, fired with the regulation charge, was at twenty-five degrees; yet, by theoretical calculation, it should be forty-five degrees; also that the usual velocity was some five hundred yards per second, whilst in vacuo it would be nineteen thousand seven hundred and ninety-two yards per second. At an angle of from four to five degrees, the real range was six hundred and forty yards; without the resistance of the air, and at an angle of four and a half degrees, it would be three thousand six hundred and seventy-four yards,

or six times greater. The retardation, or the effect
of the resistance of the atmosphere, varies with the
surface, content, density, and velocity of the shot.
The areas of spheres are as the squares of their diameters; the contents of spheres as the cubes of their
diameters. With two spherical shot of the same
diameter, the one of lead, the other of iron, traveling
with equal velocities, the retardation of the leaden
projectile will be less than that of the iron, and in-
versely as their densities, or nearly as eight to eleven;
the specific gravity of lead being eleven to three hundred twenty-five, that of iron seven to four hundred
twenty-five.

It is a well-known fact that great irregularities
occur in the path described by projectiles fired from
smooth-bore guns. If a number of spherical bullets
be fired from the same gun, under the same circumstances, with regard to charge and quality of gunpowder, and elevation, with the greatest care and from
fixed rests, very few of the shot will range to the same
distance; and moreover the greater part will be found
to deflect considerably to the right or left of the line
in which the gun is pointed, unless at very short
range. The principal causes of these deviations are
windage and the *eccentricity* of the projectile.

The effect of the rotation, originating from windage,
or from the eccentricity of the projectile, is thus ex-

plained by Robins, who says : " This whirling motion of the bullet occasions it to strike the air obliquely, and thereby produces a resistance which is oblique to the track of the bullet, and consequently perpetually deflects it from its course." The side of the bullet which moves forward experiences an increased resistance, and the opposite side which retires experiences a less resistance than it would if it received no rotation ; the consequence naturally is that the bullet is deflected in the direction of the least resistance, which will be in the opposite direction to the deflection caused by the rebound of the bullet from its last impact upon leaving the bore, or in the direction to which the leading surface of the bullet spins. Thus the track of the spherical ball is not the curve depending simply on the three forces; viz., gunpowder, gravity, and the resistance of the air; but becomes a double curve, being deflected to the right or left, according to the position of the center of gravity when the gun is loaded, or according to the rotation acquired by the ball rebounding from the side of the barrel.

The following excellent illustrations of the accuracy of Robins' theory of rotation, suggested in the Hythe Lectures, will perhaps convey a still clearer idea of this important law of projectiles:

If a wooden ball four and a half inches in diameter

be suspended by a twisted double cord nine feet long, and receive a rotatory motion as the string untwists, it will revolve in the same vertical plane. But, if it be made to spin while vibrating, it will be deflected to that side on which the action of the whirl combines with the progressive motion.

By firing through successive and parallel screens of thin but strong tissue paper, erected at equal distances along the line of the trajectory, the amount of the deflection can be observed and measured. In this experiment it will be found that the amount of deflection is not all proportionate to the increased distances of the screens.

Robins, in order to carry demonstration still further, bent a gun-barrel to the left, about four inches from the muzzle, at an angle to the axis of the piece, of three or four degrees. When a bullet from this bent barrel was fired through a number of screens, it traversed the first screen to the *left*, but finally struck the target to the *right* of the line of aim, taken along the straight portion of the barrel.

All projectiles, except those fired from rifled barrels of sufficient pitch, in consequence of the resistance they meet with from the air when they are eccentric, spherical, or elongated (and they are always one or the other), rotate naturally, the former round an accidental axis passing through the center of gravity, and the latter round the short axis, also passing through the center of gravity; so that at first sight it would appear advisable, if possible, so to construct projectiles that they might rotate round an axis in the natural direction. It must be remembered, however, that the rotation, to correct the flight of the projectile, should be round an axis coincident with its initial direction; any rotation in any other direction acts as a disturbing force, and causes irregularities.

The object of rifling is to give such a rotation to the projectile as to insure its stability for the longest ranges; the longer the bullet the less the stability, and consequently the greater the rotation required. If the rotation becomes too weak at any part of the range, the bullet will wabble, perhaps turn over, and deviation must ensue.

It was thought formerly that a rapid twist would be detrimental and decrease the velocity; but this has practically been disproved. A high initial velocity and a rapid rotation can be given without causing any injurious effects, except that the greater the velocity of rotation with the same velocity of translation, the greater will be the drift.

A quick twist will undoubtedly necessitate a stronger barrel than a slow one; but this may be arranged in small arms, without increasing the weight, by the de-

scription of metal of which the barrel is constructed.
The more rapid the twist, the more the ricochet will
deviate; the velocity of rotation, being much less than
that of translation, diminishes but slowly; while the
resistance of the air, being proportional to the squares
of the velocities, diminishes rapidly the forward motion of the shot.

The velocity of rotation to be imparted to a shot is
influenced not only by its length, but by other considerations, which we will now proceed to discuss.

The greater the density, the less will the velocity of
rotation be impaired by the air's resistance, and the
less will be the rotation required ; therefore lead will
require a less rotation than iron, as explained in a
preceding paragraph.

FIG. A.

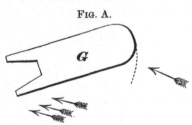

With respect to
the position of the
center of gravity,
an elongated shot
having the center
of gravity very for-
ward will have but
little tendency to turn round its shorter axis (see
fig. A).

If the resistance of the air in front of the center of
gravity caused the direction of the longer axis to be
moved, it would be counteracted by the resistance of

the air acting on that part of the bullet in rear of the center of gravity. In this position of the centre of gravity, with a weak rotation, the shot would have the greatest tendency to lower its point, and to keep its axis a tangent to the trajectory, thereby causing the resistance to be kept in the front of the projectile, and the velocity of the shot to be less reduced than if the axis of the shot were kept parallel to its initial direction, and the resistance applied to the whole of its lower surface. With a weak rotation, however, the center of gravity being forward, an irregular motion of the rear of the projectile will generally take place; hence a rapid rotation in this case is necessary.

The nearer the center of gravity is to the rear of the bullet (fig. B), the greater the rotation required to keep the bullet point first; for while the resistance on that part of the bullet

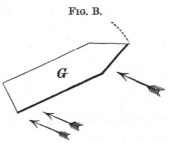

Fig. B.

in rear of the center of gravity is much reduced, the power of the direct action of the air on the front of the bullet is much increased in consequence of its distance from the center of gravity and the greater leverage. In this position of the center of gravity the bullet is supposed to retain, or nearly so, its initial

3

direction, unless the rotation is weak, when the bullet will turn over.

In the case of an elongated projectile whose center of gravity does not lie in the long axis of the bullet, an irregular rotation will take place round an axis passing through its center of gravity, parallel to the long axis; and consequently, the greater their distance from each other, the greater the rotation necessary.

In windy or boisterous weather a powerful rotation is necessary to keep the axis in its true direction; for the lighter end of the bullet is more easily acted on by the wind than the heavier. If the lighter end were in rear, this part would be pressed to leeward, and the front and axis directed to windward; from the increased resistance on the forward side, the bullet would have a tendency to be driven to windward. If its lighter end were in front, the bullet would turn on its short axis, and its heavy end would try to go first. For a military rifle to be serviceable, a rapid rotation is indispensable to keep the bullet steady under all circumstances.

When the axis of the bullet is not a tangent to the trajectory, the resistance of the air ceases to act equally on the front of the bullet. It acts on its lower surface, and the more so, the more the bullet preserves its parallelism to the line of fire, and the further it is from the muzzle; so that the bullet meets with greater resistance than if the axis is kept in the direction of the trajectory, and the range will be lessened.

The more pointed the bullet, the further is the center of gravity thrown back, and the axis is more liable to injury. If the point is injured and does not coincide with the axis of the bullet, an irregularity in the flight of the bullet must take place. The general mode of throwing the center of gravity forward is by hollowing the base of the projectile, and by blunting the point.

FIG. A.

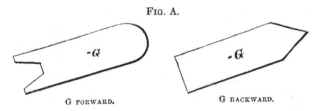

G FORWARD.   G BACKWARD.

The direction of the rotation of nearly all rifling is to the right, so that the lower portion of the bullet passes from right to left. Now, the lower half of the bullet travels on compressed air, the upper on rarefied; the result is that the bullet rotates on the compressed air and works to the right, in the same way that a top would do if made to revolve in the same direction, and placed on its edge on the ground. If the rifling were to the left (the lower part of the bullet rotating from left to right), the drift would be to the left. The longer the range and the greater the angle of descent, the greater the drift; but if the axis of the bullet was a tangent to the line of flight, this deviation would not take place.

Another cause of deviation is the unequal pressure of the air upon the front of the bullet, and the twisting of the long axis from the plane of fire. It is accounted for thus: Suppose the rifling to be in the usual direction, and the elongated bullet to have a conoidal or rounded front, the greatest pressure would be on its lower front; the rotation from right to left below will cause the point to work round to the right, and the axis consequently to be turned in this direc-

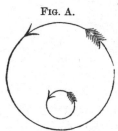

Fig. A.

tion. If pressure is exerted on the left front of the projectile, the point will fall; if on the upper front, it will work to the left; and if on the right front, the point will rise (fig. A).

Combining these effects, and supposing the air to commence acting with greater force on its lowest front, the point working round, the action would be transferred to the left, upper, and right fronts in succession, the point of the bullet describing a circle, while the center of gravity remains at rest. It is presumed that this motion is generally imparted to elongated shot, and that its axis is never a tangent to the trajectory, or in the plane of fire. In whichever direction the axis is twisted from the plane of fire, the resistance of the air passing through the center of gravity will cause the bullet to deviate in the same direction.

If the rifles were cut in the opposite direction, the movement of the axis would be also changed. It is stated by Professor Magnus, of Berlin, that a flat-headed shot would deviate, with a right-handed rotation, to the left.

It has been supposed by some that the greatest drift occurs with projectiles which are without grooves. Capt. Tamissier, instructor of musketry at the school at Vincennes, originally placed three grooves on projectiles to correct their flight, to act as the feathers of an arrow, by creating resistances on the posterior end; and as the resistance of the air acts in the direction of a tangent to the trajectory, the moment the axis of the projectile ceases to remain a tangent, the air acts directly against these surfaces on one side, and the axis is forced back to its position as a tangent to the trajectory; it was supposed that it had the same effect in correcting drift, but these resistances must reduce range.

Fig. A.

It does not appear to be clearly known what angle

to the trajectory the axes of elongated bullets preserve during their flight. It has been supposed by some that they preserve their primary direction, and by others that they form a tangent to the trajectory; theory may be cited in favor of either assertion: experiment may hereafter prove which is correct.

Sir William Armstrong says: "Experiments have been quoted of rifle projectiles having been fired with such small charges as to allow of the projectile being distinctly seen in its course through the air; and it was said to have been clearly perceived, in such cases, that the axis followed the curve" (possibly alluding to some experiments by a Royal Commission at Berlin); "but in all my own experiments," he continues, "the indications attending the graze marks, and the form of the holes made in distant targets, led to a contrary conclusion. In fact, it was easy to understand that the eye might be deceived, by the impression left on the retina, by an object thus rapidly moving, and producing the illusion of a sort of tail following the direction of the curve."

Major Owen, Royal Artillery, in a recent work, says: "Many who are constantly employed in noting the flight of shot, assert most positively that when the velocity is not too high, they can clearly see the projectiles descend with their points downward. It is difficult to say whether this is a mere optical delusion;

but the effects in targets, which can be examined at leisure, are more satisfactory evidence than that of the mere view of a shot during flight.   Now, it is almost invariably found that the holes made in targets are circular, even when elongated shot descend at considerable angles; for instance, some forty-pound shot fired recently at seven and ten degrees of elevation, the angles of descent for which would be about nine and thirteen degrees respectively, cut circular holes out of vertical targets made of thin wood covered with sheet lead.   The most probable explanation of this fact must evidently be that the point of the shot had drooped during flight; so that, on striking, the longer axis was nearly perpendicular to the plane of the target. . . . . This drooping of the point is of importance, for did the axis remain parallel, during flight, to its primary direction, the projectile would, most probably, when fired at any but a very low angle, on striking an object of hard material and solid structure, as a wall, etc., turn up against it lengthways, and therefore produce but trifling effect. This has not, however, been found to take place in the experiments hitherto made, but on the contrary, the penetrations of elongated shot at considerable ranges are always remarkably great.   There is but little fear of a shot turning up against an object unless the velocity both of translation and rotation be very low, and the angle of fire very high."

The effect of the density of the atmosphere on the flight of rifle projectiles, more especially apparent at long ranges, is now universally recognized. The denser the atmosphere, the greater the resistance and retardation : consequently the lower the bullet will strike ; the rarer the atmosphere, the less the resistance, and the higher the bullet will strike.

The initial velocity of a round shot is greater than that of an elongated one of the same diameter, taken transversely. Yet owing to the greater retardation it experiences (whereby its velocity is diminished), its flight is considerably less than that of the elongated shot, which latter travels at a more uniform speed throughout its flight.

Greater range and greater accuracy are attained by the use of the elongated shot than by the spherical ; the angle of elevation being much less, its trajectory will be lower, thereby increasing the chance of its striking the object.

Sir William Armstrong states that at certain low elevations the range of an elongated projectile is greater in the atmosphere than in vacuo, and the following is the explanation given by him: "In a vacuum the trajectory would be the same, whether the projectile were elongated or spherical, so long as the angle of elevation and the initial velocity were constant ; but the presence of a resisting atmosphere makes this remarkable difference, that, while it greatly shortens the range of the round shot, it actually prolongs that of the elongated projectile, provided that the angle of elevation does not exceed a certain limit, which in my experiments I have found to be about six degrees. This appears at first very paradoxical, but it may be easily explained. The elongated shot, if perfectly formed and having a sufficient rotation, retains the same inclination to the horizontal plane throughout its flight, and consequently acquires a continually increasing obliquity to the curve of its flight. Now, the effect of this obliquity is, that the projectile is in a measure sustained upon the air, just as a kite is supported by the current of air meeting the inclined surface, and the result is that its descent is retarded, so that it has time to reach to a greater distance.

CHAPTER II.

WHAT a rifle is, and what the object of rifling is, are questions which the young beginner will be very apt to ask, and it is necessary that this laudable desire for knowledge should be at once gratified.

The barrel of the old musket or smooth-bore was little else than a tube of iron, in which the ball fitted so loosely that when clean it would readily fall to the breech. In order to load easily it was necessary to have the ball much smaller than the bore of the gun, which caused great "windage," and occasioned considerable loss of propelling power, on account of the escape of a portion of the explosive gas on one side or other of the ball, which, at the instant of leaving the muzzle of the gun, received a direction from that side of the barrel against which it was last in contact with. No surprise will therefore be felt at the wildness of the flight of the projectile discharged from a smooth-bore. In addition to this, an almost insuperable difficulty had to be overcome in casting a spherical ball that should be perfectly solid; a slight hollow or air cavity being generally found somewhere in the interior. The center of gravity would necessarily be effected by this wherever it might occur, and in consequence cause irregularity in the flight of the projectile. Hans Busk, in his valuable "Hand-Book for Hythe," says: "This particular difficulty, it is true, was latterly overcome at Woolwich by means of an ingenious apparatus for forming bullets by compression out of cold lead. Every ball thus produced is necessarily of equal density and perfectly solid. Had it been possible to project bullets of this kind from an accurately straight and cylindrical tube, their flight, for moderate ranges, would have been tolerably true, could the windage at the same time have been prevented; but when the barrel, after a few discharges, became foul from the products of combustion, it would have been hardly possible to have fired many successive rounds." To correct this obstacle to accurate shooting, rifling was devised, but by whom is by no means certain; though the credit of the invention has generally been attributed to Gaspard Zoller of Vienna, who flourished at the end of the fifteenth century; though about the same time (A.D. 1520), Koster, a gunsmith of Nuremberg, enjoyed a great reputation for the excellence of his workmanship, and it is gener-

ally conceded that he was the first to practice the
spiral form of grooving ; but it is very doubtful
whether he was aware of the great value of the
change. To Robins, an English mathematician, is
due the credit of making the subject an anxious
study, and to his elaborate researches we are indebted for all we know; his treatise, or "Tracts on
Gunnery," published in 1745, being a standard work
at the present day. In the closing paragraph, he
records his conviction of the value of rifling in the
following words : " Whatever state shall thoroughly
comprehend the nature and advantages of rifled-
barrel pieces, and, having facilitated and completed
their construction, shall introduce into their armies
their general use with a dexterity in the management
of them, they will by this means acquire a superiority
which will almost equal any thing that has been done
at any time by the particular excellence of any one
kind of arms, and will perhaps fall but little short of
the wonderful effects which histories relate to have
been formerly produced by the first inventors of fire-
arms."   How prophetic these words have been I need
not point out, when we see that at the present day
each nation is straining every nerve to produce a
weapon that shall excel that of every other.   Vast sums
have been spent in endeavoring to obtain the object
sought, and yet perfection has not yet been reached.

Rifling or grooving the barrel, originally devised to remedy the evil previously alluded to, was found, with certain subsequent modifications, to obviate others of still greater moment.

The object of rifling is to give rotation to the projectile round its axis of progression, in order to insure a regular and steady flight.

The first attempts at rifling were of a very primitive character, and consisted simply of cutting a few straight grooves the length of the barrel; the object aimed at being to facilitate loading and provide for the escape of the residuum of the powder. Koster, as previously stated, found that by giving a spiral direction to the grooves, greater accuracy was obtained; the theory being "that the position of the axis of rotation of the ball not being dependent upon any accidental circumstances, but being rendered coincident with its line of flight, the resistance which the fore-part of the bullet encounters from the air acting equally on all sides, is evenly distributed round the center of gravity."

Another advantage is, that if there should be any irregularities on the face of the ball, they are successively presented to the action of gravity and the air by its revolution on its axis, thereby tending to correct any deflection these defects might give rise to.

I may here very properly give a slight description

of the mechanical means of cutting the rifle grooves as first practiced. On the end of a rod is fixed a cutter, with teeth like the teeth of a saw, which cut the required shape of the groove; and on the opposite side of the rod is a piece of copper to keep it steady in the barrel. The spiral movement is given to this rod by a socket, through which it works similarly to a barrel already rifled; which, together with the barrel, is fixed in a sort of bench from six to nine feet long. Sometimes the rod itself is twisted to the degree of spirality wanted; and this rod working through two square holes of its own size is of course turned while passing through. On the end of this rod being introduced into either end of the barrel, its action is regulated by a screw, raising or depressing the cutter so as to indent it more or less; it is then driven with force through the barrel, and repassed a few times, until it passes easy. The cutter is then made to cut again by a turn of the screw, and again forced through, repeating the process until the groove is sufficiently deep. The cutter is of course directed by the rod, and the groove is cut with the same degree of turn as that to which the rod is twisted.

Robins says: "Various plans have been proposed for furnishing the projectile itself with vanes, wings, grooves, or other configurations, intended to give it rotation during its passage through the air; but the only practical method hitherto adopted has been to make the barrel of a fire-arm of such a shape in its interior that the projectile while being propelled from the breech to the muzzle may receive a rotatory combined with a forward motion."

Of all the many systems of rifling proposed it is unnecessary to speak. They may be described under three general heads,—the grooved cylinder, the elliptical or oval bore, and the polygonal.

The Grooved Cylinder.—Rifling by grooves is a system that has generally been adopted by gunmakers of all countries and in all periods since the introduction of rifled arms, and is that which is adopted at the Royal Small Arms Factory, Enfield, in the manufacture of rifles for the army and navy. As far as I am acquainted, all American rifle-makers practice this system.

The Elliptical or Oval Bore.—The distinctive character of this system, as adopted by Mr. Lancaster, is that the barrel is cut in its interior in the form of an ellipse, the difference between the major and minor axes being twelve thousandths. The barrel being a smooth-bore is easily cleaned ; there are no recesses for the collection of fouling, and the bullet does not act upon the air with any sharp edges.

The Polygonal System.—This has been adopted by Mr. Whitworth in the construction of his rifle, the

bore of which is hexagonal and measures across the
flats, *i.e.*, the minor diameter, four hundred and fifty-
one thousandths inch, and across the angles, *i.e.*, the
major diameter, five hundred and three thousandths
inch; and by Mr. Westly Richards in his breech-
loader, the bore of which is octagonal; also by Mr.
Henry, of Edinburgh, the bore of whose rifle is hep-
tagonal, with a rib in each of the angles.

In considering these different systems it will not be
necessary to give any extended explanation of the
first, as it is so common that it would be a work of
supererogation.

With respect to the second system, Hans Busk, in
" The Rifle, and How to Use It," discourses as follows: " Of all the modifications of the principle of
rifling that have ever been brought out, none can be
said to exceed in simplicity the one now commonly
known as Mr. Lancaster's system of elliptic rifling.   I
say commonly known, because it is in fact merely the
revival of a very antiquated system, alluded to and
accurately described in ' Scloppetaria ' (page 87) as
' a very old invention, quite obsolete ' more than a
century ago.

"A problem, the solution of which has long been a
scientific puzzle, has been the reduction of windage to
a minimum, without too great a concomitant increase
of friction.   With the old many and deeply grooved

rifle, if by any means we could have annihilated the windage, we should at the same time, most probably, not only have greatly augmented the friction, but we should have cut or furrowed the ball to such an extent that the resistance of the air against its roughened surface would have been increased so considerably that no equivalent advantages would have been gained.

"In the elliptic rifle this difficulty is satisfactorily combated. A section of the bore is in fact so slightly oblate, that without the application of a gauge its eccentricity is hardly perceptible. The 'twist' found by experience to be most advantageous is one turn in thirty-two inches. The most convenient diameter of bore, four hundred and ninety-eight thousandths inch, is suitable for all purposes, the length of the barrel being thirty-two inches; while an eccentricity of one hundredth inch in half an inch is found amply sufficient to cause the bullet to spin on its axis to the extreme verge of its flight. It is not very material whether the bullet, which should be of the softest lead, be cast with or without a cavity at the base, though, upon the whole, a slight hollow is perhaps advisable. In either case, its lateral expansion, at the moment the gun is fired, is enough to compel it to fill the barrel perfectly; in fact, to seal the tube hermetically till the projectile has passed the muzzle.

4

The bore being as smooth as that of a shot-gun, the increase of friction is not great, and the bullet speeds upon its errand, without being in the slightest degree jagged or indented. The precise form of the fore-part of the Lancaster bullet, whether acute or obtuse, is not of primary importance, though it is essential that it should fit the barrel accurately. For this purpose, each bullet, after having been cast, is struck through a steel gauge or 'swedge,' which, correcting any superficial irregularities, gives to every bullet precisely the same external form. It matters little where the center of gravity of these bullets is situated, nor do the defects, incident to all cast bullets, appear to effect the precision of their flight. The chief objection urged against this rifle is its occasional uncertainty."

With respect to the concluding portion relating to the uncertainty, I may state that the rifle has been submitted to very severe tests, both by the military authorities and by private parties, and the result has been most satisfactory; indeed after a protracted trial at Malta in 1857, against the Enfield, it established a very high character, and conclusively proved its superiority to that weapon. At a later period, when speaking of rifles generally, I shall again advert to this gun.

We now come to a consideration of the third sys-

tem, or polygonal, which has been so identified with
Mr. Whitworth's name, that it is generally described
as "Whitworth's rifling;" though, as I have stated
above, other makers use the system.

In 1854 Mr. Whitworth, the distinguished mechanic,
was induced by the late Lord Hardinge, then general
commanding in chief of the army, to consider the
subject of rifling.   After a long series of experiments
he adopted that system in which the interior of the
"barrel is hexagonal," and which, "instead of consisting partly of non-effective lands, and partly
of grooves, consists of effective rifling surfaces."   The angular corners of the hexagon are always rounded, as in diagram.

For an ordinary military barrel thirty-nine inches
long, Mr. Whitworth proposed a forty-five hundredths
inch bore, with one turn in twenty "inches," which he
considered the best for this length.   "Either cylindrical or hexagonal bullets may be used" with this rifle.
"Supposing a bullet of a cylindrical shape to be fired,
when it begins to expand it is driven into the recesses
of the hexagon.   It thus adapts itself to the curves
of the spiral, and the inclined sides of the hexagon
offering no direct resistance, expansion is easily
effected" (fig. A, p. 52).

"While the ordinary grooved rifle depends upon
the expansion of the soft-metal projectile, in the hex-

agonal system, rifling may be effected, independently
of expansion, by making the projectile of the same
shape as the interior of the barrel (fig. B) ; in other

FIG. A.

FIG. B.

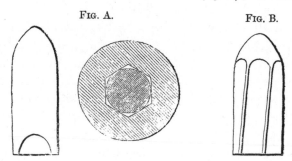

words, by having a mechanical fit between them.
The projectile may be used naked, and be made of
metal of any degree of hardness. The expansion
principle may also be combined with an easy mechanical fit, so that a projectile of metal harder than lead,
as an alloy of lead and tin, may be used, which, while
it loads easily, will expand sufficiently to fill the bore
and give more than double the penetration."

In 1857 a trial of the Whitworth took place at
Hythe against the Enfield, when the former proved
greatly superior to the latter, both as regards accuracy
and penetration. It has also been under trial before
Committees of the House of Commons, and main-
tained its reputation, as is proved by the following
extracts from their reports, under date of 26th Nov.

1862.   They state that "the makers of every small-
bore rifle having any pretensions to special accuracy
have copied to the letter the three main elements of
success adopted by Mr. Whitworth; viz., diameter of
bore, degree of spiral, and large proportion of rifling
surface.   It is not probable that any further modifications or quasi improvements that might result from
the question being now thrown open to the gun trade
would be attended with any practical advantage."
The result of this trial will be best conveyed in the
words of the committee's report, where they say:
"They think it only just to Mr. Whitworth to acknowledge the relative superiority of his small-bore rifle,
even as a military weapon, over all the other rifles of
similar caliber that have been under trial; viz., the
Enfield, Lancaster, and Westley Richards breech-
loader."   And again: "With the exception of the
defect already noticed as to wear, and the difficulty
of obtaining ammunition suitable for the rifle as well
as the service, the committee are of opinion that the
Whitworth rifle, taking all other points into consideration, is superior to all other arms as yet produced,
and that this superiority would be retained if Mr.
Whitworth could insure all the arms being made with
equal mechanical perfection."   This is high praise,
and whether altogether deserved or not will be considered when I come to that portion of my subject

which treats of the rifles of various makers, and their adaptability to the various purposes of war, the chase, or target shooting. It must be remembered that Mr. Whitworth's experiments with rifled pieces, both great and small, have cost the British Government an enormous sum, every facility having been allowed him, and the whole of the immense workshops of the nation being at his disposal; while in this country, individual enterprise has alone had to fight the battle of introducing a new fire-arm. If American ingenuity has not yet produced an arm equal to Whitworth's (which I consider an open question when the performances of Remington's new improved rifle, and others undergoing tests, are considered), I feel confident, that were the same encouragement given and

ROUND.   CIRCULAR.   ANGULAR.

facilities offered by the U. S. Government, that an arm would be produced that would meet every requirement. But to revert to the subject of rifling, as I before stated, in the majority of cases the cylindrical grooving is adopted, but the form, depth, and number of grooves used vary according to the caprice of the maker.

Three forms have been adopted. The proportion that the grooved should bear to the land or unrifled surface is unsettled, but the prevailing opinion appears to favor an excess of groove.

In all early rifling the grooves were made deep and uniform; subsequently they were made shallow and uniform, and now they are made progressive, *i.e.*, increasing in depth from the muzzle to the breech. This system was first practiced by Capt. Tamissier in France in 1846, not from choice, but as an expedient to enable the French Government to convert their old muskets into rifles. The grooves were made twenty thousandths inch deep at the breech, but were gradually decreased toward the muzzle, where, in consequence of the thinness of the metal, they were made only four thousandths inch deep. Col. Boucher, in his "Volunteer Rifleman," does not approve of this system, for he says : " There are no scientific principles involved in such a proceeding, nor was it even attempted to say there were, though good results accidentally followed the suggestion." He proceeds at great length to argue on this question, and arrives at the conclusion that the system is radically wrong, and that great evils arise from its adoption ; but I do not here propose to make any further allusion to his views, but would commend his really valuable work to the attentive perusal of the inquiring student. It is purely a scientific work. I do not propose to make mine so, and have not the space to devote to a discussion of the subject. The system has been adopted in both France and the United States, and has given good *practical* results, and this I look upon as being of more value than theoretical views.

With regard to the number of grooves employed, they vary from two to seventy, and indeed I have heard of more. I consider that from three to seven are those most likely to give good results.

The pitch of the rifling, the degree of spirality or turn, are the terms generally given to the twist in the grooving, which may be classed under three headings, —uniform, gaining, and decreasing.

The first of these is that which is in most general use in England, and is adopted by Mr. Whitworth in the construction of his rifle. Hans Busk says : " As for the degree of twist, I have never found any less rapid spiral excel that with one turn in twenty-four inches. Mr. Whitworth informs me, indeed, that with his hexagonal bore one turn in twenty inches answers best." And after condemning in the most positive manner the second or gaining twist, he lays it down as a maxim that " the twist should be *uniform,* from breech to muzzle, and should not make less than one entire turn in two feet." On the other hand, the gaining, or, as it is better known, the "gathering twist," and which is believed to be of American origin, receives the unqualified approval of that most accomplished writer, John R. Chapman, in his "Improved American Rifle." At page 135, after laying down certain general principles regarding the "twist," he says: "It has been proven by a great number of experiments, to my satisfaction, that at a distance of two hundred and twenty yards a caliber of ninety to the pound, and the barrel eighty-five calibers long, using a flat-ended picket weighing one hundred and forty grains Troy, with about six calibers or sixty grains of powder, of *moderate strength*, with a gaining or increasing twist ending at one turn in three feet six inches, will project its bullet with less variation in a side wind than any other combination of caliber and twist. To produce the greatest effect at four hundred and forty yards, it is necessary to have the caliber eighty to the pound, and the twist end at one turn in three feet three inches; and at six hundred yards, a caliber of seventy to the pound, and a twist ending at one turn in three feet. For long ranges and large calibers, the powder ought to be weaker in general strength, and the grain much larger than is now used in our best forty-rod rifles." Again, a little further on, he says:

" The *increasing* or *gaining* twist was introduced into
the combination of the improved American rifle by
Edwin Wesson. I am not aware that any one in particular claims its invention, or I would award him all
the praise it deservedly merits. I venture to assert, in
the face of those who are sticklers for a regular, nay,
a decreasing twist (here he takes a fling at Greener,
author of ' The Gun and the Science of Gunnery,'
who advocates a decreasing twist), that a rifle with a
gaining twist, in a windy day, at two hundred and
twenty yards, will make a string one-third shorter
than a rifle with a regular twist. I consider at that
distance that a rifle with a regular twist of one turn
in four feet, with a caliber of eighty to the pound,
performs better than any other; and I know that
such weapons, with a charge of two inches of the
caliber of powder, will, when fired, twist over sideways in spite of all you can do, and also ' kick ' or
' recoil ' very severely. Surely, if such recoil and
twisting can be felt and seen, the tendency for the
bullets to scatter and strike the target in a circle, and
not in a straight line, is easily accounted for; for remember that this twisting motion is generated and
commences at the very instant that the bullet is put
in motion, and consequently the axis of the barrel at
the breech end must shift its position, and point,
when the bullet leaves the muzzle, in a direction dif-

ferent from what it did when the trigger was pulled;
for it must take some length of time (about the one
thousandth part of a second), however infinitely short,
for the bullet to move from the breech to the muzzle
of the weapon.

" The circle of error of these weapons at two hundred and twenty yards is never less than six inches;
whereas, in an increasing twist, it will not be more
than two inches, and sometimes only one. Any one
may convince himself by experiment that a rifle with
a regular twist of one turn in six feet has but little
tendency to twist sideways, even with a charge of two
and a half inches of the caliber of powder. Assuming
then from experience that four feet is as much as a
bullet of eighty to the pound ought to make one turn
in during its flight, and that a bullet can be projected
out of a twist of one turn in six or seven feet without
any injurious twisting of the weapon; then these degrees of rotation can be given to it at the breech and
the muzzle, just as well as starting and driving it the
whole length of the barrel through a regular twist of
one turn in four feet. Is it not reasonable that if the
bullet can be started and driven along the four feet
regular twist at all, it will be started and driven with
much less friction along the increasing twist commencing at one in six and ending at one turn in four
feet? Assuredly so; and practice shows that the

twisting of the rifle can scarcely be perceived, and the recoil not worth noticing. I should not dwell so long upon this point did I not know that an erroneous opinion is entertained by some respectable mechanics. It is not generally known by rifle-makers and others than an increasing twist is a true geometrical line formed by the application of an arc of a large circle to the surface of a cylinder; and the radius of this circle must of necessity be longer for a slow, and shorter for a quick gain. The usual method of laying out this line on a rifling cylinder is by means of compasses and measurements, which, at the best, is only a rude and unsafe approximation to truth, and the curve on machines so made abounds in crooks and irregularities. The radius of the large circle generally ranges from thirty to forty feet, according to the notions of the rifle manufacturers."   Hans Busk, who is well known as a writer on rifles and a recognized authority, says : "The principle in question is obviously unphilosophical, for besides altering the shape of the bullet, it causes increased resistance at the muzzle, the very place that relief is wanted," and considers it altogether a waste of time and money to pursue any further experiments with rifles of that principle.

The decreasing twist was advocated by Mr. Greener, because the motive gas does not propel the bullet as fast at the breech as at the muzzle. Many rifle-makers in this country coincided with Greener in this opinion, and manufactured their rifles on this principle, but I believe that all, or nearly all, have seen the error of their ways, and are keeping up with the spirit of the age by adopting the " gaining " twist.

It is held by the advocates of a uniform twist, that the bullet, in a barrel with a gaining or decreasing spirality, receiving its expansion at the breech, is moulded into the shape of the barrel at that part; but in proceeding down the barrel under the force of the powder, it is obliged, in order to make its way out, to alter its shape. It is never, therefore, from the instant it is put in motion, at any two points, of the same form. This increased resistance to the passage of the bullet cannot take place without loss of power, loss of initial velocity, and consequently, loss of rotation.

As a matter of curiosity, I append a list of old rifles in the Artillery Museum at Paris:

19 with straight grooves.

131 with grooves uniformly inclined.

87 with an increasing twist near the breech.

29 with an increasing twist toward the muzzle.

83 with an increasing twist toward the middle of the barrel.

67 had grooves making half a turn and under in the length of the barrel.

219 had grooves making from half to a whole turn in the barrel.

55 had grooves making from one to two entire turns in the length of the barrel.

The calibers of the above arms were, three hundred and eleven of sixty-eight hundredths inch and under, and thirty-two above sixty-eight hundredths inch.

It may now be interesting to consider the various systems suggested, and those rifles which have been presented from time to time to meet the various requirements for good shooting and adaptability for sporting and military purposes ; for it must be borne in mind that a great number of rifles have been at various times brought forward that their inventors fondly hoped would prove *excelsior*, but when submitted to the test, sadly disappointed expectations. Many arms were perfect in *theory*, but sadly deficient in practice. The requirements of sporting, military, and target guns are very dissimilar, and many an arm that would answer well for sporting purposes, or target practice, would be utterly useless as a military weapon, and therefore the principal endeavors have been to produce such a piece as would combine *all*, in sufficient degree to recommend it to notice, yet keeping in view the absolute requirements for military purposes. Some of the new breech-loaders, such as Colt's, Spencer's, the Ballard, etc., are claimed to be every thing requisite; but as I shall have something to say respecting each of these a little further on, I will at once proceed to the consideration of the several changes in the construction of rifles. The earliest rifle of which we have any knowledge is a hunter's wheel-lock rifle, dated 1613; the barrel has seven grooves, with double lines between the grooving. A few years subsequent to this, the first patent for rifling small arms ever granted, was issued in England; it is dated 24th June, 1635, and reads as follows: " The gunsmith undertakes to rifle, cutt out, and screwe barrels as wide, or as close, or as deepe, or as shallowe as shall be required, and with great care." An arm known as " Baker's Rifle " was issued to the Ninety-Fifth Regiment of the British Army in 1800. This rifle weighed nine and a half pounds. The barrel was two feet six inches in length, and had seven grooves making a quarter of a turn in the length of the barrel,

with a caliber of twenty bore. It was loaded with great difficulty, a small wooden mallet being used to make the bullet, which was larger than the bore, enter the barrel; this forced the projecting ribs into the ball, and so kept it in contact with their curvatures during its expulsion. However, after a short trial, this system was discontinued. This was the first method adopted, and, as may well be believed, was of so rude a nature as completely to deform the ball, and thereby destroy any chance of *good* shooting. Another method was loading at the breech, but the great difficulties encountered prevented it being generally adopted; though the improvements since effected in breech-loading arms leads us to hope that in time all difficulties will be overcome and it will be generally adopted. In loading at the breech, a ball, *larger* than the bore of the piece, was used. This ball, under the action of the powder, was forced into the grooves, and thus obtained the rotatory motion necessary to ensure accuracy of flight. This process, though simple and easy, had to be abandoned on account of the difficulty of preventing the escape of gas at the breech, and the very complicated nature of the mechanism.

BELTED BULLET

Another method was by using the "belted bullet," or a ball with a rim which fitted the two-grooved or Brunswick rifle, and, following the grooves, obtained its rotation.

No great results could be expected from this system.
Robbins describes another method in use on the Continent. He says : " But in some parts of Germany
and Switzerland an improvement is made by cutting
a piece of very thin leather or fustian, in a circular
shape, somewhat larger than the bore. This being
greased on one side, is laid upon the muzzle with its
greasy part downwards, and the bullet being placed
upon it, it is then forced down the barrel with it.
The riflings should for this purpose be shallow, and
the bullets not too large." This method of loading
took up a great deal of time and was not satisfactory.
Indeed, so unsatisfactory was the state of rifled arms,
that they found very little favor in England or on the
Continent, France, indeed, about this time, having
abandoned them entirely, after a long and careful series
of trials. Capt. Wilcox, in his excellent treatise on
" Rifles and Rifle Practice," alluding to these difficulties, says : " None of the above methods of loading
fulfilled the conditions required of an arm for soldiers,
—the first being too slow; the second offering breech-
loading defects ; the third not giving any marked
superiority over the musket; the fourth, also, being a
slow method of loading. The rifle, as an arm for
infantry, would probably have fallen into disuse in
Europe, and been forgotten there, had not a new
method of loading been discovered by M. Delvigne, a

5

French infantry officer of the Royal Guard." The method of Delvigne, alluded to by Wilcox, was the placing at the bottom of the breech a small chamber having an abrupt connection with the bore. The charge of powder nearly filled this chamber, and the ball, which was spherical in form and fitted the barrel loosely, rested on it, and was forced into the grooves by several sharp strokes with a heavy rammer having a conical head, in order that it might receive a spiral motion during its projection from the barrel. This hard ramming also forced the ball into the chamber, to the injury of the powder.

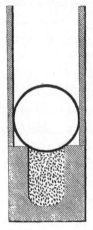

SYSTEM DELVIGNE.

Although this system gave easy loading and increased accuracy of shooting, the defects were so great that it was soon abandoned. The fouling was so bad, that after a few shots the powder did not go down into the chamber, but rested on the grooves, which necessitated such hard ramming to force the bullet into the grooves, that its shape was destroyed and its flight became exceedingly irregular.

Col. Thouvenin, of the French Artillery, brought out in 1828 a rifle on the tige principle, and which was known as the *carabine á tige*, or pillar rifle. In place of the chamber, as in Delvigne's rifle, a small cylinder or pillar of steel was fixed in the bottom of the bore. The powder lay around this pillar, and the bullet, which was cylindro-conical, rested on it. By this means the bullet was more easily expanded, and with less detriment to its shape. In marching, or any ordinary movements, the ball was not liable to be displaced ; but being spherical, it received obliquely the impulse of the charge, and was consequently propelled with diminished force. The tige system did not come into general use, though in 1844 another effort was made to introduce it, with Delvigne's elongated bullet, he

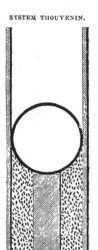

SYSTEM THOUVENIN.

(Delvigne) having about this time discovered that elongated bullets, hollowed at the base, were expanded and forced into the grooves of the rifle by the gas evolved in the explosion of the powder. He accordingly obtained a patent for a bullet consisting of a cylinder terminated by a cone. Col. Poncharra suggested that a "sabot" of hard wood be placed at the top of the chamber, in which the ball (with a greased patch) should rest ; but from the complicated

nature of the ammunition, and the liability of the
" sabot " to be broken by the ramming necessary to
force the bullets into the grooves, it was not adopted.
Numerous other expedients were resorted to, but
without any success, until 1847, when Capt. Minié, an
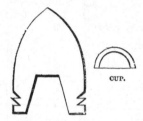
instructor of the musketry
school at Vincennes, suggested the placing of an iron cup
in the cavity of Delvigne's
bullet (see figure). This was
found to answer admirably,
and the construction of rifles
on the tige or stem system was discontinued, the
Minié rifle (so called, but which was an ordinary rifle
firing a Minié bullet) becoming the favorite weapon.
By this means the old smooth-bore musket was by
this simple process converted into a long-range rifle.
It was now considered that the solution of the principle of expansion had been obtained. Gen. Jacob,
however, did not so consider, for he pursued his
experiments (which may be said to have been on a
gigantic scale) in India, and on testing the Minié
bullet he pronounced it a failure, the iron cup,
fitted into the hollow at the base, being liable to be
blown though the bullet. After many thousand experiments, he decided that a bullet of the following
form was the most suitable.

It was claimed by him that "this projectile was effective up to twelve hundred yards, and probably to much greater distances. The effect of its shape in

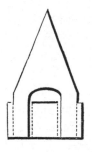 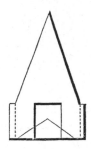

overcoming the resistance of the air is so great, that after a flight of twelve hundred yards its progressive velocity is but little diminished, and even at fourteen hundred yards the percussion shells made of the above shape explode well."

Having now instructed the beginner in the principles of rifling and the theory of projectiles, I think that some account of the various rifles at present in use will be acceptable.

CHAPTER III.

THE RIFLE IN ALL ITS VARIOUS FORMS.

I SHALL now proceed to a description of the rifles of the different makers in this country, England, and the Continent, both muzzle and breech-loader, which latter has been so much improved that for sporting and military purposes it bids fair to completely supersede the former. Nearly all the objections formerly urged against it have been overcome; and doubtless, ere long, from the numerous experiments being conducted by every nation, an arm will be produced that will meet every requirement.

I shall first speak of Wesson's "Improved American Rifle," which has been highly commended, and particularly so, by so competent an authority as Chapman, who, in his excellent work on the rifle, speaks thus of it:

"The barrel is made of cast steel, not very highly carbonized, thoroughly annealed in an air-tight oven, the bore being drilled out of th solid bar, straightened, ground, cut, or planed outside into an octagonal shape, the bore being left perfectly central. The length of this barrel, breech inclusive, when the muzzle is off, is two feet eight inches, and the loading muzzle, to be in proportion, is as long as its outer diameter. The outside of the barrel tapers a little from breech to muzzle, the difference in diameters being one-fourth of an inch, and its weight is ten pounds. It is indispensable that the barrels of target rifles be made of cast steel, and not of iron. The wear and tear of usage is hardly ever seen in a cast-steel barrel fixed off with a patent muzzle; whereas, in an iron one, it is soon perceptible, and its good shooting qualities quickly disappear. The barrel is not furnished with a rib, except the short tube at the breech end may be so called, the peculiarity of stocking precluding its use. The patent breech is made of wrought iron, case-hardened, and is joined to the break off by the old fashioned hook, with the addition of a half-lap joint, secured by a square-headed screw, which is turned by the cone-driver. Such a mode of fastening the barrel to the stock does away with the wood forward of the breech, and gives a peculiarly elegant and striking appearance to the weapon. The false or loading muzzle is put on by means of four steel wire pins, about one-eighth of an inch in diameter, and three-eighths long, and the holes for these pins are drilled before the muzzle is cut off, and as near the outside as practicable. The muzzle piece is cut off and the pins firmly fixed into it, and then held by a cramp to its place, when the rifling or cutting is done, by which a perfect fitting of the creases and bands at the junction of the muzzle with the barrel is secured. The bevel of the muzzle ought to be turned out in a lathe to insure accuracy, and to this the attention of a good maker is particularly directed, for the perfection of the bevel affects the patching and the uniform filling of the creases with lead. A small globe of steel is fixed upon the upper part of the muzzle to prevent the front sight being seen when the muzzle is on the barrel, so that there be no danger of firing it away. The bore of the barrel, in the first instance, is scant three-eighths of an inch, or about ninety round bullets or forty-three pickets to the pound. It is then worked out with lead and emery until it be parallel and round, and then cut with what is called a 'gaining twist,' starting at the breech at about one turn in six feet, and ending at the muzzle at one turn in three feet six inches. There are six cuts or creases, and the sides of the lands are cut square to their surface, giving a slightly dove-tailing appearance to the cuts. The cuts are not quite so wide as the lands, and great care is taken in cutting them of an uniform depth, which ought to be no more than will insure sufficient lead and patch for the firm holding of the bullet to the twist of the weapon. It is then what is technically called 'freed' from the breech to within one and a half inches of the muzzle, so as materially to reduce the friction of the bullet and patch in passing out when the weapon is fired. The communications to the seat of the cone are free and open, and the breech furnished with a vent or breathing nipple, about the diameter of a common pin, and bushed with platina. The lock has back action, furnished with a single or French set, which I prefer to the English or double set, I presume from education. The guard is of a peculiar shape, so as to allow the marksman to hold his weapon firmly ; the stock is of black walnut, straight from the butt to the break-off, and there forms a considerable angle with the barrel. (I have endeavored to prevail on Mr. Wesson to give the stock less crook, being convinced that a rifle with a very crooked stock can not do as good shooting as it is otherwise capable of.) It is furnished with a patch-box of elegant shape, and a small box for the insertion of a wiper end, which screws into the ramrod, to be used in case of emergency. A globe sight is fixed into the stock just behind the break-off, and a bead sight at the muzzle end of the barrel. The front or bead sight is so called from its peculiarity of shape. A bead somewhat smaller than a pin's head is filed on a piece of steel wire, and the stack left as flat and thin as practicable ; this stands up about three-sixteenths of an inch from the barrel, and is shaded by a thimble about three-eighths of an inch in diameter and one inch long. The bead, stalk, and thimble are attached to a piece of beveled steel, which is moved sideways for counteracting the wind by sliding along a dovetail cut across the barrel about one-twelfth of an inch deep and three-eighths of an inch wide ; a pointer filed on the front end of the thimble serves to denote how many divisions of the index the sight has been moved from the center. This index is cut on the top of the barrel, and is left polished and divided into thirty-seconds of an inch. The globe sight at the breech end is made of steel, the top part being circular, with a small hole through the center, countersunk on each side, to take away reflection. It is desirable that the center of this hole be in the plane of the axis of the stalk, so that half turns may be used. One side of the stalk is flatted down with a file, so that the different ranges can be marked upon it. The stalk is cut with a thread of sixty-four turns to an inch, one turn corresponding to half a division on the front index."

I have tested Wesson's gun, and from my experience I can confirm Chapman's good opinion of it. If any man wants to make fine shooting, he can not go astray in getting one of Wesson's best. But I would not advise him to follow Chapman's idea of a straight stock. The more crook there is, the less will the recoil be felt.

I do not deem it advisable to note the peculiarities and excellences of rifles made by the different makers in the States, but to give a description of what may be considered a good style of gun, and leave it to each individual's taste to select the kind most suitable for himself. I will not give any account of the old Kentucky rifle, the barrel of which was nearly four feet long, very heavy, with small bore, as it has gone entirely out of fashion, but will confine myself to the kind at present in general use. The American Target Rifle is, as I have elsewhere stated, only to be consid-

ered in the light of ordnance, and only valuable for
experimenting, being, as I consider, of no practical
use whatsoever.   Doubtless, I will bring down upon
my head some severe remarks for so cavalierly disposing of it; but as my object is to guide and instruct the
beginner in obtaining such a knowledge of rifle-shooting as will enable him to put it to some useful purpose, I will pass the target rifle over, referring him to
Chapman, or some other writer who has gone fully
into this subject.   So many changes are taking place,
and opinions are so diversified upon this subject, that
it is rather difficult to say what is the present style ;
but I think it will be found that a barrel of from
thirty to thirty-four inches, with a bore from thirty-
eight hundreths inch to forty-four hundreths inch,
will be found to answer as well as any. If for sporting purposes, I would counsel the shorter length,
though I believe that the great hunters of the plains
use rifles with barrels of from thirty-five to forty
inches, and of a caliber so small as to enable them to
make sixty balls out of a pound of lead!   It is very
clear that such a rifle could only be useful on horseback, as the bullet would not be effective at long
range, and moreover, from its lightness would not
make good shooting in windy weather.   How different
this from the ponderous double-barreled rifle used by
Gordon Cumming in his African campaign, that took

a two ounce ball, and which was such a favorite with him that when it burst he "mourned over it as did David over Absalom!" The requirements of the prairie hunters demand that they go as light as possible, and therefore they have reduced the weight of the ball to a minimum. I would not counsel the novice adopting their method, but get a gun that throws a good heavy ball, as by that you will not only be able to fire more accurately, but you will secure many an animal that would carry off the lighter ball, even if planted in its very vitals. I may here mention that it has been found by experiment that a barrel of twenty-six inches is the maximum for strength of shooting, and one of thirty-four inches for accuracy. Therefore a barrel must range between these two to insure the great desiderata of strength combined with accuracy. The bullet has varied with the rifle, and the picket bullet of oval shape, that was in vogue years ago, has given place, through many gradations, to the conical bullet, with a flat base. It has been found that slightly flattening the apex, so as to form a vacuum, improves the shooting. Tamissier, in his experiments, made use of bullets flattened at the front, in order to enable him to carry the center of gravity as far forward as possible. It is very difficult to lay down particular rules as to what a rifle shall be, as marksmen and gun-makers are both whimsical, and each one has his set idea as to what a rifle should be. Some advocate a long barrel, while others maintain that any thing beyond thirty-three inches militates against good shooting. The best firing I have ever seen was made by C. Sheppard, of Toronto, with a rifle made by W. P. Marston, of that city; it is of fifty bore, thirty-three inch barrel, pitch of rifling one turn in thirty inches, six grooved, cut square the width of the lands; depth of groove fifteen thousandths inch, and slightly freed at the breech; charge of powder, two and a half drams; weight of rifle, from nine to ten pounds. These proportions are about as good as can be hit upon. The shooting made by Sheppard was at three, four, and five hundred yards; fifty shots at each range, fired on previously fixed days without regard to the weather, which was sometimes very bad. His average for the one hundred and fifty shots was at three hundred yards, six and one-quarter inches; at four hundred yards, eight inches; at five hundred yards, nine and three-quarters inches. It must be understood that this was done with open sights and without *any* rest. A Capt. Boustead in Hamilton made three shots at four hundred yards that aggregated only eight inches. This of course, can not compare with the strings fired from a dead rest, with telescope sights, from that ponderous machine, the "target rifle," but it shows what can be done with open sights. And I maintain that such style of firing and the use of such sights is the only way to make any practical use of the rifle. Any man that can fire one hundred and fifty shots, in all weather, at three, four, and five hundred yards, each one of which would have killed a man, must be counted a wonderful shot; and I estimate the performance as being vastly greater than seven, eight, or nine-inch strings at forty rods, from a piece of light ordnance like the target rifle. I may be severely criticised, by the advocates of the heavy rifle, for expressing these views, but I do so as I honestly believe that it is the only way to make a man serviceable in the field or the forest. I find that Frank Forrester coincides with me, for he says, at page 111, speaking of fancy target practice, that it is "what may be called the fripperies and frivolities of the art. Target shooting from rests, with telescope sights, patent-loading muzzles, and other niceties, is very neat, and doubtless telling also in the practice ground, *but wholly useless and ineffective in the field.*"

I have also been informed, by a gentleman in whom I have great confidence, that at a meeting of a target club in Ohio, held just before the commencement of the late war, thirty men put ten shots each within the circumference of a nine-inch circle, at a distance of three hundred yards. This is almost marvelous; yet

I have good reason for believing it. I hope to see the
English method of rifle practice—viz., with light guns
and heavy balls, at long ranges, depending upon *firm
holding* for their success—supersede that in vogue in
America, where heavy barrels and light balls at short
ranges and from rests are most in fashion. A friend,
who is a great authority on rifle matters, writes me,
giving his views in the following language:

" The old-fashioned rifle, for accuracy of shooting,
can not be excelled, with Curtis' patent muzzle and a
brass starter.

" The improvements in the conical ball for rifle-
shooting sportsmen, consists in flattening the point, as in diagram, and
swedged with a steel die.

" The length of barrel not to exceed from thirty to
thirty-four inches; weight from ten to twelve pounds;
ball, thirty-four to forty-four hundredths inch diameter. A twenty-six inch barrel for the strongest shooting, and thirty-four for the truest carriage; but thirty
inch is recommended for general utility. The old
Kentucky rifles were from forty to forty-four inches in
length of barrel."

I have had, and shall again have occasion to speak
of the great shot and veteran sportsman, Seth Green,
of Mumford, Munroe County, N. Y., and it may be
well in this connection to mention that at the last

sportsmen's convention at Leroy, N. Y., he proved himself the best shot in New York State. He fired with a rifle made by William Billinghurst, of Rochester, who, besides being a thorough sportsman and good shot, is one of the best, if not the *very best*, riflemaker in the United States. He is quite a Solon among the sports of that section, and his shop is "the headquarters" for all shooters. The rifle that Green shot with was a regular American target rifle ; barrel, thirty-one inches long, exclusive of the patent muzzle, and weighing twenty pounds; caliber, sixty, and carrying twenty-eight conical balls to the pound; the charge of powder was three and one-quarter inches in the barrel. Billinghurst had practiced with the rifle a good deal previous to the match, and in a letter to me, speaking of its performances, he says : "In reasonable fair weather we have been in the habit of making strings of from ten to fifteen inches, ten shots at two hundred and twenty yards, or forty rods, measuring from the center of the bullet holes to center of mark ; sometimes they would measure a little more and sometimes a little less, according to the weather." This, it will be admitted, is very fair shooting, but is quite eclipsed by some practice he made last year when experimenting with a new rifle of his own make, thirty-two inch barrel weighing twenty-eight pounds, thirty caliber taking fourteen conical bullets to the

pound. Between four and five hundred shots were
fired by various parties during the trial, which lasted
some ten days and was at forty rods; the shortest string
measured seven and one-eighth inches, and the longest nineteen and one-eighth inches. This is most extraordinary shooting; but that it was done, nobody
who is acquainted with Billinghurst can for a moment
doubt. I give two of the best targets made on that
occasion, for which I am indebted to the courtesy of
Mr. Billinghurst.

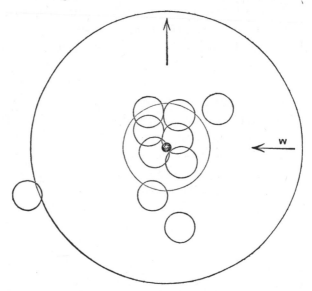

TEN SHOTS—FORTY RODS—SEVEN AND ONE-EIGHTH INCHES.

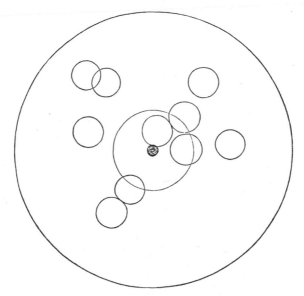

TEN SHOTS—FORTY RODS—EIGHT AND SEVEN-EIGHTHS INCH.

In addition to these, a number of strings nearly as good were made, but they were carried off by the parties that made them. Nevertheless, a record of ten strings was preserved, on the back of a target, which show an average of fourteen and five-sixteenths inches, varying from ten and three-eighths inches to nineteen and one-eighth inches. I forgot to mention that the rifle was eight grooved, with a "gaining twist" commencing with one in six feet and ending with one in three feet. All the shooting was done with Billing-

6

hurst's combination bullet, full particulars of which he
will supply to any gentleman applying to him. I have
not mentioned telescopes, as I have very little actual
experience with them. The beginner will not need
them, and the " old hand " probably knows far more
about them than I do myself. I understand that
William Malcolm's are the best in use. It would be
impossible to mention and treat of the rifles of all the
makers in the States, and I shall not attempt it,
merely mentioning the name of Lewis, as I have seen
and tested his guns, which are of first-rate make and
possess good shooting qualities.

The Canadians, who are eminently a sporting people, have a number of good rifle-makers among them,
—such as Booth, of Ottawa ; Grainger and Marston,
of Toronto; Soper, of London, who made a rifle for
the Prince of Wales when in this country, and others
of merit. Marston, of whose rifle I spoke when mentioning Sheppard's shooting, makes a very excellent
gun at a moderate price. I was desirous of obtaining
a sketch of it to insert in this work, but in reply to
my application he writes : " Were I to send you a
sketch of my rifle, I think it would be of little service,
as its general appearance is so much like other 'small
bores,' and they so like the short Enfield, that a reduced copy would look like them." This, no doubt,
is very true. He further says : " I use six grooves,

cut square the width of the lands; depth of groove, fifteen thousandths inch, slightly freed at the breech, thirty inch regular twist, fifty bore, thirty-three inch barrel; weight of gun, nine and one-half to ten pounds; and these I hold to be the best proportions for a ten pound gun up to fifteen or sixteen hundred yards in wind and weather. The charge is two and one-half drams of powder and one ounce of lead." His experience as a rifle-maker extends over a period of thirty years in England, Canada, and the United States, and being a well-informed man, his opinion is entitled to weight. However, as it is not my intention to specially commend any particular maker, I shall take leave of this portion of my subject, leaving the choice of the gun to the individual fancy of the purchaser, believing that sufficient has been said to assist him in choosing a suitable weapon. I shall now proceed to the consideration of breech-loaders, to which I purpose devoting considerable space, as I believe the importance of the subject demands it. I have no doubt but that, ere long, the muzzle-loading rifle, for all but *fancy* target practice, will be completely superseded by the breech-loader.

BREECH-LOADERS.

It seems to be unquestioned that the breech-loader, for military and sporting purposes, will very soon supersede the old-fashioned and trusty muzzle-loader. Nothing but certain defects prevented this long ago; but the recent war between the North and South, and, still later, the terrible struggle between Austria and Prussia, wherein the latter triumphed by means of the needle-gun, or *zundnadelgewehr*, showed that troops armed with muzzle-loaders, no matter how good they were, had not the slightest chance against those armed with the deadly breech-loader. The terrible destructiveness of this arm will be more fully demonstrated when I come to speak more particularly of the merits of the various arms that have been put forward as candidates for popular favor. It is singular that nearly three hundred years elapsed from the time that we first have any account of this kind of weapon, before any improvements were made in it. It has been claimed that the breech-loader was the invention of a French king (Henry II., in 1540), but I think that is disproved by the account given by Hewitt of the various rifles and guns deposited in the armory of the Tower of London. In his work on the Ancient Armor and Weapons of Europe, he says: "The barrels are of several varieties,—breech-loading and muzzle-loading, bell-mouthed and cylindrical. Two examples of the breech-loading arm, both of which appear to have belonged to King Henry VIII., are in the Tower collection. One of these, No. $\frac{12}{1}$ of the catalogue, has the royal initials H. R., and a rose crowned, supported by lions, chased on the barrel, where also is the date 1537. The No. $\frac{12}{3}$ has the rose and fleur-de-lis carved on the stock, and it is remarkable that the movable chamber which carries the cartridge has exactly the form of that in vogue at the present day. These two examples appear to be the arms named in the Tower inventory of 1679,—'carbine 1, and fowling-piece 1, said to be King Henry the Eighth's.'"

Robins appreciated the value of the breech-loading principle, as the following extract will prove: "As this mode of loading took up a good deal of time (alluding to the spherical ball and patch), the rifled barrels made in England (for I do not remember to have seen any foreign rifles so constructed) are contrived to be charged at the breech, where the piece is made larger, and the powder and bullet are put in through an opening in the side of the barrel, which, when the piece is loaded, is filled up with a screw. Somewhat of this kind, though not in the manner now practiced, would be *of all others the most perfect method* for the construction of these sort of barrels,"—thus, in a

manner, predicting that which has now come to pass.
Very little attention was paid to this subject until
Col. Colt devoted himself to the perfection of a rifle
charging at the breech.   True it is that from time to
time some rude attempts were made in this line, but
to him I think is due the credit of perfecting an arm
on the breech-loading principle, and truly a terrible
arm it may be considered.· I do not think that the
repeating principle is one that can as yet be successfully applied to a military weapon, but for sporting
purposes it is invaluable.   To show that I am not
biased in my opinion, I will quote Hans Busk, who, it
will be admitted, is a competent authority.   In "The
Rifle and How to Use It," he thus speaks of Col.
Colt's rifle : " I have already (at page 42) adverted to
the principle of repeating fire-arms, as introduced
and successfully carried out by Col. Colt in the manufacture of his celebrated pistols.   The rifles he has
more recently produced are similar in construction,
equally handy, but of course are more effective still
than the smaller arm.   They are of different patterns,
and vary in bore and length, the barrels being respectively eighteen, twenty-one, twenty-four, twenty-
seven, and thirty inches long, according to the purposes for which greater or less range may be required.
Their power, efficiency, and applicability to military
use have been severely tested and satisfactorily proved.

In addition, indeed, to previous contracts, the American Government have lately ordered several thousands for the equipment of a picked body of men, the Secretary of War having reported upon this particular arm in the following eulogistic terms : ' The only conclusive test of the excellence of arms for army purposes is to be found in the trial of them by troops in actual service. Col. Colt's arms have undergone this test, and the result will be found, in some measure, by reports from Gen. Harney and Capt. Marcy, who used them in Florida against the Indians.' These reports relate only to ' the rifle,' but are clear and satisfactory; and as that arm has been much less used than the pistol in our service, they become important. . . . . But to return to Colt's repeating rifle, an engraving of which I annex. It will be seen that its appearance is neat, while, as regards weight and portability, it is not one whit more cumbersome than the obsolete military rifle of former days. By a very simple arrangement, the cylinder containing the chambers can, after firing, be instantaneously detached and replaced by a loaded one, so that a dozen rounds may be delivered with the utmost requisite rapidity."

In its internal construction this rifle, as well as the latest made pistols, differs somewhat from those of earlier make. The catch which causes the breech cylinder to revolve, instead of acting against ratchet teeth cut on the cylinder itself, works in grooves cut in its circumference in such a manner that a pin, by traversing the grooves, not only makes the cylinder rotate, but also locks it when required. This is an obvious improvement.

The Government of the United States have taken great pains to test the comparative value of different breech-loading arms, and the result of their investigations may be briefly summed up in the words of Col. May, one of the principal members of the scientific board instituted for the above purpose. He expressly states that, having in view not only Sharp's rifle, but all others that have been used in the American cavalry service for the last twenty years, he considers Colt's rifle "far superior to them all in every respect."

Allusion having been made to

SHARP'S RIFLE,

I think that a short description will enable the intelligent reader to judge for himself as to the relative merits of the two guns.

These arms have now attained the highest perfection in every respect. The proprietors have adopted all the improvements that ten years of experience could suggest. The primers are carefully prepared, are waterproof, and *sure fire;* the arms and thin parts are of new and most approved patterns, the gas-check shuts off every particle of escape, and the manufacturers challenge the world to produce an arm of superior material, strength, accuracy, force, safety, or rapidity and certainty of fire. They are self-priming, with Sharp's primer, and adapted to the use of the army percussion cap. The barrel is of cast steel, and its chamber or ball seat is counterbored, slightly conical, the exact shape and diameter of the ball, so that the ball, when properly forced to its seat, has its axis exactly coincident with that of the bore; the rear of the bore contains an adjustable bouching, and the space between its forward end and the base of the ball admits the clamp and rod with which the bouching is driven back in adjusting it.

Numerous reports from the ordnance and other army boards, and letters and certificates on file in the Ordnance Office at Washington, attest the superior quality and efficiency of Sharp's rifles and carbines, which have withstood every test, and—the most satisfactory of all—ten years' service in the field in the hands of United States troops, and on board our ships of war. They have also been supplied, in large quantities, to the British, Mexican, Peruvian, Chilian, and Venezuelan governments, and are highly esteemed in the service. More than this, it is the *only breech-loading arm* of any account in which *loose powder and ball* can be practically used with effect or safety; others requiring a very expensive and peculiar kind of fixed ammunition, which can not be prepared in the field, and is of no service except it be used in the particular style of arm for which it was prepared.

Our arm was fully tested, in this country, during the late war.

It is the arm demanded by and furnished to the *sharpshooters*, after fully testing the various other styles presented, not without injury to themselves in some cases, and it is the first choice of the masses of both infantry and cavalry as a service arm.

Sporting rifles have been sold in such great numbers that their merits are fully appreciated. The recent improvements having removed the only defect, —the escape of gas at the joint,—these arms are now recommended as being the most perfect arm of the times.

In point of material, workmanship, and accuracy or rapidity of fire, as compared with any other muzzle-loading, breech-loading, or revolving fire-arm that can be produced, we say try it, and if the trial does not attest its superiority we shall be disappointed.

At the siege of Arequipa, Peru, in March, 1858, over six hundred of Vivanco's men were shot down at the barricades by Castilla's attacking forces, armed with Sharp's rifles, they sustaining only a trifling loss.

In April, 1858, Colonel Suasue, at the head of one thousand men of Vidauri's force, armed with Sharp's carbines, attacked Governor Manero, in command of three thousand men of the Government forces at San Luis, in Mexico, and achieved a most signal victory, killing upward of six hundred men, taking the city, and making prisoners of Governor Manero and three of his colonels, with a slight loss.

About the 1st of September, 1858, Colonel Wright's command, principally armed with Sharp's carbines, were engaged with the party of Indians that had previously defeated Colonel Steptoe's forces, when armed with the old muskets and carbines. The engagement resulted in a most disastrous rout and defeat of the Indians, with a loss of fifty warriors killed and wounded, while of Colonel Wright's forces not a man was harmed.

This is the description of the gun and its adaptability for a military weapon, as put forth by the company which are engaged in their manufacture. Many testimonials have been given in favor of this gun, which is probably more widely known than any other breech-loader. At one time it enjoyed immense popularity, but whether it has not answered the expectations that were formed of it, or from the introduction of so many new guns on different principles have captivated the public taste, it certainly does not enjoy the popularity it once did. It is most unquestionably a good arm, and very well adapted for sporting purposes. At recent trials before military boards at Springfield and Washington, it performed well; and having been adapted to use metallic cartridges, it gave such satisfaction, that I understand that the United States Government have ordered the conversion of a large number of arms on this principle. If the Sharp does not now occupy the same prominent position that it once did, it is not owing to any inferiority on its part, but to the stimulus given to the production of breech-loading fire-arms by the recent great military events having brought forward a large number of competitors, each one having a host of friends. I will close this notice of Sharp's rifle by giving an opinion from a gentleman who, I think it will be admitted, is a competent authority :

" Colonel Berdan, who has had more than a year of active service on which to base his opinion, considers the Sharp's improved rifles to be far superior to any other thus far. In all *essential* points they are superior to muzzle-loading rifles for active service. The only point in which any muzzle-loader has the superiority is with those in which the ball takes the groove, and finds its center while being rammed down."

THE MAYNARD RIFLE.

This was one of the first breech-loaders introduced to the notice of the American public, and by its fine performance did much toward removing the prejudice that was at one time entertained against breech-loaders. I am indebted to Cleveland, in " Hints to Riflemen," for the following excellent description of this sporting and target gun :

" The Maynard rifle, which was first patented in 1851, and of whose peculiar construction a very good idea may be obtained from the annexed representations, was invented by Dr. Edward Maynard, of Washington, D. C., and is certainly one of the most ingeniously contrived instruments of the kind which have yet been produced. Indeed, it combines so many ingenious arrangements, which, together, result in the production of a weapon whose efficiency and strength are quite as remarkable as its perfect simplicity, that it is only by a careful examination and study of its various parts and their workings that one can properly estimate the amount of brain-work involved in its construction. The fact which first presents itself, upon a cursory examination, is that it is of extremely compact form, in which every feature is reduced to the smallest possible occupation of space, without giving the slightest ground for any apprehension of deficiency in strength. The motion of the guard by which the breech is raised for the reception of the cartridge, is so easy, that the first feeling which it excites is one of doubt lest an accident should cause its displacement at a moment when mischievous consequences might ensue. But an examination of its working reveals the fact that the mechanical arrangement of its joints is such as to insure the strength of a solid mass of steel, which is not affected by any strain to which it can possibly be exposed, and that this is attained without the use of a single spring, bolt, or catch, but simply by the movement of the parts, which work with mathematical precision, and derive their strength from their relative positions, which may be compared to those of the supporting bones in the animal system.

"A very simple but very important improvement has been recently introduced, by which the empty cartridge, after being fired, is started from its place by the act of raising the breech for reloading, so that it may be easily withdrawn. This is one of those apparently trifling arrangements, the value of which can only be appreciated by one who has seen a deer bounding away from him, while he was fumbling with his finger-nails to start a cartridge which happened to stick, as such things always *happen* to do at such times.

"The removal of a single pin disconnects the barrel from the stock, and the whole gun may then be packed in a space of twenty inches in length by six wide and one deep, so that it may be carried in a trunk, or an easily portable case. Barrels of different calibers, either for shot or rifled, may be fitted to the same stock and changed in a few seconds.

FIG. 1.

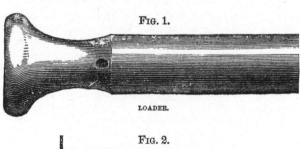

LOADER.

FIG. 2.

THIRTY-FIVE HUNDREDTHS INCH CARTRIDGE.

FIG. 2. FIG. 1.

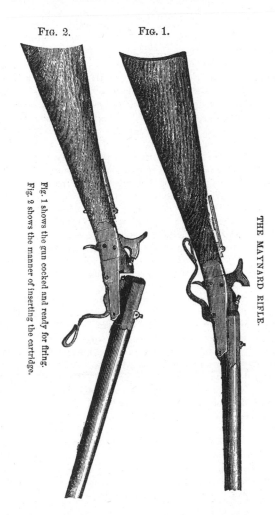

THE MAYNARD RIFLE.

Fig. 1 shows the gun cocked and ready for firing.
Fig. 2 shows the manner of inserting the cartridge.

" The ammunition is contained in a metallic cartridge, having an aperture in the base through which the fire is communicated from the cap. As these cartridges constitute a very important feature of Dr. Maynard's invention, they demand something more than a passing notice. Theoretically, the charge delivered from a metallic cartridge should be more certainly accurate than that from one of paper or cloth, and especially in breech-loading guns, where the cartridge rests in a chamber, from which the ball is driven through the caliber, which is of less diameter. For, supposing the point of the ball to be entered perfectly true in this caliber, its base, when a paper cartridge is used, is unsupported at the moment of explosion, and may be turned to one side or the other by the unequal pressure exerted by the gas. With a metallic cartridge, provided the ball is fitted perfectly true in the end, and the cartridge is made to fill the chamber, the base of the ball is held in its place as firmly as the point till the whole has entered the rifled caliber. The ordinary self-exploding metallic cartridges are compressed about the base of the ball after its insertion, which would seem to involve a risk of untrue delivery, owing to unequal friction upon the base while forcing itself loose. In practice, however, I have certainly found no cause of complaint on this score. Dr. Maynard's cartridges are constructed in such a manner that, when charged, by means of a very simple implement which accompanies every gun, the ball is not only, of necessity, mathematically exact in its position, but is held, *without compressing the cartridge*, by simply being exactly fitted to it, so firmly that it can not be moved, after being placed in the chamber, in any direction, except with a perfectly true delivery through the caliber. The cartridges may be used over and over again for an indefinite period, and, being loaded by the gunner himself, he is relieved from the apprehension of being unable to provide himself with ammunition, as well as from the fear of accidental explosion, which must always exist with the cartridges having the fulminating composition in contact with the powder. There is also a very simple arrangement for using loose ammunition, the ball being first inserted at the breech, and followed by a cartridge or charger, which is simply filled from the flask for each shot. I have been thus particular in describing the Maynard cartridge, because its merits, which are really very important, are liable to be overlooked by a casual observer, and because Dr. Maynard is entitled to the full credit of its invention, having obtained a patent for his mode of manufacturing them, and securing the bullet with a flat base in a perfectly true position in the cartridge, and holding it there without compressing the cartridge about its base, as long ago as 1856.

" The barrels are of two sizes,—one being of half an inch caliber, carrying twenty elongated or thirty-five round bullets to the pound ; the other of thirty-five hundredths inch caliber, carrying forty-six elongated or ninety round bullets to the pound. To the latter I am ready to accord the fullest praise. I know of no breech-loader which I consider its superior ; and, indeed, in accuracy and force, I have never seen it surpassed by any gun fit for field service.

" Of the large barrel I can not speak in the same terms. It is too light for the charge it has to carry, and the recoil is so severe as to neutralize the effect of the increased charge , so that its penetration at forty yards is little, if any, more than that of the small barrel whose charge is one-fourth less.

" In the shaping of the stock, the object of reducing the whole to the most compact form possible has led to a sacrifice of fullness, which gives it a lank appearance, as if sawed from a board, which, I think most men will agree with me, is by no means atoned for by the capacity it gives of being stowed in half an inch less depth of case. A new model, however, has recently been prepared, in which this objectionable feature has been removed, and it is to be hoped that in future its beauty of form will be in keeping with its intrinsic excellence.

" In connection with this gun, I ought not to omit to mention the Maynard primer, which is another invention of Dr. Maynard's. It consists of a narrow strip of varnished paper of double thickness, having deposits of fulminating powder in cells between the two, at equal distances apart. Each strip contains three dozen of these cells, equivalent to the same number of caps. The strip is coiled in a magazine concealed beneath the lock-plate, and brought up by a motion of the wheel in the act of cocking, so as to bring a cell directly upon the top of the nipple. The fall of the hammer explodes it, and at the same time cuts off the paper behind, so that it is not seen again till the gun is again cocked.

" My own experience in its use has been but small, but, so far as it has gone, it has been entirely satisfactory. It secures the same advantages which are possessed by the metallic cartridges which have the fulminating composition in their base, without being liable to the danger of explosion from an accidental blow. . . . .

" I am quite confident that no gun has done so much as the Maynard to remove the prejudice entertained against breech-loaders by many old riflemen ; and indeed no sportsman, after convincing himself, as he may very readily do, of its accuracy and force, can fail to perceive the very great advantages it possesses over any muzzle-loading rifle."

Mr. Cleveland gives some diagrams of the shooting made by this gun in experienced hands, but as he does not tell us under what circumstances it was fired, whether *off-hand* or from a rest, I do not think it worth while to include it here. In my experience, I have never known any good shot who could not, with any decent rifle, at some time or other, make some extraordinary shooting. I prefer, therefore, to take the experience of that veteran rifle-shot and hunter, Edward Stabler, who, in a letter to Cleveland, gives his opinion of what the Maynard is, and likewise some illustrations of what may be considered its ordinary shooting. He says :

" I first saw Dr. Maynard's rifle five or six years

since (1863), and in the hands of a friend, while hunting in the Alleghany Mountains. It had the short barrel, only twenty inches in length, and a large caliber; it was literally an object of derision to our hunting companions, who were all advocates of and used the long, old-fashioned muzzle-loaders. Yet, when we came to compare the 'pop-gun,' as they called it, with theirs of the greatest repute, at any distance over one hundred yards, all their guns were beaten. The penetration was nearly double; and when, at long range, the little gun was always 'in,' or close to the mark, the big ones were as often as otherwise 'nowhere.'" A little further on, he says: "As good, if not the best, shooting I have ever witnessed, has been done by my thirty-two inch small-caliber 'Maynard.' After properly arranging and adjusting the sights, and attaching a hair-trigger, firing with a rest, *four successive* balls at sixty-six yards, all breaking into the first hole, and all covered by a York shilling, a dime covered three entirely, and nearly all of the fourth ball; at three hundred yards (also with a rest, and the only sure test of the accuracy of a rifle), *three successive* shots were all within the compass of a visiting-card, or less than a two-inch ring; the nearest within half an inch of the center.

"The Maynard barrels are all made of steel, which I consider far preferable to iron. It admits of boring and rifling with more precision, is clearer of flaws, and is more durable in the grooves, especially for breech-loaders, using no patch. It is probable that much of the superiority of the Maynard rifle is owing to the arrangement of the sights,—three of them front, middle (open with leaves), and rear or 'peep' sight; the last raising and sliding with perfect accuracy, giving any desired range, and having a very fine aperture, affording, at the same time, a shield to the eye, and giving a *long* range of sight to a very *short* gun.

"To be explicit and direct, I will add that the rifle referred to weighs eight and one-quarter pounds; length of barrel, thirty-two inches; the conical ball, one hundred and fifty grains; the ordinary charge of powder, thirty grains; and the cartridge, when properly loaded, is absolutely waterproof. The rifling is with three broad grooves, the lands and grooves being equal; the small caliber has one turn in four feet, the larger caliber one turn in about five feet. Taken as a whole, length and weight of barrel, size of ball, and shooting qualities, together with true scientific principles in construction, and superior workmanship and finish, all combined, it excels any rifle I have ever seen for hunting purposes; for it is light enough to carry all day without fatigue, yet has both length and weight for steady off-hand shooting.

With a rest, the aim is almost unerring at any reasonable distance.

"The opportunity has not yet occurred to test it, but I feel very confident that, with a clear, still atmosphere, and a standing shot, a deer could be killed twice out of three shots at five to six hundred yards."

He proceeds to give some further illustrations of the performances of the Maynard, with which he seems completely in love, and says that "the Maynard is considered entirely efficient at *more than twice the range* of ordinary muzzle-loading rifles; the greater the range the more marked the difference." Now I do not know what Mr. Stabler considers "ordinary muzzle-loaders," but I must certainly dissent from any such doctrine as this; indeed, I think that it is very much the other way. Speaking of ordinary muzzle-loaders, one may be supposed to understand Purdy, Wesson, Fish of New York, Billinghurst of Rochester, the Springfield and Enfield rifles. Now I feel pretty sure that the makers above named would feel somewhat astonished to be told that *any* breech-loader had *double* the effective range of their guns. If the Maynard is as effective at the *same* range as either of the guns mentioned above, it is a most extraordinary weapon. Another statement is that "they can be fired with almost unerring and deadly aim, eight or ten times a minute, at a range of many hundred yards." This is speaking of the performance

of the "Maynard" in the hands of a Confederate
regiment at Ball's Bluff. Now, though a practiced
and skilful rifleman might, under favorable circumstances, discharge eight or ten shots with tolerable
accuracy, it is preposterous to suppose that a regiment of men in the heat of a bloody contest could do
so ; true they might discharge the gun that number
of times, but the "unerring and deadly aim" would
be wanting. I find that at the last Wimbledon meeting (a report of which lies before me) a very thorough
and exhaustive trial of breech-loaders was made ; the
Westley Richards, Spencer, Remington, Berdan converted Enfield, Craig Needle, and Benton were all
tested in the hands of the *very best* shots in England,
and that under the most favorable circumstances an
average of eight shots was all that was realized*
(though the Berdan was fired thirty-six times in
three minutes, and the Enfield thirty-eight times in
the same time) ; and that the accuracy was not of the
very highest order, is proved by the fact that out of
four hundred shots only three hundred and seven
struck the target—the size of which varied from two
feet by six feet at two hundred yards to six feet by
eight feet at five hundred yards, that being the longest

---

* This was written before the result of the meeting this year
(1867) was made known, and the splendid firing made then by
the Snider Enfield, alluded to in another place, shows the improvement that is taking place.

distance fired. I am not unfriendly to the "Maynard," but I do not like to see such rash assertions.

I have been induced to give such an extended notice to the "Maynard," from the fact that it has been for a long time a very favorite weapon among sportsmen, and if it is now losing its position, it is not from the defects that have been discovered in it, but that the pressure of the times has set the very best mechanical skill to devise better breech-loaders than those in use up to the time of the breaking out of the fratricidal struggle that has lately so nearly rent our country asunder. Dr. Maynard has introduced a new pattern of his rifle, making it more like other breech-loaders and doing away with the primer. Not having seen a specimen of it, I am not able to make more than this passing allusion to it.

MERRILL'S RIFLE.

"The simplicity and strength of construction arrived at in the Merrill rifle are only equaled by its extraordinary range and accuracy of fire ; and the efficiency of the arm not being based on any patent metallic or India-rubber cartridge case, but using the simple paper cartridge or loose powder and ball, and the ordinary percussion cap, gives them great advantages over arms depending on fixed or regularly prepared ammunition, and makes them justly preferred, not only on the frontier, but wherever a rifle is required.

Another advantage the Merrill plan possesses is that it can be easily applied to muzzle-loading arms at small cost, without restocking, altering the lock, or changing the general appearance or diminishing the strength of the arm. The alteration of muzzle-loaders to the Merrill plan of breech-loading has been practically tested by the United States Government with the most entire success, and has placed in the hands of the troops an arm that can not be surpassed, and also at small cost.

"For sporting purposes or target shooting the Merrill rifle can not be equaled, as it has attained the highest perfection in every respect. The barrels are of the best material, and the chambers are bored out to the exact size of the conical ball which they use, so that the plunger which puts the cartridge in its place forces the point of the ball firmly into the grooves or rifling of the barrel, thereby insuring its going straight to the mark, and not turning, as conical balls frequently do, when fired from other rifles.

"The sporting rifles are fitted with globe sights of the most approved pattern, which insures fine shooting. These rifles have been fired *five hundred times* without cleaning, and any number of shots can be discharged without any change taking place in the working of the machinery. This is owing to there being no escape of gas, which, when escaping, causes what has been termed clogging in other breech-loaders, but which can never occur with the Merrill rifle, as the plunger or breech-pin is reamed out so as to make an expansive spring, and the cavity being filled up with copper, upon which the force and heat of the explosion act at the moment of discharge, causes the plunger to expand as much as the barrel will allow it, or, in other words, to keep up with the expansion of the barrel or surrounding surfaces, and thereby prevent escape of gas, which not only clogs up the working parts of a gun when escaping, but causes great loss of power. Thus, no gas escaping from the Merrill rifle, accounts for its having more penetration than other breech-loaders."

After reading the above (which is the manufacturer's account of it), one would suppose that he had the prospect of a *perfect* arm for all purposes of target shooting, sporting or military use, and that it would be unnecessary to look any further; but experience has shown that this arm is quite unfitted for military purposes, though it has received high testimonials from military men. It is a noteworthy circumstance that no sample of this rifle was submitted to the Board of Officers that sat at Washington in April and May, 1866, under Special Order No. 40 from the Adjutant General's Office, dated Jan. 30, 1866, to test all weapons that might be submitted, and to report upon the one most suitable for arming troops with. It seems to me that the mechanism is of the clumsiest and most primitive sort. Fancy a soldier having to work a great long arm or crank during the heat of battle, or a sportsman being obliged to do the same thing when charged by a wounded Buffalo bull or a grizzly in the Rocky Mountains. Another great objection to it as a breechloader is the use of the ordinary percussion cap and loose powder and ball ; for though this is claimed by the inventor as a great merit, I look upon it as a fatal objection ; so much time would be lost, that troops armed with Sharp's, or any other of the improved arms using cartridges carrying their own ignition, would play desperate havoc with an enemy armed with them.

THE BURNSIDE BREECH-LOADER.

This gun was considered the best of fifteen or twenty arms that were submitted to a Board of Officers convened at West Point in 1857, and consequently was adopted into the United States service to a very great extent. It was not found, however, to answer the expectations formed of it, as it was open to the same objection urged against Sharp's,—that it was on the "trap-door" principle. The next arm that claimed public favor was

THE SPENCER BREECH-LOADER.

The construction of the gun is much simpler than that of the needle-gun, but is still complicated. The

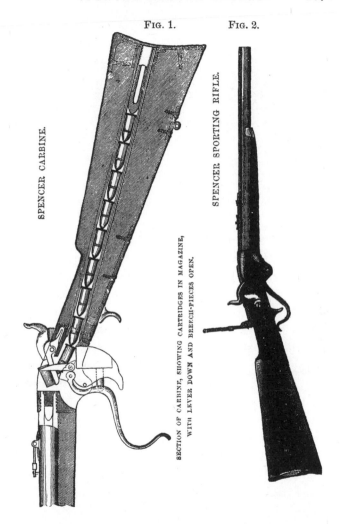

FIG. 1.

FIG. 2.

SPENCER CARBINE.

SPENCER SPORTING RIFLE.

SECTION OF CARBINE, SHOWING CARTRIDGES IN MAGAZINE, WITH LEVER DOWN AND BREECH-PIECES OPEN.

FIG. 1.   FIG. 2.

FULL SIZE.

CARTRIDGE FOR ARMY AND NAVY
RIFLES, AND LARGE CARBINE.

CARTRIDGE FOR LIGHT CARBINE
AND SPORTING RIFLE.

breech is formed of two pieces, one of which is the
breech-pin and the other the block on which the cartridges are carried. The breech-pin is attached to
the lever, which forms the trigger-guard, and the
carrier-block is pivoted into the breech-receiver by a
pin which is situated below and in rear of the hinge
of the lever. Between the block and the breech-pin
is a pin which presses the latter upward, and behind
the breech-pin is a curved piece of steel, which guides
the cartridge to the breech. This guide is worked by
a spring situated near the hammer, and in front of it
is the shell-ejector, which also works by its action.
On the left side of the breech-pin is a slide upon
which the hammer strikes to fire the priming. The

magazine is situated along the entire length of the interior of the butt stock, and is composed of a stationary outer tube and an inner tube which slides in and out. The inner tube is simply a steel box, with a spiral spring for pressing the cartridges forward to the barrel as soon as the breech is opened. To operate the gun the following motions are required: Supposing that the magazine is already filled with the cartridges (of which there are seven) and secured in the butt stock by turning the handle to a longitudinal position with the hammer, First, the lever is pulled down, which first throws the breech-pin below the chamber of the barrel, and then makes the carrier-pin and block slide back, ejecting the exploded shell and enabling the fresh cartridge to pass over the breech-pin; the cartridge being, of course, pushed forward by the spiral spring, which becomes relieved from confinement the moment the lever is pulled down, and the block and breech-pin swung backward. The cartridge is then directly in front of the chamber of the breech, and as soon as the lever is moved back it is forced into the barrel by the breech-pin, which presses it up from the rear. The chamber and magazine are thus effectually closed by the block and breech-pin, and it only remains to cock the hammer and draw the trigger. While this gun has been successfully used in the United States Army, it does not appear to be considered by the military authorities advisable to adopt it as the regular arm. The danger of injury seems great from the delicacy of the movements. Some improvements have been made in it, as noted in the report of the Washington Board, and though open to the objection that all repeaters are, it is nevertheless a *most serviceable arm*. As a repeater it has no equal. The fact that it stood the practical test of very rough usage in the American war tends greatly to overcome *theoretical* objections to it. Over one hundred thousand carbines and rifles have been furnished to the U. S. War Department of this pattern, and few complaints have been made. From a mass of testimonials in its favor, I subjoin the following letters :

FROM LIEUTENANT-GENERAL U. S. GRANT.

HEADQUARTERS ARMIES OF THE UNITED STATES,
City Point, Va., Oct. 10th, 1864.

Dear Sir,—In reply to your letter of the 20th ult., requesting my opinion in regard to the merits of the Spencer Repeating arms, I have to say that it is the prevailing opinion amongst officers whose commands have been furnished with these weapons, that they are the best breech-loading arms now in the hands of troops, both as regards simplicity and rapidity in firing and superiority in manufacture.

Respectfully, your obedient servant,

U. S. GRANT, Lieutenant-General.

WARREN FISHER, Jr., Esq., Treasurer Spencer
Repeating Rifle Company.

FROM MAJOR-GENERAL JOS. HOOKER.

HEADQUARTERS NORTHERN DEPARTMENT,
Cincinnati, Ohio, Oct. 12, 1864.

WARREN FISHER, Jr., Esq., Treasurer Spencer Repeating Rifle
Company :

Sir,—I had a few of the Spencer Rifles in my corps during
the campaign which resulted in the fall of Atlanta, and feel no
hesitation in pronouncing them to be the most effective arms
now in use. Perhaps my estimate of the value of this description of rifle will be better understood when I state it as my conviction, the result of long experience, that a regiment armed
with it is fully equal to a brigade armed with the muzzle-loading rifle, and can put as much lead adrift in a given length of
time It is in no way inferior to the muzzle-loader in accuracy
or length of range, with the very great advantage of not clogging by over-use, and is less likely to become unserviceable
from the wear and tear of a campaign. With these weapons I
have never failed to silence the fire of the enemy's sharpshooters. They were quick to discover them in the hands of my
pickets, and took especial care to avoid them. As an evidence
of the effect these arms had on the *morale* of the men, I may
state it as a fact I have repeatedly observed in the course of the
campaign that my men would make interest to go upon the
picket line, losing sight of the danger to which they were exposed in the satisfaction of witnessing the triumphs of their
weapons, and that I consider an unerring test of their superiority. Several regiments applied to me for permission to arm
themselves with them at their own expense. I am thus explicit
that I may expose the folly of manufacturing muzzle-loading
arms instead of breech-loading repeaters, or even the single
breech-loader.

> Your obedient servant,
>
> JOSEPH HOOKER, Major-General.

FROM MAJOR-GENERAL WM. T. SHERMAN,
Commander of the Army of the Southwest.

HEADQUARTERS MILITARY DIVISION OF THE MISSISSIPPI,
St. Louis, Dec. 23, 1865.

WARREN FISHER, Jr., Treasurer Spencer Rifle Co., Boston, Mass.:

Sir,—Yours of Dec. 18 is received. The Spencer Repeating Rifle was used by both cavalry and infantry in my army, and was universally preferred over all other breech-loaders.

We used this rifle to great advantage by infantry at Griswold Station, near Macon, Georgia, also at Bentonville, N. C. ; and Kilpatrick's cavalry were so impressed with its adaptability to cavalry uses that the General made every effort to procure it to the exclusion of all other carbines.

I am, with respect, etc.,

W. T. SHERMAN, Major-General.

FROM MAJOR-GENERAL GEO. H. THOMAS,
Commander of the Army of the Cumberland.

HEADQUARTERS MILITARY DIVISION OF THE TENNESSEE,
Nashville, Dec. 26, 1865.

Mr. WARREN FISHER, Jr., Treasurer Spencer Repeating Rifle Co., Boston, Mass. :

Sir,—I received your letter of the 18th instant yesterday. I have seen the Spencer Repeating Rifle tried under the most difficult circumstances, and have become convinced that it is one of the best repeating rifles which has been in use during the war. Although apparently complicated in its machinery, it is very easily understood by the men, and can be kept in as good order as easily as the old smooth-bore musket ; nor is it any more liable to damage by the accidents of service than the common musket.

Its repeating qualities render troops armed with it three times as efficient as when armed with the old-pattern musket. I sincerely hope that the Government may adopt it for both infantry and cavalry.

Very respectfully, your obedient servant,

GEO. H. THOMAS, Major-General, U. S. A.

Letters from distinguished generals of the Union Army, and newspaper articles, commendatory of the "Spencer" as a military weapon, might be furnished to any extent; but surely nothing could add weight to the testimony of the generals whose letters are given above. That it was not injured by constant use and hard service is amply proved by the following letter from Col. Barber after three years' use of Spencer Rifles:

HEADQUARTERS 197TH OHIO V. I.

C. M. SPENCER, Esq.

Dear Sir,—

*　　*　　*　　*　　*　　*　　*　　*

Your rifle has more than met my expectation in regard to it. The best thing that I can say in its favor is that I have over two hundred of them in steady use through all the campaigns of the Army of the Cumberland for nearly three years, *and never had a single one condemned as unserviceable.* Nearly every man of my command will buy the sporting rifle when they go out of the service, if they can raise the money.

*　　*　　*　　*　　*　　*　　*　　*

Yours very truly,

　　(Signed),　　　　G. M. BARBER,

　　　　　　　　　　Lieut.-Col. 197th Ohio V. I.

In addition to all this, the Board that sat in Washington in October, 1867, spoke in the highest terms and pronounced it the *best* magazine gun they had had submitted to them.

But it is more particularly as a sporting gun that I wish to consider it. The question of military weapons is, at the present time, so closely engaging the attention of the various governments of the world that we may hope, ere long, to see the problem of "what is the best breech-loader" definitely settled. The new pattern of sporting rifle (model 1867) now turned out by this company is certainly a very handsome and effective weapon, and one that I can confidently recommend. I recently took occasion to test this gun, in company with a party of sporting friends, and it gave the greatest satisfaction. The practice was very good indeed, though the day was unfavorable to *fine* shooting. In this connection I may be permitted to quote the opinion of a first-class shot and accomplished sportsman—not only as to the merits of the Spencer, but also as to its excellence over the other repeating gun (the Henry) that has been prominently before the public :

"I have given the Henry rifle an exhaustive trial, and have fully proved the disadvantages of that arm, not only as a military, but as a sporting gun. The Henry rifle is *full cocked* by turning forward the trigger guard during the same motion which raises the cartridge from the magazine to the level of the barrel. This is the first grand error ; because the consequence of this self-cocking principle is that the mainspring has to be made weak, the consequence of which is that the detonating powder in the rim of the cartridge must be of a very explosive character, so that a very slight blow may fire off your gun, so slight a blow, or even pressure, sufficing, that I have known several instances in which the charge was ignited by the simple following of the breech pin while pushing the cartridge to its place in the barrel while the hammer still stood at half-cock !

"I have never yet seen a fire-arm, the mainspring of which is controlled in cocking by any other motion than that of raising the hammer by hand, which is either safe or reliable. Then, again, the pin does not close the breech perfectly, the proof of which is that after a few discharges the yellow metal in its rear is burnt black by powder, not to mention the still more convincing fact that several parties have had their eyes injured by the ejectment of gases on firing. Another objection to this patent, for field use, is the open space in the ' body ' and the long open slit in the ' tube,' as well as the peculiar fitting of the catch and joint at the muzzle, all exposing the gun to the almost certainty of hopeless rusting in a soldier's hands in a campaign.

" There are so many repeating and breech-loading rifles inviting attention just now that space will not permit me to notice them further than that the ' F. Wesson ' single breech-loader appears to be for sporting purposes almost faultless. But in so far as my judgment goes, all must give way to the 'Spencer.' I believe the gun known as the ' Spencer Sporting Rifle ' to be the best repeater at present known, whether for military use or for game. I take the sporting rifle because it is the one I shoot with, and because the military weapon is not finished well enough to suit me. This gun is of the same caliber as the ' Henry,' forty-four hundredths, but carries a charge about one-third heavier, and I find its range to be proportionably greater. The barrel is of fine and very soft steel ; the body of best wrought iron, case-hardened, and the whole immensely strong and durable. The breech is closed by a solid block of iron, which renders any escape of gas impossible. After firing three hundred rounds, no mark of powder is to be found in the cavity of the ' body.' It is made an objection by some that in the heat of action, or while charging the magazine hurriedly in pursuit of game, the ' tube ' might be dropped. So it might, but your gun is just as good as ever, for by depressing the muzzle it is charged quite as readily as when the cartridges are pressed forward by the spring ; and any kind of a stopper will do to close the entrance to the magazine. This gun is very easily cleaned and kept clean, and a child may take it to pieces and put it together again in half a minute. The lock (an excellent one) is altogether apart from the loading apparatus, and bids defiance both to damage and moisture.

"As to shooting, the capability of this rifle is really astounding, considering its weight and caliber. Its penetration at one hundred yards is nine-and-one-half-inches dry pine boards, and its range may be judged from the fact that a few days since I fired at a bird on the top of a high tree, in the direction of this village, and the bullet in its descent penetrated obliquely the weather-boarding of a house a little over one mile and a quarter from where I fired!

"Take it for all in all, I consider this the best, safest, and most reliable rifle I have ever seen or heard of."

THE BALLARD BREECH-LOADER.

This gun is one of the simplest and most effective of American breech-loaders that we have seen. It is made of four pieces,—the hammer, mainspring, trigger, and double spring; the mainspring being encased in the lock, and thus protected from being broken.

One distinguishing characteristic of this gun is that the whole of the lock is contained in the movable breech-piece, B, which has both a slight longitudinal movement and a rising and falling movement within the receiver, A.

Fig. 1 is a side view, with a part of the receiver broken away to expose the breech to view, and represents the breech open for loading. Fig. 2 is a central

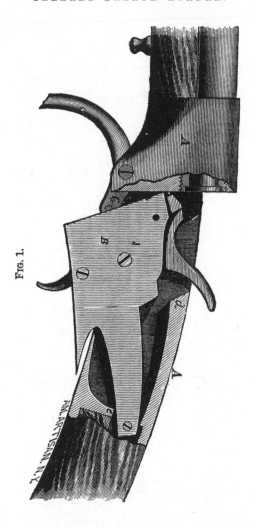

Fig. 1.

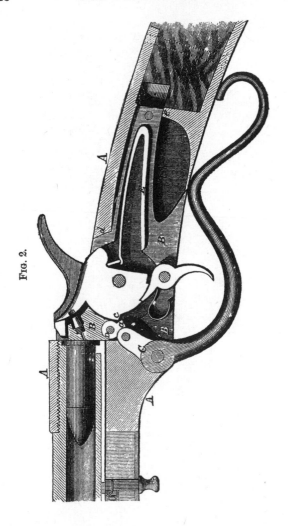

FIG. 2.

longitudinal, vertical section, showing the gun loaded and half-cocked.

The breech-piece, B, is fitted snugly, but so as to slide freely within a mortise in the receiver, A. In order to provide for the insertion into it of the several parts of the lock ; viz., the hammer, trigger, trigger-spring, and mainspring, E, all of which are shown in fig. 2,—it is divided vertically and longitudinally into two equal parts, which are secured firmly together by two screws besides the hammer-pin. These screws hold the two parts together so firmly that the breech is as strong as if made of a solid piece. The front part of the breech-piece is connected by a short link, D, with the upper and shorter arm of the trigger guard-lever, C, by the downward movement of which the breech is opened for loading, as shown in the first figure, and closed for firing, as shown in fig. 2. The hammer is half-cocked in the act of opening the breech by the action of a projection, a, on the link, D, against a shoulder, c, on the front of the tumbler. In firing, the recoil is received mainly against a shoulder, d (fig. 2), in the receiver, but to some extent upon the shoulder, e.

The principle on which this gun is made is simple, and but for one defect, which shall be mentioned, it would stand the equal of all competitors. The lever which protects the trigger being pulled down, the lock, including the hammer, falls below the breech, leaving the chamber of the barrel exposed. Under the chamber and about two inches from the breech is a small knob attached to a spring, which, being pushed toward the breech, ejects the exploded shell entirely from the piece and leaves the chamber free for the insertion of another cartridge. When the lever is pulled down the hammer is half-cocked by the action, so that on the lever being drawn up and the breech effectually closed, all that remains is to complete cocking the hammer and to fire the gun. In addition to its adaptability for metallic cartridges the Ballard rifle can be fired with paper cartridges and percussion caps. Directly in front of the hammer, and on the breech-block, a nipple is fixed, so that, in the event of metallic cartridges giving out, the old system can be followed, still loading by the breech or muzzle with loose powder and ball. As will be seen by the above description, the weapon is free from all complicated machinery, and can be fired with great rapidity. Experiments with this gun have been made on several occasions with various results. As many as twenty shots per minute have been fired from the carbine, and the inventors claim that in the hands of an expert twenty-five shots can be fired. Last year fifty-one breech-loading rifles were examined at Springfield by order of the United States Govern-

ment, and of this number six were selected as being
the best adapted to army use. The "Ballard,"
"Peabody," "National," and "Berdan" rifles, with
two others, were the ones selected. Notwithstanding
the many merits of the Ballard rifle, it still has one
defect. As the gun is made at present, the ejector
and the lever require two motions to work them. By
attaching them together, and thus causing the shell
of the cartridge to be ejected, the instant the lever is
pulled down and the breech is opened, the last fault
in the weapon would be removed. It is understood
that this improvement will be made, and when it is,
the rifle will be a most dangerous arm in the hands
of a well-drilled soldier. The Ballard rifle is well
made and elegantly finished, possessing great strength,
united with lightness. The carbine weighs about
seven pounds, and the army gun, when made, will
weigh about nine pounds. It is estimated that at a
distance of one thousand two hundred yards, with a
load of forty-five grains of powder and two hundred
and eighty-five grains of lead, the rifle is accurate,
retaining its initial force throughout that distance.

This rifle is deserving of very high praise, and if it
has a few slight imperfections, they are such as will,
I think, be soon overcome. As a sporting gun it is
certainly excellent, as good as the best; and in proof
of this I publish a letter from Theo. R. Davis, of New

Mexico. Whoever has the pleasure of that gentleman's acquaintance knows that he is perfectly competent to speak upon the subject. Whether the gun is as well adapted for purely military purposes as the Peabody, Remington, Spencer, and some European arms, is a question that can not by any means be considered settled. Certainly it is a good weapon, and the hunter, scout, or Indian fighter, who is armed with a Ballard, may confidently meet all comers. The following is the letter alluded to above :

SANTA FE, NEW MEXICO,
Jan. 21st, 1866.

Dear Frank,—I shall give you now the long-promised rifle letter. You must remember what a determined advocate the old-fashioned muzzle-loader had in me. Its load was certain and the affair was balanced. Many is the loose ball I've dropped from my mouth down the throat of my reliable Lewis rifle. The old friend has an honored place on the antlers of a two hundred and fifteen pound buck that he spoke to while we were out together among the hills and streams of your Adirondacs.

But we are a progressive as well as an aggressive people. The breech-loader was evidently an improvement, the copper ammunition alone being an immense advantage. The question was, Which is the best of all the breech-loaders? You know my love for a good rifle ; a poor one has never been in my possession for more than two days, or until some one could be found that would accept it as a gift. Rifle after rifle was tried and thrown aside ; one was too clumsy, another had no balance whatever, and all were to me inferior, as hunting-rifles, to the trusty muzzle-loader.

Soon after this a friend loaned me a breech-loader of which he spoke highly. " Try it, old fellow," he remarked ; " see how you like it, and let's hear your opinion."

I liked the gun from the first; it came up right; there was no jar, and it worked like a clock. Of course I went through the lock; it was simplicity itself, and as strong as it was well made. I have owned that rifle (108) from that day. Over four thousand bullets have been sent through its bright barrel, in which there is not the first show of lead, and the rifling is as true and sharp as the day on which I got it. The lock has not been repaired, and simple wiping out has served to keep it in a first-rate condition for close shooting either at sixty or three hundred yards. I have killed deer in the Adirondacs with it, and taken the top of a partridge's head away many a time. In a close bush fight it has never failed me. For buffalo hunting it is magnificent. More than one antelope has been brought down at three hundred yards. During our Indian fights it was the treasure of our party.

Do you wonder, my dear fellow, that I am an enthusiastic believer in the Ballard rifle? There are other rifles that can be discharged more rapidly, but they are unbalanced and so liable to get out of order that a man needs a gunshop with him to be sure that he will have something to shoot with. Beside this, you know as well as I that a rifle can be fired too rapidly. I have yet to meet a good shot that cares to discharge a rifle more than six or seven times per minute. I can send fifteen balls out of my Ballard in that space of time. I am convinced, and you are at perfect liberty to say so, that the Ballard is the *ne plus ultra* of breech-loaders for hunting purposes.

We go to the Apache Canon to-day to give the wild turkeys a rattling. If you were here you should take the pet, when you would be convinced that a good breech-loader is the thing after all. At all events, that is the case of your friend,

THEO. R. DAVIS.

The above recommendation is of great value. It is not, like many published by proprietors and agents of guns, obtained by the practice of a special gun purposely prepared for the trial and fired under favorable circumstances. But this is the candid opinion of one gentleman to another after a long, and it will, I think, be generally admitted, a severe trial. An arm that will perform well under all circumstances against large and small game,—man, buffalo, bear, antelope, turkey, and partridge,—must be acknowledged to be nearly perfect.

I shall conclude this account of the Ballard by giving the following notice of an important rifle match that came off at Point St. Charles, Montreal, Dec. 5, 1866. The match was to test the relative endurance and rapidity of firing of the Ballard and Palmer rifles. At the three hundred and sixteenth round the Palmer rifle gave out, the Ballard having then fired about five hundred shots, and it continued to be fired till one thousand and twenty-three rounds had been fired in one hour and forty-five minutes, or an average of about ten shots a minute—a feat of consecutive firing perhaps unprecedented.

THE PEABODY RIFLE.

The Peabody rifle being constructed on somewhat similar principles to the Ballard, I will next speak of it.

This breech-loading rifle was invented by Mr. Henry O. Peabody, of Boston, Mass., who was several years

in perfecting and completing this superior arm. In
its form, the Peabody is compact and graceful, and
its symmetry is nowhere marred by unseemly projec-
tions. This symmetry is preserved in the act of loading, as the whole movement of the breech-block is
performed within the stock, the end of the trigger-
guard falling but little more than an inch. In most
other breech-loaders the guard must describe a curve
of ninety degrees, and assume a position at a right
angle with the line of the barrel, while the breech-
block itself drops below the stock. No movement of
the barrel, or any other parts, except those immediately connected with the breech-block, is required
in the performance of any of its operations. The simplicity and ingenuity of the mechanism with which
these operations are accomplished are such as to pre-
clude the possibility of their being impeded by the
effect of friction, rust, or exposure to the influence of
dust, rain, or continued service. Some of the supe-
riorities of construction are: 1st, That the formation
of the breech-block, when the guard is drawn down,
is such as to form an inclined plane sloping toward
the breech of the barrel ; and the groove on its upper
surface, corresponding precisely with the bore of the
gun, facilitates the entrance of the cartridge, so that
it slides directly into its proper position without the
necessity even of looking to see that it is properly

inserted. 2d, The removal of the empty cartridge-shell is effected by the action of an elbow-lever, which throws it out with unerring certainty the instant the guard is lowered. This lever derives its power simply from the action of the breech-block itself, and can not become deranged, as it is not dependent upon any spring, and is of such strength as to render breakage or derangement from use or exposure simply impossible. 3d, The gun can not be discharged till the breech-block is in its proper position; and this breech-block is of such strength, and so firmly secured, as to insure its perfect safety, as has been proved by the severest tests. 4th, The rapidity of fire is equal, if not superior, to that of any other single loader. In a trial before the American Board of Officers at Spring-field, it was fired twenty times a minute, and out of sixty-five guns presented for examination, was the only one that endured all the trials, and the report recommended its adoption. In this trial it was fired with eighty grains of powder and five balls (two thousand two hundred and fifty grains of lead), a test which no other gun stood, three out of the four, to which the whole number was reduced at the conclusion of the trial, being shattered at the breech with a charge of eighty grains of powder and four balls, while the Peabody, with the additional four hundred and fifty grains of lead (the weight of each ball), re-

mained uninjured. The conclusion of the American
war prevented, however, any action upon the report
of the Board of Ordnance. The only difference of
construction between the Ballard and Peabody is that
in the latter the opening of the breech and the ejection of the exploded shell take place simultaneously.
The breech-block is a solid piece of steel, hollowed
out at the top to receive the cartridge. When the
lever is pulled down this block falls below the chamber, and exposes the breech ; the cartridge is then
inserted, the lever pulled back, and the breech closed.
And here is the only objectionable feature in the Peabody rifle. Unless the cartridge is inserted into the
chamber, flush up with the breech, there is great
danger of a premature discharge from the sudden
contact of the breech-block with the fulminate. As it
now stands, the utmost care is needed in loading the
piece. It seems to me that by giving the end of the
breech-block a slight incline the danger would be
removed ; for if even the cartridge was not shoved
home, instead of a sudden shock there would be a
gradual pressure which would force it into its proper
position. · The finish of the Peabody is not quite as
good as some other guns, but this is no defect, and
can be easily remedied.

The first figure of the illustration is a side view of
the breech part of the gun, with part of the breech-

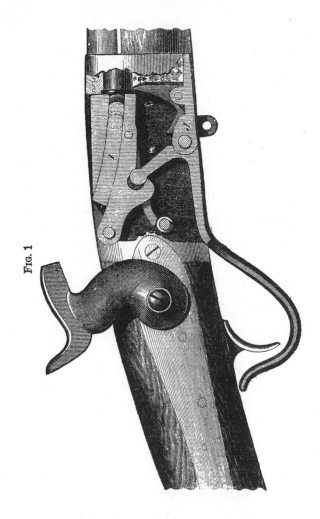

FIG. 1

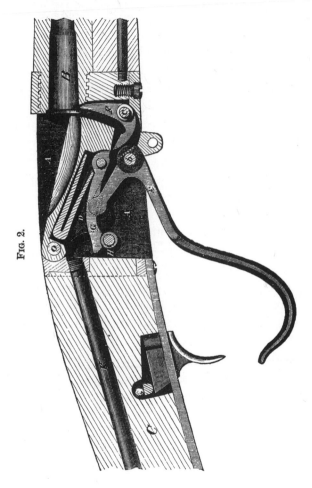

Fig. 2.

receiver, A, broken away to expose the breech-block D, and its operating mechanism to view in a position for firing. Fig. 2 is a central longitudinal section. The breech-block is pivoted at its rear end on a pin, *o*, which passes through it and the receiver ; and it has a concave recoil bearing in the back of the receiver. It opens the chamber of the barrel for loading by a downward movement, as shown in fig. 2. Its upper side is hollowed out to form a channel leading directly into the bore of the barrel when open. The movement of the breech-block is effected by the trigger-guard lever, E, which works on a pin, *b;* and its upper and shorter arm, which is directed toward the joint-pin, *o*, of the breech-block, terminates in a notch in the under side of the block, the end of the said arm being rounded to allow the necessary play. Under the breech-block, and partly contained within a mortise in the same, there is pivoted to it a brace, G, the rear end of which bears upon a roller, H, which is fitted to turn on a stationary pin inserted through the breech-receiver. A spring arranged within the mortise of the breech-receiver presses the brace down upon the roller. This combination of the brace, spring, and roller serves to securely fasten the breech-block and guard-lever when the arm is ready to be fired.

F is the cartridge-shell extractor, made in the form

of an elbow-lever, and pivoted to a pin, c, inserted through the breech-receiver. This is so operated upon by the forward end of the brace, when the breech opens, as to throw the discharged cartridge case entirely out of the gun. J is the portion of metal upon which pivots the trigger-guard, and between which and the opposite side of the metal framework of the breech-frame is pivoted the lever which extracts the empty cartridge shell. The firing of the cartridge, B, is effected by the hammer striking upon the rear end of the firing-pin, I (fig. 1), which slides in a groove in the right side of the breech-block, and the forward end of which is made with a beveled edge to strike upon one side of the head of the cartridge shell and explode the priming.

The Canadian Government having determined on arming the volunteers with breech-loaders of American manufacture, owing to the delay experienced in obtaining a supply of Enfield rifles converted to breech-loaders on the Snider principle, invited the various makers of the United States to submit patterns of their arms. After careful consideration of the merits of the various weapons submitted, they decided in favor of the Peabody as the best, it seeming to combine in itself, in the greatest degree, the essential requisites of simplicity of structure, accuracy and rapidity of fire, strength and general efficiency.

I attach two reports on the performance of this gun,—one at Montreal before the Inspector of Musketry of the British forces in America, and the other the report of the Royal Commission in Denmark :

Tests at Montreal, on the 24th August, 1866, under the supervision of Captain T. J. GRANT, Inspector of Musketry, by order of Lieut.-Gen. Sir JOHN MICHEL, commanding the forces in British North America.

TO TEST THE ACCURACY WITH CONTINUOUS FIRING.—For this purpose sixty rounds were fired collectively by myself and three non-commissioned officers of the Twenty-Fifth Regiment, at a target six feet square, at three hundred yards distance, aim being invariably taken on the same spot, and no allowance for wind, defective sighting, etc. There were but three misses, which I conceive to have been due to the firers. The gun was not cleaned during the trial.

TO TEST RAPIDITY OF FIRE COMBINED WITH ACCURACY.— In the trial I succeeded in firing nine shots, at a target six feet square, at one hundred yards distance, in one minute. All the shots hit the target ; the time was marked by Capt. Campbell, Thirtieth Regiment.

There was no hitch in the working of the gun during the trial, nor any perceptible falling off as regards accuracy ; and it possessed this decided advantage over the Spencer Repeating Rifle, which I had tried on a previous occasion, that there was no escape of gas from the breech.

(Signed),   THOS. J. GRANT, Captain,
Inspector of Musketry,
Superintending Officer.

To the Deputy Adjutant-General, etc., etc.,
      Montreal.

ROYAL DANISH LEGATION AND CONSULATE GENERAL,
New York, 15th October, 1866.

To the President of the Providence Tool Co., Providence, R. I. :

Sir,—His Danish Majesty's Government has instructed me to

communicate to you the report on the "Peabody Gun," made by the Royal Commission for examining and trying experiments with breech-loading arms.

REPORT.

The breech-loading system of the Peabody gun is simple and convenient, and under the whole firing its mechanism has acted very satisfactorily.

It was subjected to the following trials :

1. 100 shots from rest, distance 600 feet.
2. 75 quick shots, with and without rests, distance 400 feet.
3. Three days later ; 25 shots from rest, distance 600 feet.
4. 210 shots at target, distance 200 to 2,400 feet.

During these trials the gun was not cleaned. Incessant quick firing did not influence the hitting quality, and the mechanism continued to act perfectly to the last shot.

Twelve shots were fired in one minute.

No change was perceptible in the different trials ; good hitting shots were obtained at a distance of two thousand four hundred feet. The Commission, composed of the officers of the Royal Artillery, close their report thus :

"The Peabody gun has, on the whole, given a very satisfactory result, and must be considered the best single-shot breechloading weapon with which copper cartridges are used."

I have the honor to be

Your obedient servant,

(Signed), H. DOLLUER,

Charge d'Affaires *ad inter.*,

and Acting Consul General.

In consequence of the satisfactory nature of the above report, the Canadian Government gave an order for five thousand guns of this principle.

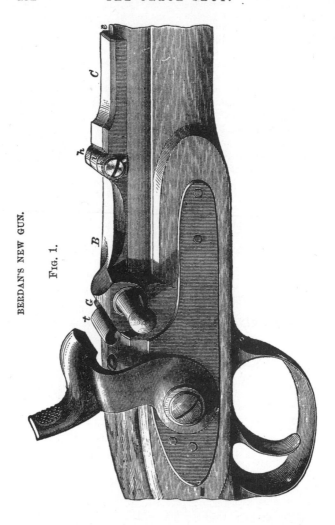

BERDAN'S NEW GUN.

FIG. 1.

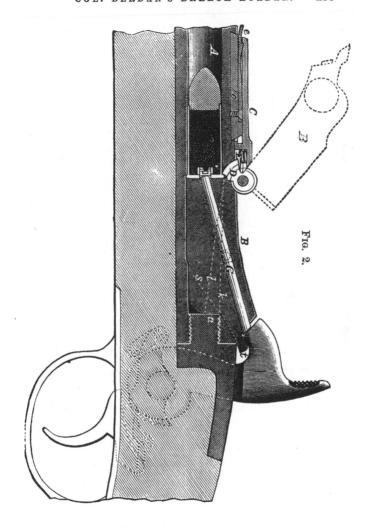

FIG. 2.

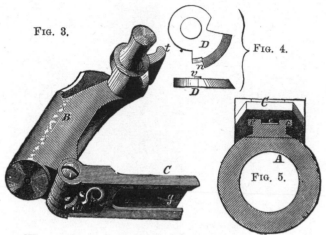

FIG. 3.   FIG. 4.   FIG. 5.

The next gun that I shall describe is

COL. BERDAN'S BREECH-LOADER.

This invention is for the conversion of muzzle-loaders into breech-loaders, and it is claimed by the inventor and his friends to be one of the best before the public. The manner in which the conversion is effected is as follows: About three inches of the upper part of the barrel in front of the breech-pin is cut away, leaving the breech-pin intact, so that it may form the recoil bearing for the breech. The breech is composed of two pieces of steel, one being in front of the other. The front piece constitutes the breech-piece proper, and the rear one a brace which sustains the breech-piece against the recoil in firing. The breech-piece is hinged to a band which is clamped around the barrel, and a brace is hinged to it. The rear end of the brace and the recoil bearing are so formed that the breech can not rise until the brace rises by a movement in the hinge. In opening the breech for loading, a knob on the right-hand side of the brace is pressed upward with the finger, thus relieving the brace from the recoil bearing, against which it was pressed by the force of the recoil. The brace is lifted up from the recoil bearing until a stop upon it comes in contact with a stop on the breech-piece, above the hinge. The breech-piece and brace are then moved together from their position, and thrown forward in the direction of the muzzle, thus exposing the chamber of the band. The firing-pin is made of two pieces which meet at the hinge joint, so that the pin does not prevent or interfere with the opening of the breech, which it would assuredly do were it constructed of one piece. To eject the exploded shell, there is a small spur upon the hinged part of the breech-piece. This catches hold of the end of the fulminate, and as soon as the breech-piece is thrown forward, the shell is thrown completely out. For the purpose of preventing the escape of gas into the breech-piece from the charge after it is fired, there is a projection upon the right-hand side of the brace, behind the knob, so arranged that the hammer must pass over it as it descends. This is an excellent arrangement, for, should the brace not be in its proper place, the head of the hammer slides over the projection, forcing the brace down, and effectually closing the breech. The description of Berdan's rifle, as given here, is taken from drawings published in the "American Artisan," and prepared under the personal supervision of Colonel Berdan, the inventor. As we stated before, the gun possesses considerable merit, and if the breech-piece could be so improved as to simplify it, and thus do away with a portion of its mechanical arrangement, the weapon would become more valuable.

Fig. 1 of the engraving represents a side view of the breech part of Colonel Berdan's new gun; fig. 2 is a central longitudinal section of the same; fig. 3 is a perspective view of the breech-block and its appurtenances; fig. 4 represents a side view and an edge view of the cartridge-shell ejector; and fig. 5 is a transverse section of the barrel and the strap which attaches the breech-block thereto.

Colonel Berdan has contrived a number of different systems of converting the Springfield musket into a breech-loader. At the late trial of arms at Washington, no less than four modifications of his plan were tested, and were found to work so well that the report of the Board was in favor of the Berdan system, though they desired that some slight alteration should be made in it. I shall allude more fully to this report at the conclusion of this chapter.

It is not correct, however, as stated in the "American Artisan," that "it showed itself so superior to the Snider gun, that it is probable that the order for the conversion of one hundred thousand Enfields on the Snider plan, which was given before the arrival of Col. Berdan's agent, would never have been given." The patent for the conversion of the Enfield on the Snider principle is the property of the British Government, for which they paid seventy-five thousand dollars. And instead of giving an order for converting one hundred thousand, they have converted in the Government workshops nearly four hundred thousand, and are satisfied that they have got a good arm for the present. Col. Berdan has modified certain inventors' principles, and produced a gun that has obtained the recommendation of a board appointed to inquire into these things ; let him and his friends rest satisfied.*

---

* Since the above was written, Col. Berdan has brought out still another breech-loader, differing in many important particulars from the one above described, and which I will endeavor to notice in an addendum.

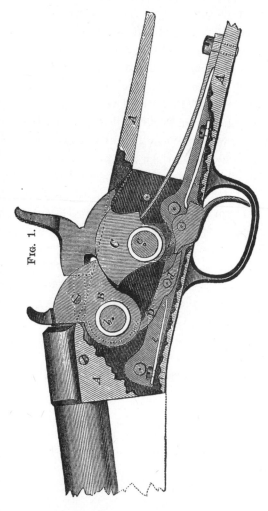

REMINGTON'S IMPROVED BREECH-LOADER.

FIG. 1.

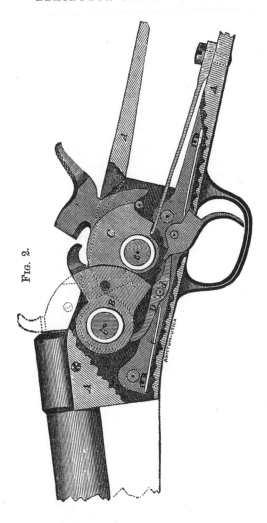

FIG. 2.

REMINGTON'S BREECH-LOADER,

having claimed a great deal of attention both in this country and on the continent, where it has been, in a measure, adopted by Austria, I shall present a description of it. It is so called from being manufactured by the Messrs. Remington & Sons at Ilion, N. Y. It is made under the patents of Leonard Seiger and Joseph Rider. It can load at half or full-cock, and can be fired with great rapidity, as is proved by Mr. Kerr having fired it forty-seven times in three minutes, at the great rifle match at Wimbledon in July, 1866. As an instance of its strength, it may be stated that it has been fired with a charge of one hundred and twenty grains of rifle powder and eighteen hundred grains of lead without any injury to the arm. It stood all the tests of putting it in water, rolling in sand, etc., to which the arms were subjected by the Board of Army Officers that recently sat at Washington. The breech-piece and the lock, excepting the mainspring, can be taken apart and " assembled " twice in a minute.

" The peculiarity of this gun is the breech-piece, which has a swinging movement on a pivot below the barrel, opening the chamber for loading by a movement of its face backward and downward from the barrel. The great merit of this gun is its extreme simplicity.

" Fig. 1 is a side view of the breech part of the gun with one side of the breech-receiver, A, broken away to expose to view the breech and lock, which are shown in the position they occupy at the time of firing. Fig. 2 is a view similar to fig. 1, except that it represents the parts in position for loading. The breech-piece, B, is fitted snugly to a mortise in the receiver, A, which attaches the barrel to the stock, and the pivot, *b*, upon which it swings, is inserted through the breech-receiver. The breech-piece is braced against the recoil at the time of firing by means of the tumbler, C, of the hammer, which is made thick enough to fill the mortise provided in the receiver for the breech-piece. As the pin, *c*, on which this tumbler and the hammer swing, and which is inserted through the receiver, forms the recoil bearing, it is made very strong, seven-sixteenths of an inch in diameter. The breech-piece and tumbler, C, are so formed that when the breech piece is closed the rounded upper portion of the tumbler works in a concavity in the back of the breech-piece, and when the hammer is drawn back to half-cock or full-cock the rounded part of the breech-piece works in a concavity in the front of the tumbler. This mode of matching the breech-piece and tumbler prevents the possibility of the hammer falling until the breech-piece is perfectly closed, and so obviates the possibility of premature explosion of the charge. The hammer strikes upon a firing-pin—shown in dotted outline —working through the breech-piece. The extractor by which the discharged cartridge shells are drawn out from the chamber of the barrel works between the receiver and the breech-piece, and is operated by the opening movement of the latter. The breech-piece is operated by applying the thumb of the right hand to a comb like that of a hammer provided on its upper part. This allows the trigger-guard to be made a fixture.

" To prevent the trigger from being drawn when the breech-piece, B, is open, there is arranged under the breech-piece and tumbler, C, a small lever, D, called the ' trigger-lever,' which works on a pivot, *d*, and to the front part of which there is applied a spring, *e*, which presses it upward against the hub of the breech-receiver. The rear end of this lever is situated under the sere or point of the trigger, and when the breech-piece is open its hub holds the said lever in such a position that the

sere can not be drawn out of the notch of the hammer, but
when the breech-piece is closed the front end of the said lever
slips into a groove, shown in dotted lines, provided in the hub,
and so permits the trigger to be drawn. The spring, e, by
pressing the front end of the trigger-lever against the inclined
entrance of the said groove, effects the perfect closing of the
breech, should this fail to be quite accomplished by the forward
movement of the breech-piece effected by the application of the
thumb to the comb. Besides thus insuring the perfect closing
of the breech-piece, the lever, D, also holds the breech closed
until the tumbler of the hammer is in place to lock it; and it
also prevents the wearing off of the front corner of the rounded
portion of the tumbler, and rear corner of the rounded portion
of the breech-piece, as these pass each other, which would
otherwise take place in case of the hammer being liberated
from the trigger before the breech-piece was quite closed."

Many objections have been urged against the Remington rifle, the principal of which was the liability
of the breech-block to jam. To properly understand
this objection, it will be necessary to describe more
minutely the working of the breech-block, which
works backward and forward with the hammer, thus
necessitating a full cocking of the gun before the
piece can be loaded. The breech-block is a solid
piece of steel, pierced by a firing line and acting in
conjunction with a tumbler attached to the hammer.
At the lower part of the chamber of the barrel is a
spur for ejecting the exploded shell, which is connected with the breech-block by a spring. The mode
of operation is as follows: The hammer is first cocked
to its fullest extent, then the breech-block is pulled

backward to the hammer, which catches it by a nip, and thus keeps the breech open. On the cartridge being inserted, the block is pushed forward, and the breech closed. Nothing then remains but to fire the piece. It is objected that this system will not work, and one writer, in speaking of this arm, says :

" The defects in the gun are these : In the first place, unless the breech-block is kept thoroughly well oiled, the greatest difficulty is experienced in pulling it backward with the fingers. Now, as in active service soldiers have no time to take out the block and ' grease ' it every day, it will be seen that a great delay in loading must ensue. In the next place, the spur or shell ejector is entirely too small, and will not eject the shell unless it (the shell) is also thoroughly well greased. In the presence of the writer one of these guns was operated with, and the result was that even with the shell well greased the spur failed to eject it oftener than once in five times. A great deal of trouble was experienced in forcing back the breech-block, in consequence of the inability of the spur to eject the shell. When the block was at last forced back, it was found that the spur had merely cut through the metal without ejecting the shell. We are thus minute in mentioning the defects of the Remington gun because of the claim for superiority made by the inventor. How the defects can be remedied it would be difficult to explain. The breech-block is really the stumbling-block. Without a shell in the chamber, it is pulled back with comparative ease ; but with the exploded shell resisting the forward action of the spur, it requires a finger of uncommon strength to operate it. So far as the ' greasing ' of the cartridges is concerned, the statement that such greasing is a necessity only renders the gun more objectionable. In nearly all of the other breech-loaders now prominently before the public, it is immaterial whether the metallic cases of the cartridges are well greased or not, the spurs possessing sufficient

10

width and bottom to eject the exploded shells entirely from the chamber of the barrel. It is stated that the Austrian Government has adopted this weapon; but the statement has not been authenticated. Austria has not yet adopted any particular breech-loading fire-arm for her army."

There was a great deal of force in this objection, and likewise in the opposition that was shown to this gun on account of the weakness of the breech-piece. The inventors set themselves to work to remedy these defects, and so successful have they been that they have now produced an arm that is apparently perfect in its construction, and most probably destined to play a great part in future warfare. Under this new condition, the Remington was submitted to the Board of Officers that assembled at Albany early in 1867, in accordance with instructions from the State Legislature to report upon the "best breech-loading arm." It was highly approved of, and is spoken of in the following terms by the same writer who penned the foregoing paragraph condemning it:

"This weapon (the Remington Improved) is essentially different from, and is in every respect superior to, the breech-loading rifle of the same name described by me some months ago, and on which it is an improvement. Instead of the double ears which formed the lever of the breech-block, it (the lever) is opened and shut by means of a single ear on the right side of the ear of the breech. The opening of the breech causes the empty cartridge shell to be rapidly ejected from the barrel, and, unlike that of its predecessor, the hammer has no connection with the breech-pin. Altogether this weapon possesses many excellent characteristics, and, should the State decide upon making new guns instead of altering old ones, must prove a formidable competitor of the other breech-loaders. The gun which was tested had been fired over one thousand times before, often at the rate of eighteen shots per minute, and without the slightest injury to any part of its mechanism. It is elegantly finished, is very light, and has immense strength. Its construction is very simple, the breech-block being composed of only three pieces, which can be pulled to pieces and put together again in a few seconds."

This is the rifle that is now known as the "Remington Improved Breech-loading Rifle." As a matter of interest, I subjoin an account of a series of trials had at Vienna (Austria), in October last, before the Archduke Wilhelm, Field Marshal; Count Ryland, President of the Royal Commission appointed to ascertain the "best form of breech-loaders" with a view to choosing one for the army :

The trials on the Remington gun marked No. 1 were chiefly made with the object of testing the breech-closing arrangements, in order to ascertain its fitness for military purposes, and also to determine its efficiency and durability when exposed to the vicissitudes of war. The question of accuracy in firing was not specially attended to at this trial, as other experiments on this subject are now being conducted apart from those on the breech-closing arrangements. In accordance with the above-mentioned object a series of experiments in firing were undertaken with the Remington gun on several days. Accounts of these experiments follow in the order they were made :

First Experiment on the 20th September, 1866.—The commission had the gun first taken to pieces, and then examined the parts composing the breech-closing arrangements and the lock, and also the mechanism of the breech-closing. It was then determined to fire from the gun—the simplicity of which in its arrangements and mode of use is particularly remarkable—first, sixty shots with the cartridge containing the greatest amount of gunpowder, *i.e.*, seventy-five grains English ; then forty shots with cartridges containing sixty grains of gunpowder each, at a target three hundred paces distant ; and also forty shots, quick firing, with sixty-grain cartridges. Not the slightest interruption occurred during these one hundred and forty shots ; the breech-closing arrangements worked perfectly well ; the target firing confirmed the accurate firing of the gun ; and in quick firing from the shoulder thirteen shots per minute were made. In the examination of the gun when taken to pieces after this firing, no fouling, charge, or damage could be detected in the breech-closing arrangements. The gun was finally put together again without cleaning the breech-closing arrangements, and laid aside for further experiments.

Second Experiment on the 21st September, 1866.—The firing to test the durability of the breech-piece was continued as follows :

(*a*). *With cartridges containing sixty grains gunpowder each,* eighty shots were fired continuously. One of the cartridges split up all along, without, however, in any way hindering the opening of the breech or fouling the breech-pieces. After cooling the barrel by pouring cold water through it, thirty shots more were fired, and after these—

(*b*). *With cartridges containing forty-five grains gunpowder each,* the following five series of continuous firing were made : Forty-eight shots, forty-two shots, eighty-four shots, thirty shots, one hundred shots,—altogether three hundred and four shots, during which there was no interruption. The cooling of the barrel after each series of shots was accelerated by pouring water through ; and finally, after four hundred and fourteen shots had been fired on this day, water was poured over the gun and the breech-closing arrangements, and the gun then laid aside in this condition, so that at the next trial the amount of rusting might be ascertained, and the influence this would have upon the breech-closing.

Third Experiment on the 22*d September*, 1866.—The gun which had been wetted with water on the previous day and laid aside in that state was taken to pieces and examined. It then appeared that all the parts composing the breech-closing arrangements and the lock were much attacked by rust, but notwithstanding this the proper work of the lock was not prevented. The gun was then put together without any cleaning of the breech-pieces, and subjected to further experiments in firing, so as to obtain convincing proofs as to whether the rusting of the breech-closing arrangements and lock would not disturb or injure their proper working. For this purpose there were fired under the same conditions as in the former experiment, and with cartridges containing forty-five grains of gunpowder each, three hundred and forty shots in seven series of forty-two shots each, and one series of forty-six shots. During this firing two cartridges missed fire, but exploded properly on being shifted in the barrel; forty shots were also made with the hand free and without taking aim, for which three minutes thirteen seconds were required. During all this firing the breech-closing arrangements worked perfectly well, and when the breech-pieces and lock were finally examined there was no perceptible change. Thus up to the present, the Remington gun had fired altogether sixty shots with cartridges containing seventy-five grains gunpowder, one hundred and ninety with sixty-grain cartridges, and six hundred and eighty-six with forty-five grain cartridges,—altogether nine hundred and thirty-six shots,—without any cleansing of either the barrel or the breech-closing arrangements. The commission now determined to have this cleansing performed, with a view of continuing the experimental firing on the arrival of a fresh quantity of cartridges, and of ascertaining whether the removal of the rust would cause any deterioration in the strength of the breech-closing arrangements and their perfect working order. It was also determined to further test the Remington gun by firing altogether two thousand shots, and employing for this first all the sixty-grain cartridges which were to be supplied to the commission for the experiments.

Fourth Experiment on the 27th September, 1866.—On this day three hundred and sixty-one shots were made with sixty-grain cartridges in the following series: Thirty-nine shots; one cartridge missed fire, but on shifting it in the breech and firing again, it exploded properly. Forty shots, forty shots, and one hundred and twenty shots, continuously and without interruption, the barrel being cooled after each series. Six shots fired to estimate the amount of recoil in a machine; the recoil was found to average forty-eight pounds (German). Thirty-two shots; quick firing, not from the shoulder, and by an expert; this took one minute fifty-two seconds, which is equal to seventeen shots per minute. Thirty-four shots continuously from a rest, and after the opened breech-closing arrangements had been strewed with road dust. Finally, fifty shots continuously, during which there was no interruption. The gun was then again strewed over with dust, and laid aside exposed to the damp night air.

Fifth Experiment on the 28th September, 1866.—The gun was first examined, when it was found that the lock did not permit of the hammer being raised to full cock; however, on taking the gun to pieces, it was found that the obstruction was caused by the presence of some grains of sand between the spring of the lock and the adjoining breech-piece. After removing this sand and putting the lock together, it was found to be in perfect working order, although still uncleaned. The testing of the breech-closing arrangements was then continued as follows:

(*a*). *With cartridges holding sixty grains gunpowder each,* forty shots were fired against a target about three hundred paces distant, in order to compare the present accuracy in firing with the results obtained in the first experiments. No difference was found in the results of the target shooting. Then ten shots were fired at a target six hundred paces distant, and with good accuracy; and one hundred shots in two series of fifty shots each, against boards (Traver's) to determine the power of penetration of the shot.

(*b*). *With cartridges containing forty-five grains gunpowder each.*—There were fired six series,—one of forty-nine shots, four of forty-two shots, and one of eighty-four shots; altogether, three hundred and one shots. One cartridge missed fire, but on shifting it in the breech and firing again it exploded properly. During all the four hundred and fifty-one shots fired on this day there was no interruption. The gun was laid aside uncleaned.

Sixth Experiment on 29*th September.*—On examining the gun it was found that the breech-closing arrangements were unchanged, although covered with dust and a little powder smoke, and the gun could be manipulated as well as before. For the further testing of the gun the following concluding series of firing with forty-five grain cartridges were made: First, four series of forty-two shots, each continuous, during which firing ten cartridges were employed which had been lying for a quarter of an hour in water; then forty-two shots were fired continuously, eight of which were directed against a wooden chest filled with cartridges, in which the latter were placed in various positions; some with their lower ends (the percussion ends) facing the spot from whence the shots came; others with the ball end toward it; others, again, with their sides in that direction. Of these shots, fired from a distance of one hundred and fifty paces, the eighth hit the chest and passed through the side. Among two hundred and sixty cartridges contained in the chest, partly in pasteboard boxes, and partly distributed between the latter, five exploded and blew off the top of the chest, which was fastened on with only two nails; ten of the rest of the cartridges had their exterior cases distorted and rendered incapable of fitting into the barrel; twenty-six cartridges were blackened by the smoke, and all the rest remained intact. After this there were fired forty-two shots continuously to make up the number of shots fired to two thousand; and, finally, seven shots with cartridges purposely filed thin at the rim, and split in different parts, in order to cause the cartridges to burst, and ascertain the effect of this upon the breech. During this experiment the gun was placed in a safety apparatus. Five of the cartridges prepared in this manner were split up partly at the bottom, and there was, in consequence, a slight flash of flame at each side of the breech, rather like what occurs when a cap splits on the touchhole of an ordinary gun. The breech-closing arrangements did not undergo any change in consequence, and both the breech and the hammer preserved their normal position. On subsequently taking to pieces and examining the gun, it was found that the breech-loading arrangements and lock were not perceptibly worn, that the breech closed as firmly as ever, and that a little powder-smoke was only deposited on the surfaces of the lock-case and on the spring of the lock, which, however, would not have hindered the continued use of the gun. The two hundred and fifty-nine shots made on the sixth day of experiment without any interruption concluded the testing of the Remington gun, so that altogether there were fired, with good effect, sixty shots with cartridges containing seventy-five grains gunpowder each ; seven hundred and one shots with sixty-grain cartridges ; and twelve hundred and forty-six shots with forty-five grain cartridges, making altogether two thousand and seven shots.

(Signed), {
ARCHDUKE WILHELM,
    Field-Marshal Lieutenant.
COUNT ARTHUR BYLAND,
    President of the Royal Commission.
MAJOR F. KREUTZ.
}

VIENNA, Oct. 3, 1866.

This must be considered satisfactory, and it is a test that should certainly satisfy any reasonable man of the great value of this arm. I have dwelt at great length on this arm, as I consider that it and the Peabody and Berdan are the best American single breech-loaders for military purposes.

The Messrs. Remington have reason to be proud of the high character their gun maintains. The American Government have purchased a very large number; the factory is driven to the utmost to supply an order of twenty thousand for Denmark; Norway and Sweden have adopted it, and doubtless France will be glad to have it again submitted, since the vaunted "Chassepôt" has turned out a failure.   I may appropriately wind up this notice of this weapon in the words of a very competent English journalist who writes thus:

" We were shown yesterday a handsome specimen of the new or Improved Remington American Breech-loading Rifle,—a weapon apparently perfect in its construction, and most probably destined to play a great part in future warfare. As a military breech-loader, so far as our judgment goes, it is unequaled. Whether we consider it as an efficient fire-arm, judging it solely by its likelihood to stand the tear and wear of campaigning, and its comparative safety from derangement of parts by the enemy's shot, we can come to but one conclusion,—that it is the most remarkable military breech-loader the world has yet seen. It can be made of any reasonable caliber, and to take any necessary charge of gunpowder, fulfilling in these great essentials two most desirable requirements. Its simplicity of mechanism is so great that Mr. Remington's agent, in our presence, took separate and put together (or, to use his phrase, ' assembled ') the lock in less than a minute. The peculiar feature of novelty in this invention consists in the application of a swinging breech-piece, pierced by a firing-pin, to a barrel bored ' through and through,' and acting in combination with a tumbler attached to the hammer, so that the curved edges of the tumbler and the breech-piece will correspond and interlock to brace against the recoil. It has been advanced by some that the movable breech-piece might be driven open by the recoil of the cartridge. This in the new Remington is shown to be a mechanical impossibility, and has been practically tested by filling the barrel to the muzzle with clay, in front of one hundred and twenty grains of the quickest electric gunpowder, bulging out the steel barrel at the point where the powder and clay met, but not dislodging the breech-piece. To handle the breech-piece and hammer is like handling solid iron weights, indestructible by any common usage , and the whole of the parts are put together so as to protect what little there is to injure in the most complete attainable manner. For rapidity of firing the Remington can not be excelled. It was fired at the last Wimbledon meeting fifty-one times in three minutes."

F. WESSON'S BREECH-LOADER.

This gun is constructed on different principles from any of those I have previously enumerated, in having a solid breech, and the barrel tilting up to receive the cartridge.

The inventor of this gun, Franklin Wesson, who is noted as a rifle-maker, and of whose muzzle-loading rifle I have spoken in another place, was the first to manufacture a breech-loader for using the fixed ammunition. It at once attained a great degree of popularity, and has always retained it. I am not aware of its being used to any extent as a military arm, its chief use being for sporting purposes, and for which it is admirably adapted. I used one in my deer-hunting expeditions last fall, and wish no better; its simplicity, portability, and accuracy strongly recommending it to the sportsman. It is so well known

WESSON'S BREECH-LOADER,

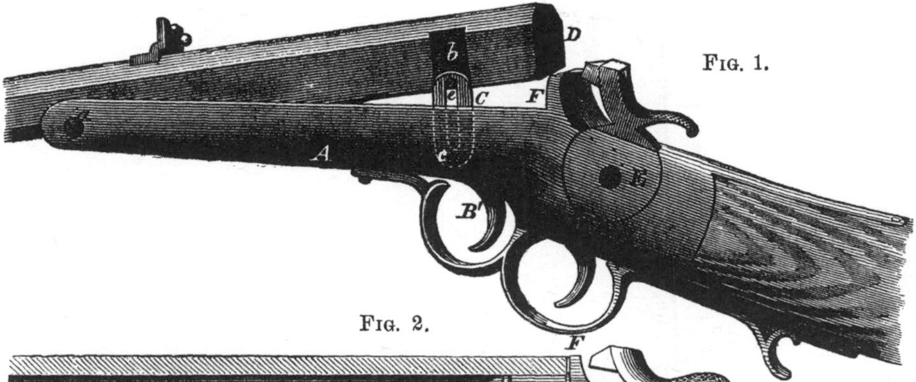

Fig. 1 is a perspective view of the left-hand side, showing the barrel in position for loading.
Fig. 2 is a longitudinal section, showing the piece loaded and half-cocked.

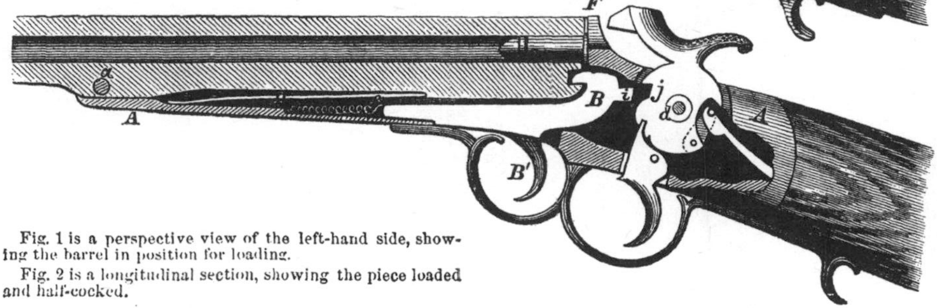

FIG. 2.

FIG. 1.

Fig. 3.

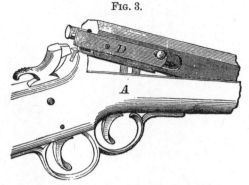

Fig. 3 is a perspective view of the right-hand side, showing
the cartridge-shell extractor.

that a description seems almost unnecessary; yet a
few explanatory remarks of the cut may be interesting.
The barrel works on a pivot at *a*, and is thrown up by
a small trigger, B, to receive the cartridge; it is prevented rising too much by a link, C, which catches on
a small pin, *e*. This link works in a groove cut in the
side of the barrel. The hammer, which can be taken
out by removing the plate, E, strikes the cartridge
through a small nick cut in the breech, F. The shell
is extracted by a slide, on the right-hand side of the
barrel, working in a groove. It is worked by a small
knob, and after performing the operation is returned
to its place by a spiral spring.

Mr. Wesson, the inventor, still continues the manufacture of this gun at Worcester, Mass. He claims to

be able to fire as rapidly as any breech-loader yet invented, and faster than any repeater for fifty shots. In a trial at St. Louis, Mo., for a stand of colors, the Wesson distanced all competitors; out of one hundred shots, fired at a target of the size of a man, fifty-six hit; and again, at Kentville, Mass., out of twenty shots, all were hits, while none of the others made more than thirteen.

COCHRAN'S BREECH-LOADER.

This weapon does not rank among the first of American inventions, but it contains merits which are peculiarly its own. The housing is light, but strong, and into this the barrel is screwed. The breech-block, having a rolling bearing at its rear end, is fitted to the housing, with a pin inserted into the bearing for the purpose of keeping the breech-block in its proper place. The front of the breech-block against which the cartridge rests, when the breech is closed, is a spherical convex, and is so positioned with the barrel that the pressure of the shell aids in keeping it firmly locked. The operating lever of the breech-block forms the trigger-guard, and is somewhat similar in appearance to the Ballard rifle. There is one feature in it, however, which no other breech-loader's lever possesses. The end of the lever, instead of resting near

or on the stock, is turned up and enters the stock, so
that when the breech is open there is no possible
chance of its lever catching against any thing. The
piece in the stock is elastic and has a kind of hook at
the top, which catches hold of a notch (in the stock)
and serves either to keep the breech effectually locked,
or to prevent the lever from coming out of the stock
entirely when the breech is opened. The lever being
pulled down, the breech-block is forced upward by
the action of the hinged end of the lever against the
rear portion of the block. The breech is thus exposed
and the cartridge is inserted into the barrel, under
the breech-block, or if not under, the gun must be
turned over. This is a very awkward manner of
loading, and, notwithstanding its originality, is the
most objectionable feature of the gun. It is true that,
to facilitate loading, the under part of the breech-
block is made hollow, but this only weakens the
block, while it does not, to any great extent, facilitate
loading. It is urged by the inventor that one of the
advantages arising from this method of loading is,
that, should there be a premature discharge, the powder will escape downward, and not upward, so as to
injure the face. This is very doubtful, inasmuch as
that all explosions have an upward tendency, and the
result of a premature discharge of the cartridge would
be the blowing out of the breech-piece directly toward

the face of the soldier.   The shell-ejector is, perhaps, the best feature in the gun, although it is not equal to the ejector of the Peabody rifle.   It consists of a straight piece which slides on a guide formed between the lower portion of the barrel and the breech-receiver.   A rod of steel connects it with the operating lever, which is contained in the breech-receiver, to the right of the block.   On the lever or trigger-guard being pulled down, the rod is pushed backward, carrying with it the ejector, and consequently the exploded shell.   On the lever being liberated the spring at the end of the ejecting rod straightens itself, throwing the ejector forward and drawing the lever back to its proper place.   By means of a notch under the breech-receiver the ejector can be operated with the finger and independently of the lever; but as this would only increase the time required for firing, it will seldom be used.   Should the connection with the lever become destroyed, it would then be of use, but not otherwise.   As stated before, the Cochran rifle possesses merits, but as a military arm it can scarcely become a favorite.   The difficulty, or rather discomfort, of loading from beneath the breech-block is a most serious objection.

I have never seen this gun, but should not imagine it was one that would ever become popular, though as manufactured by Daw, the eminent London gunsmith, it has attracted considerable attention in England. The "Land and Water," in its account of a trial at Beaufort House, under the auspices of Lord Ranclagh, claims it to be the best in use. Some modifications have been made from the description above, and the central-fire has been substituted for the rim-fire cartridge.

POULTENEY BREECH-LOADING MUSKET.

This is an arm that has only recently been brought forward, and as no public trial has been had of it, as far as I am aware, no opinion can be formed of its merits, though its advocates claim great excellence for it. The following description of it will doubtless prove interesting. It is taken from an article on "Breech-loading Arms," published in the "New York Herald" some time since:

"Through the kindness of Colonel S. Crispin, the efficient Ordnance Officer of this State, we are enabled to furnish a description of the above-named weapon. It is of recent invention, and although not yet known to the public at large, promises to become one of the most popular fire-arms in the United States. While the gun is made on the principle of rotation, it is almost devoid of mechanical work. The breech-block consists of a solid piece of steel, connected with the lever, which forms the trigger-guard, and swinging on an axis. Attached to the lever is the only spring about the gun, and it is merely the lock that keeps the breech-block properly closed up against the chamber of the barrel. Attached to the block is a spur, which ejects the exploded shell entirely from the breech simultaneously with the pulling down of the lever. The block, as stated before, swings upon an axis, but instead of falling downward when the lever is pulled down, it moves backward, thus exposing the breech. This system of operation is very superior, for should the shell not be pushed into the breech sufficiently, as soon as the lever is pulled back the face of the block comes in contact with the cover of the cartridge and shoves it home, without the slightest danger of a premature discharge. Another source of safety in the Poulteney rifle is that by the opening of the breech the hammer is half-cocked, thus preventing an accident. When fired, the hammer strikes against a pin which runs through the block, and the blow is transmitted to the fulminate. The gun is light, but immensely strong, and is well finished. The following is the mode of operating it : First motion, pulling down the lever, and by so doing expose the breech and eject the cartridge ; second, inserting a fresh cartridge ; third, pulling back the lever, and effectually closing the breech ; fourth, cocking the hammer ; fifth, firing. The only defect in this gun is that the spur or shell-ejector is not quite wide enough to insure a positive certainty of ejection, should the metal of the shell be of inferior quality."

I have seen it stated that the average number of shots that can be discharged from this arm is sixteen. I understand that the cartridge is made of India-rubber, which I should esteem very objectionable. But I will not discuss the merits of this gun, as I am not particularly acquainted with its merits or defects, and it has not as yet gained any considerable notoriety. The references to it in the report of the Washington Board are so meager that one is quite unable to arrive at any conclusion respecting it.

11

SMITH'S CARBINE.

This weapon has been largely used in the United States Cavalry service, and there is a likelihood that it will be permanently adopted for that branch of the army. The carbine is composed of two parts, one being the barrel, and the other the stock, with the lock attached. These are secured by an axis of rotation, or hinge, with a locking spring of great strength on the top of the barrel, and a catch in the rear of the hammer to retain it in its proper position. Attached to the axis of rotation is the spur, which is under the chamber of the breech, so that as soon as the barrel is thrown forward the shell is ejected. The method of operation is as follows : The barrel of the carbine is thrown upon the left arm, near to the axis of rotation, and the catch in the rear of the hammer being pressed down with the finger, the locking spring is released, and the barrel falls downward, and thus exposes the breech. A slight motion of the right hand on the stock brings the barrel and it (the stock) on a level, and the locking spring is instantly fastened to the catch. All that then remains is to cock and fire the piece. The Smith carbine is very simple in construction and possesses considerable strength. The great merit it undoubtedly has, is the ease with which it can be loaded and fired. Any ordinarily drilled soldier can, at a full gallop, load and fire it six or eight times per minute, and still guide his horse with the left hand. Although as a cavalry arm it may answer well, it is very doubtful if it would be effective for infantry. The method of loading, which would expedite the cavalryman, is very likely to delay the infantry soldier.

At the test in Washington in 1866, it does not appear to have given satisfaction, for I find that it was one of those that was set "aside" by the Board on the twenty-sixth day, under the following resolution : " That all arms *not considered suitable for further trial* be set aside."

THE "NATIONAL" BREECH–LOADING RIFLE

is constructed on the sliding-block system, and is made as follows : In the rear of the breech-block and below it is a recoil bearer, composed of iron, in the shape of a three-sided parallelogram. In front of this and above it is a solid breech-block attached to the lever. On both sides of the lower portion of the front of the block is a spur which enters a small cavity on either side of the chamber of the barrel, and these spurs eject the shell completely from the breech when the lever is pulled down. The lever forms the trigger-guard, and is secured in its place

FIG. 1.

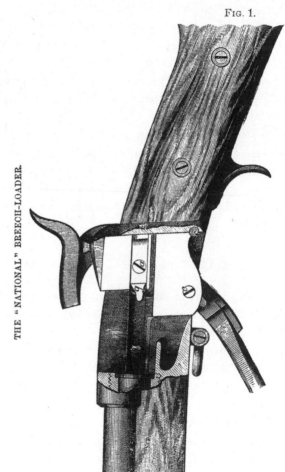

THE "NATIONAL" BREECH-LOADER.

Fig. 1 shows the gun ready to receive the cartridge, which is dropped into the receiver in front of the breech-block.

FIG. 2.

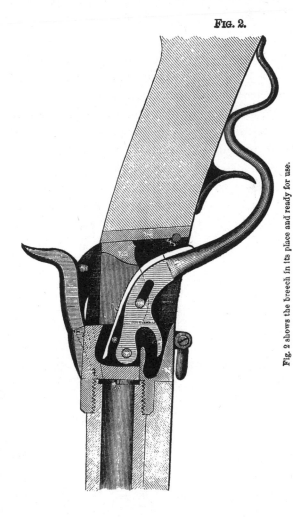

Fig. 2 shows the breech in its place and ready for use.

by a spring attached to its fore-part, which enters the stock, and rests under the breech-block. The lock is contained in a solid chamber, and has no connection with the breech-block, as in many others of recent invention. Through the upper portion of the breech-block is a pin upon which the hammer strikes, and which transmits the blow to the fulminate of the metallic cartridge. The manner of operating the rifle is as follows: The lever being pulled down, the recoil-bearer falls sufficiently low to permit the breech-block to slide over it, and the shell is rapidly ejected. As the breech-block slides backward the hammer is forced to a half-cock by the action, thus insuring absolute safety in loading. The breech being now open, the cartridge is dropped into the open space between the chamber of the barrel and the block; the lever is pulled back, and the face of the block pressing against the rim of the cartridge, forces it into the barrel. The gun is then fully cocked and fired. The National rifle is very simple in its construction, and its principal merits are that it has no dependence on springs, levers, fulcrums, nor circular bearings for resisting the discharge. The resistance is obtained by perfectly square, solid blocks, which move at right angles. Again, there is not the slightest danger of a premature discharge, so well arranged is the breech-block in the chamber. The weapon is light, but possesses immense strength. Charges, consisting of one hundred grains of powder and eighteen hundred forty-eight grains of lead, have been fired from the shoulder with but little or no recoil. As a military arm—and it is only intended for such—the National rifle must eventually hold a high position. It has been fired with ease sixteen times in a minute.

This rifle doubtless presents many advantages, but considerable modifications must take place ere it becomes fit for a *military* arm. At the tests in Washington, already alluded to, it was found that after it had been sprinkled with fine dust that it did not work freely. In the words of the report, "it was disabled by the test until the dust was removed, when it again worked well." Again, a few days later, when the arms had been sprinkled with water and laid away to rust for three days, it worked very imperfectly, though firing easily. In both these tests the Peabody, Remington, Spencer, and some others operated most satisfactorily. It performed better at the State trial at Albany, giving good results as to precision and rapidity. It also showed great penetration : one hundred shots were fired out of it in seven minutes forty-five seconds. On the whole, it worked infinitely better than when tried at Washington. This principle can not be applied to the conversion of muzzle-loaders.

THE LAIDLEY CARBINE.

This breech-loader is the invention of an officer of the United States army, and is of recent date. It is made on the same principle as the Remington gun, the only difference being that the breech-block and the hammer are pulled back together, whereas in the Remington they are pulled back separately. Another slight difference is in the locking of the hammer after it is cocked. This is done by a catch at the side of the stock, instead of by the breech-block, as in the other mentioned arm. It does not appear, from the description given, that the Laidley is near as good an arm as the Remington, from which it was copied; it has all the original defects of that arm; viz., that the distance from the axis of rotation to the finger, ears, or top of the breech-block are not long enough, and the difficulty of opening the breech, when the exploded shell is resisting the action of the block, remains the same. These defects, as previously stated, have been completely overcome in the "Improved Remington." I have seen it stated that the Austrian government have given the Colt Manufacturing Company an order for one hundred thousand of these guns, but I rather doubt the statement, as they are manufacturing breech-loaders in their own armories on an entirely different principle.

THE HENRY RIFLE (REPEATER).

A great deal of prominence was given to this gun some time ago, and every exertion was made to puff it into notice. True, it enjoyed a certain degree of popularity, from the fact that seventeen shots could be fired from it without re-loading, and this, no doubt, was very fascinating, but the most cursory examination shows that it is utterly unfit for either military or sporting purposes. The mechanism is altogether too delicate, and if once out of order,— and the great length of the spiral spring renders it, in my judgment, peculiarly liable to accident,— you are left with a very ordinary rifle. It is constructed on the same principle as the Spencer. The magazine is composed of a tube running under the barrel from the breech to within five inches of the muzzle, and is partially open along its entire length at the bottom. At the top of this magazine and up to the muzzle is a tube which moves on hinges to one side, exposing the chamber of the magazine, so as to admit the cartridges. This tube contains a follower, which is pressed forward by a spiral spring, thus forcing a cartridge into the breech as fast as

the lever is pulled down.   On entering the breech
the cartridge is forced into the barrel by an upward
movement of the main-spring.   The shell is ejected
by a spring catch, which seizes it by the rim and
ejects it, room being left in the barrel for it to rise
over the rim.

At the trial in Washington (Sept. 1866), its performance was very unsatisfactory, it failing in nearly
every instance, showing clearly that the objection
above taken is well founded.   I have seen very high
testimonials in favor of this arm, and one man in the
West (St. Louis), in his enthusiastic admiration for it,
goes so far as to say, "I will take the Henry rifle and
shoot against any living man at one thousand yards
with any other gun, and give him one hundred yards,
if his gun was made in Europe."   This is sheer "bun-
combe."*   It never, as far as I have been able to learn,

---

* This would-be "crack shot" can never have seen a European gun, or if he has, it must have been some of the "cheap
John" trash from Birmingham or the continent, which are generally more dangerous to the shooter than to the thing shot at.
The Whitworth, Rigby, Metford, etc., are the best rifles for
long range in the world, being, in the hands of a good marksman, tolerably certain up to two thousand yards, and are as
superior to the Henry as that gun is to the old " gas-pipe."
I may have more to say on this in another place.   I merely
mention this to show how absurdly some men talk on rifle
matters.

made even respectable practice at any long range;
its shooting was not in any respect
to be compared to the Ball, Ballard,
Peabody, Remington, Spencer, Sharp,
or any one of the many guns that
I have seen tested. Cleveland makes
the same remark at page 188. "In
speaking of its accuracy, however, although several of the writers" (alluding
to the testimonials in the advertising
pamphlet) "praise it highly, I find that
they allude to it only in general terms,
and without specifying its performances. I am bound to say that in this
particular the shooting of the only one
I have had an opportunity of testing,
and which was sent to me from the
manufactory for the purpose, was any
thing but satisfactory. I could not, on
an average, put three shots out of five
into a circle of two feet in diameter at
one hundred yards, and at two hundred  HENRY BREECH-
they varied four or five feet, wandering LOADER, REPEATER.
in every direction. . . . . I tried the gun repeatedly,
and called in the aid of two experienced riflemen who
succeeded no better, though one of them assured me
he had seen good shooting done with it at two hundred

yards. It is likewise very liable to get leaded, and in the test of it, at the Ordnance Department in 1862, proved this, as the report says it was 'found to be considerably leaded and very foul, the lands and grooves not being visible. In other respects it was found in perfect order.'" I have seen much better firing than Cleveland. In the spring of 1866 I formed one of a committee to test the gun; a number of crack shots fired with it from two hundred, four hundred, and six hundred yards. The practice at two hundred and four hundred was fair, but at six hundred very wild, many of the shots missing the target altogether (it was six feet by six feet), and the others scattered all round. In addition to the objections already urged against it, I have also to state that there is great danger of explosion of the cartridges, even in the act of loading. I am aware of an instance where the cartridge exploded on being dropped into the magazine.

THE WINCHESTER BREECH-LOADER (RE-PEATER).

An improvement, or rather, an alteration on the Henry, has been recently made, and the new weapon is called the "Winchester." Instead of the magazine being partially open, it is entirely closed up, and instead of loading from the top, the cartridges are inserted into the magazine from the breech, thus enabling the gun to be used either as a single loader or as a repeater. By this manner of loading the cartridge last inserted is the first one fired. The cartridges are inserted in the magazine through an opening in the side of the frame, back of the lower block. A spring lid, grooved on the top, and of a length to correspond with the size of the cartridge, opens inward by a slight pressure of the cartridge, which is then pushed forward, and as it drops in its place is held there by a shoulder; the lid then rises to its place and closes the aperture. If the Henry rifle was condemned for its complications, the "Winchester" has certainly not improved the defects. However terrible both weapons would be in the hands of experts, they are totally unfit for military service. The charm of being able to fire sixteen rounds of ammunition without cessation would be quickly dispelled by the slightest injury to any one part of the delicate and complicated machinery contained in the Henry and Winchester rifles.

The inventor is Mr. Winchester, president of the company by which the Henry gun is manufactured, and, having observed some of the glaring defects of that arm, he has modified them and set it before the public bearing his name.

BALL'S BREECH-LOADER (REPEATER).

I shall now proceed to give some account of the only other repeater with which I am acquainted; viz., the Ball, which was also tried before the Army Board at Washington in 1866, and on the twenty-sixth day set aside as "not worthy of further trial."

It has a magazine under the barrel, from which the cartridges are fed by a follower, J, pressed back by a spiral spring into the receiver, A, whence they are carried into the chamber of the barrel by the breech-piece, E, which is connected at its forward end with the trigger-guard lever, C, to the rear part of which is hinged a tail-piece or brace, E, by which the breech when closed is braced firmly against a shoulder, e, in the rear part of the receiver, as is shown in the figure spring, above the main-spring of the lock, presses up the brace, E, to this position.

The filling of the magazine is effected by inserting the cartridges, one at a time, through an opening at the right-hand side of the receiver, the follower, J, being at the time drawn forward to the front of the magazine by an attachment of the ramrod, and locked there until the magazine is full, when it is liberated and left under the influence of the spiral spring to force the cartridges back and feed them one at a time into the receiver as fast as required for loading and firing.

It will be perceived in this gun that a portion of the chamber is formed in the breech-piece by being cut away, as is shown at *a*, a portion of the barrel being cut away at *b* to receive the breech-piece.

It is necessary to full-cock this gun before it can be loaded, which is a great drawback, though it is claimed by the inventor that no accidental discharge can take place, as the hammer is prevented from falling by a cam. For a very full account of this arm, I must refer the reader to the same source as I am indebted for some portion of the foregoing particulars; viz., "The American Artisan" of Nov., 1866, though I do not find that it stood the test at Washington, as there stated, it being dropped by resolution of the Board on the 26th day, and when subsequently tried for strength of construction, did not give satisfaction, as the following extract from the official report of the Board shows:

"Ball's patent repeating carbine. First round, sixty-five grains rifle-powder, with two balls (four hundred grains each); second round, seventy grains rifle-powder, with three balls; lever was blown back, throwing the breech-block down, and the stock was split; third round, seventy-five grains rifle-powder, with four balls; chamber blown open as before, and tail of guard broken off; the shell breaks around the part supported by the extractor."

It can also be used as a single breech-loader by means of a check, which consists of a pin turned by a small lever.

FIG. 1.

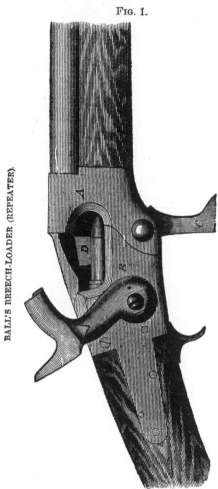

BALL'S BREECH-LOADER (REPEATER).

FIG. 2.

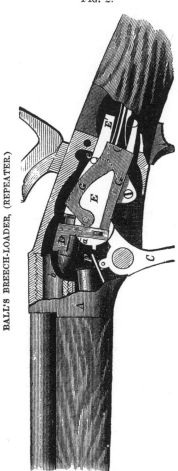

BALL'S BREECH-LOADER, (REPEATER.)

I shall now, having minutely described and commented upon all the prominent weapons, give short descriptions of a number of others that have been brought forward. The particulars are taken from an account, in the "New York Herald," of the proceedings of the Board that assembled at Albany, to choose a breech-loader for the use of the State troops. I have not seen any of the arms, and therefere can not offer any opinion on them.

THE EMPIRE CONGRESS.

This weapon differs in construction from all other breech-loaders. It is merely an alteration from a Springfield rifle, and consists of two parts—one being the barrel and the other the stock. By means of a spring, which the inventors claim to be a secret, the action of cocking the trigger throws open the breach, and ejects the shell at the same time. The breech is thrown open by the muzzle of the barrel falling downward. It was fired with remarkable rapidity, not less than eighteen shots having been fired in one minute, and of this number several struck the ring of the target. Its penetration was through the eleventh and into the twelfth board. Afterward one hundred rounds were fired in four minutes and forty seconds, being an average of nearly twenty shots per minute.

The gun was then sanded, with a view of testing its powers, and the result was that it worked with just as much ease as before. In its construction, the Empire is very simple, and, as an alteration, is certainly an excellent gun. It is strong, and apparently capable of much service. The rapidity with which it was fired created quite a sensation for a little while.

THE HUBBELL BREACH-LOADER.

This is an alteration from a muzzle-loader, and is somewhat novel in its construction. On the trial for rapidity, it fired one hundred rounds in thirteen minutes thirty-two seconds, but this slow action was stated to have been caused by the fact that the party firing was not an expert. The cartridges used not being lubricated, the gun fouled rapidly, thus testing the strength of the breech-piece and barrel to their fullest extent, and satisfying the board that the weapon was strong enough for all practical purposes. On the test for accuracy, eight shots were fired in one minute, of which three entered the target, the gun being fired by a gentleman who had never before handled it. Its penetration was through the eleventh and into the twelfth board.

THE MEIGS BREECH-LOADER.

This breech-loader is an alteration, and differs from all others in its construction. It fired one hundred shots in five minutes forty seconds, part of the time being tied down, and afterward from the shoulder. On the test for accuracy being applied, sixteen shots were fired in one minute, of which number six entered the inside of the target. Its penetration was through the eleventh board. While the gun can be fired with much rapidity, it is not simply constructed, nor does it possess the strength of many of the others. It is quite complicated, being made of several small parts, each of which is exposed, and liable to accident at any moment. After the gun had been fired one hundred times, it became so hot that the woodwork under the barrel partially burned, and time had to be given for it to cool.

A number of others, such as the Page (Magazine), Morganstern, Roberts & Simpson, Fitch-Allyn, Millbank, Lamson, etc., etc., were tested; but, not presenting any particular features of novelty, I do not consider it necessary to enlarge upon them. It may be interesting to present, in a concise form, the general qualities of the various guns tested at the Albany trial, as claimed by their inventors.

"The Allyn gun was taken apart in four minutes, and re-assembled in five and a half minutes. The inventor claims that his alteration being made by reducing the gun from fifty-eight to fifty caliber, the re-enforcement renders it stronger, and gives it a great advantage in range and accuracy.

"The Poultney breech-loader was taken apart in two minutes, and put together again in three and a half minutes. The inventor claims general superiority of construction and ease of use.

"The National rifle was taken apart in one minute and a half and re-assembled in three minutes. The advantage of the gun consists in its simplicity, strength, and durability of construction. It is very light, has no superior in range and penetration, and has no dependence upon springs or fulcrums to resist the discharge. It can fire with ease fifteen shots per second, and as the gun becomes heated it works easier. By removing a single pin with the finger, the soldier can render the gun useless. Accidents while firing are utterly impossible, as the movement of the lever in loading, half-cocks the gun, and relieves the hammer from the detonating pin. In strength it is equal to any breech-loader in the world.

"The Milles gun was taken apart in five minutes and re-assembled in nine minutes. The claim for this weapon is, that it has no springs, but consists of a breech-block and lever, worked by a gear, the gear working the extractor.

"The Meigs gun was taken apart in one and three quarter minutes, and put together again in one and one quarter minutes. The inventor claims the advantage of pulling down the guard, and with it the breech-block, thus exposing the breech.

"The Gray gun was taken apart in thirty seconds, and re-assembled in forty-five seconds. The inventor claims the advantage of a breech-pin and lever drawn back toward the stock when opening the breech. This gun has a sliding breech.

"The Empire gun was taken apart in thirty seconds, and was re-assembled in forty-five seconds. The inventor claims that the gun is simple in construction, and very strong, and can be fired as rapidly as any.

"The Hubbell gun was not taken apart. The inventor claims that it is simple and strong, and can be fired with ease and rapidity.

"The Berdan gun was taken apart in eighteen seconds and re-assembled in forty-two seconds. The inventor claims that the safety of the gun does not depend upon a lock, the whole strain of the discharge being borne upon a solid block of iron. The breech-block rotates upon a center and slides backward when closed.

"The Lamson gun was taken apart in one and a quarter minutes, and put together again in one minute twenty-two seconds. The weapon is somewhat similar to the Berdan, with the exception that the breech-block is composed of two pieces, through which the firing-pin passes."

FOREIGN RIFLES.

I do not purpose describing all the Rifles in use among Continental nations, but only those that may be considered the best, and that are known on this side of the Atlantic, and from the prominent position it holds, I shall first proceed to describe

THE WHITWORTH RIFLE.

The performance of the Enfield rifle, during the Crimean war, having proved that it was vastly superior to any arms with which the Russians were supplied, the English Government determined on at once

arming the troops with this weapon ; but the means
at their command being insufficient, partly from the
incapacity of the Board of Ordnance, and partly from
the demoralization of the gun trade at Birmingham,
owing to the combinations of the makers there, they
were compelled to apply to Parliament for means to
establish a small-arms manufactory, that would be
able to meet the demand. A select committee was
appointed, and sat for two months, in 1854, and
propounded eight thousand questions, but their
labors were of no practical value of themselves ;
though incidentally they led to the invention of the
rifle about to be described. Among other witnesses
examined was Mr. Whitworth, a celebrated ma-
chinist of Manchester. He proved that it was
possible to measure sizes with the greatest nicety,
mechanically, up to the millionth of an inch ; he
likewise showed that no steps had been taken, by
means of difference gauges, to test he accuracy of the
interior of rifle barrels, and upon which their performance so entirely depends. He also proved, that
no conclusions, on which dependence could be placed,
could be arrived at for determining the true form of
bore until that was done. It being clear that any attempt to establish a small-arms factory, without this
knowledge, would be dangerous, and there being no
unanimity among the leading gun-makers upon the

subject, Mr. Whitworth's offer, to conduct a series of experiments for the purpose of elucidating this question, if his expenses were paid, was accepted by the government, and a sum, stated to be sixty thousand dollars, granted for the purpose. Mr. Whitworth had a covered gallery, five hundred yards in length, erected in his grounds, where the series of experiments could be carried on and registered under precisely the same circumstances. I shall now proceed to give, in the words of Hans Busk, a few particulars of the rifle that was the net result of these experiments. It would occupy a vast deal of space to follow Mr. Whitworth through his experiments, which were very interesting, and demonstrated the truth of his statements: that no means existed for measuring the accuracy of gun-barrels, and that any attempt to construct arms on a large scale, without this knowledge, would end disastrously.

"The bore, as already stated, is hexagonal; and, instead of consisting partly of non-effective lands and partly of grooves, is composed entirely of effective rifling surfaces. The angular corners of the hexagon are always rounded, and either hexagonal or cylindrical bullets may be used indifferently. If one of the latter form be fired, it is immediately forced into the recess of the hexagon, and is thus compelled to adapt itself to the curves of the spiral. The inclined sides of the hexagon offering no direct resistance, expansion is easily effected. If an hexagonal projectile, accurately fitted, be used, metals of all degrees of hardness, from lead, or lead indurated by an admixture of tin, up to steel, may be used without detriment to the bore.

" An exceedingly quick turn may be given to the rifling on this principle, as with the most rapid twirl the projectile never strips.   To prove this fact, and to try the effect of extreme velocity of rotation, a short barrel was constructed, in which the rifling completed *one turn in every inch*.   Bullets made of an alloy of lead and tin, fired from this barrel with a charge of thirty-five grains of powder, penetrated through seven inches of elm planks.

" Mr. Whitworth, finding that all difficulty arising from length of projectiles could be overcome by giving sufficient rotation, and that any weight that might be necessary could be obtained by lengthening the projectile, adopted for a bullet of the service weight (five hundred and thirty grains), an increased length and reduced diameter.   He thus obtained his comparatively low trajectory.   This is obviously a great advantage, for the lower the trajectory, or the nearer the path of the projectile approaches to a horizontal line, the greater is its probability of striking an object of moderate height ; thus, in some measure, correcting errors that may have been made in the estimation of distances.

"For instance, if a rifleman, erroneously estimating the distance of an enemy's column, elevate his sight too much, his bullet will probably pass entirely over the men, and fall harmlessly in their rear.   But supposing the weapon he uses to have a low trajectory,—in other words, to move more nearly in a horizontal plane,—an error in elevation will of course be of less consequence, for his shot will most probably strike some part of the approaching column.

" An objection is frequently urged against the Whitworth (as well as the Jacob) on the ground that the friction of the missile is enormous.   Whether it be so or not, it is unnecessary at present to determine ; nor is it practically very material, if we but look at the results.   At Hythe, in 1857, it struck the target, with force, at eighteen hundred eighty yards (or one hundred twenty yards more than a mile).   At eleven hundred yards its accuracy was equal to the Enfield at five hundred yards.   With seventy grains of powder at five hundred yards it sent a bullet through thirty-three half-inch planks, and the projectile was then only stopped by a solid block of oak behind them. . . . In addition to these merits of the polygonal bore, the barrels rifled upon that principle possess great durability, showing no symptoms of deterioration after many thousand rounds.   Indeed, steel bullets have been repeatedly driven through three-quarter inch wrought-iron plates without causing the smallest damage to the barrel.

" As is seen by the previous description, the great peculiarity of the Whitworth consists in the polygonal groove-form of the bore, the gauge number of which is about forty-eight, the length of the barrel thirty-nine inches, and pitch of rifling one turn in twenty inches; so that the bullet makes nearly two complete revolutions before its departure from the muzzle; though he has made some in which the ball makes six or seven complete turns in the barrel.

WHITWORTH BULLET.

" The projectiles, as shown in the annexed cut, are conical for about the length of half a diameter from the foremost end, and hexagonal for the remainder of their length (or two and half diameters); the sides of the hexagon having an inclination corresponding precisely with those of the bore.   The interior of the barrel is bored and rifled with a degree of precision not long ago considered unattainable, and the exact fitting of the projectile is secured beyond the possibility of error."

The great objection to the Whitworth is its great cost, the plain, regulation arm costing from sixty to eighty dollars while the Enfield can be made at about one-fourth of that sum.   This is a very serious consideration, when the arming of large bodies of men is taken into account. Is it not very strange that after spending eighty thousand dollars of government money on experiments, Mr. Whitworth was not able to produce as good a gun as a private maker? A better gun than the Whitworth has been found in the Rigby, manufactured by the Messrs. Rigby of Dublin. At least, I am led to believe that it is better from the fact that it has been selected in preference to the Whitworth for firing the last stage of the Queen's prize at Wimbledon. The selection is not made by favoritism, but by open competition, the *best* gun being selected. Mr. Whitworth's gun has not answered the expectations formed of it as a military arm, and, as a sporting gun (in its present shape), would be useless.

GENERAL JACOB'S RIFLE.

The gentleman who invented this rifle probably devoted more time and money to experiments with rifles than any man that ever lived. For twenty-five years he devoted all his leisure hours to this subject. His means for testing rifles and projectiles were on the largest scale. He had a range of over two thousand yards, and on this were erected targets at all distances, from one hundred to two thousand yards. These targets were walls of sun-dried bricks; the two thousand yards wall was forty feet high, fifty feet long, and three feet thick. Here, during a great number of years, he prosecuted his researches, and after trying every possible system of rifling and every kind of rifle, he settled upon what is known as "Jacob's Pattern Rifle," which is thus described by that officer : " Double, thirty-two gauge, four grooved ; deep grooves (of breadth equal to that of the lands), to take four-fifths of a turn in the length of the barrel ; barrels the best that can be made, twenty-four inches long ; weight of pair of barrels alone, about six pounds, not less ; the ends of the lands to be rounded off at the muzzle ; patent breech, no side-vents ; first sight exactly parallel to the bore, the muzzle-sight being raised if necessary for this purpose ; folding-sight attached to the barrel, twenty inches from the muzzle, five inches long ; secured by spring below ; protected by projecting wings when lying flat on the barrel ; the slide of this sight to be well secured by springs at its back, so as never to work loose ; the slide to come down quite low on the sight ; the top of the sight and bottom of its slot to be notched." With this rifle and Jacob's shells, some very extraordinary practice has been made, as, witness the following, taken from Hans Busk's " Hand-book for Hythe:"

" I will now cite one or two instances of the precision at long ranges of the Jacobite rifle.

" On the 23d August, 1856, General Jacob, Captain Scott, Mr.

Gibbs, and Captain Gibbard met on the practice-ground at Kur-rachee, to try the effect of General Jacob's rifle-shells, at a range of twelve hundred yards. An ammunition-wagon was extemporized out of an old cart, and a charge of one hundred pounds of powder was stowed in it, in a deal box, measuring only four feet by two feet; an object which could but have appeared a mere speck at such a distance. The morning was cloudy, the outline of the butt beyond the cart was dim and hazy, and the weather altogether so unfavorable, that it required a practical eye to discern the butt at all; and it was even proposed to defer the experiment. The ninth shell, however, from Mr. Gibbs' rifle—one made by Daw, and only thirty-two gauge—exploded the powder with most brilliant effect.

"On the 5th September of the same year, a similar experiment was tried at one thousand eight hundred yards, with a box ten feet square, containing five hundred pounds of powder. The twenty-first round from General Jacob's rifle (twenty-four gauge), fired by Captain Scott, exploded the powder.

"The rifles were on each occasion fired from the shoulder, without any extra support, the shooter standing up."

One would have thought that this rifle would have answered all the requirements of a military arm, but the government would not give General Jacobs the least encouragement, but spent one hundred thousand dollars on producing a rifle in every respect its inferior.

Major Nuthall's and General Boileau's rifles are intended as improvements on the Enfield, and doubtless possess very considerable merit; but as they have never come into use, and are probably unknown on this side of the Atlantic, I will not discuss them. Boucher, who also has given much attention to the subject of rifling, brought forward an arm in many respects similar to Major Nuthall's. A few particulars, as to the price, weight, bore, form of bore, projectile, etc., etc., of the principal muzzle-loaders in use in England mav prove of interest.

WHITWORTH.

Price, from $60 to $200.

Weight of rifle, 9lbs. 5½oz.

Weight of barrel, with sights, 4lbs. 14oz.

Length of barrel, 39 inches.

Form of bore, hexagonal.

Size of bore, .564 inch across the flats ; .568 inch across the center of the flats ; .600 inch across the rounded.

Spiral, one turn in 20 inches.

Ammunition.

Powder, 75 grains Curtis & Harvey's, No. 5.

Wad, wax and tallow.

Projectile, cylindrical, pure lead, .559 diam.; 600 grains weight ; increased length being obtained for the given weight of bullet by substituting in its fore part wood for lead.

RIGBY.

Price of rifle, from $25 upward.

Weight of rifle, 8lbs. 10oz.

Weight of barrel, with sights, 4lbs. 5oz.

Length of barrel, 39 inches.

Form of bore, Rigby's rifling, 6 ridges.

Size of bore, .570.

Spiral, 1 in 4 feet.

Ammunition.

Tube cartridges.

Ninety grains, Curtis & Harvey, No. 6.

Wad of tallow (6), and wax (1).

Projectile, Eley's Metford.

Percussion on an improved system to prevent misfires or back flash.

TURNER.

Price of rifle, $20 to $30.

Weight of rifle, 8lbs. 12oz.

Weight of barrel, with sights, 4lbs. 8oz.

Length of barrel, 3 feet 3 inches.

Form of bore or rifling, " Turner's patent."

Size of bore, .568.

Spiral of rifling, 4 feet.

Ammunition.

Powder, quantity and quality, 75 grains Laurence's No. 4 grain.

Wad, none.

Projectile, regulation pattern, .55 diam., weight 600 grains.

BOUCHER.

Price of rifle, about $22, which includes a *patent steel* barrel. Mounting similar to the Enfield. This rifle can be changed in ten minutes from a muzzle-loader to a breech-loader, and *vice versa*, by merely unscrewing one nipple and inserting another, at a cost of $5.

Weight of rifle, 8lbs. 12oz.

Weight of barrel, with sights, 4lbs. 10oz.

Length of barrel, 3 feet 3 inches.

Form of bore, hexagon, with the angles rounded off, so as to form very shallow grooves, .008 inch deep in the center.

Size of bore, .570 inch.

Spiral, one turn in the length of the barrel.

Ammunition.

Powder, quantity and quality, 2½ drams of Curtis & Harvey's " improved."

Wad, none, made up like the military cartridges, but with the rose at the base cut off, and a disc of paper pasted on instead.

Projectile, lead, cylindro-conoidal, hollow, with iron disk at the base.

I will now give some account of

EUROPEAN BREECH-LOADERS.

The Needle-gun being the only one that has as yet been tested on a large scale in warfare, I presume that some details of it can not fail of being interesting.

The needle-gun, to a passing observer, is like a street-door bolt; at the breech end of the barrel, it has the same nob to slide it by, and a catch to keep it from sliding out. The bolt contains a spiral spring, and the needle, which screws in, and can be removed at will if damaged or broken. The handle of the bolt runs up and down in a slot (fig. 2), and by giving it a quarter turn, it closes the breech and draws back the needle, which starts forward into the cartridge when the trigger is pulled.

Fig 1 is the exterior view of the gun. The barrel has four grooves, the spiral of rifling being one turn in forty inches, almost twice the spiral of the Enfield rifle. The length of it with bayonet is six feet four inches (the longest in Europe); weight of solid ball, shown in fig 3, four hundred fifty-one grains; charge of powder, sixty-five grains.

IE ZÜNDNADELGEWEHR, OR NEEDLE-GUN.

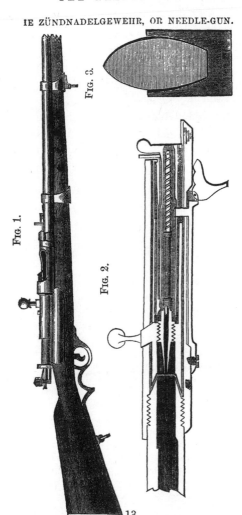

FIG. 3.

FIG. 1.

FIG. 2.

13

This arm, having proved so terribly destructive in the late war between Prussia and Austria, has attained great celebrity, and yet it is not to be compared to the Snider-Enfield, Remington, Peabody, or Berdan-Enfield. It is a most complicated piece of mechanism, being but an improvement on, or alteration of, Pauli's, which was invented in 1809, and, on being tested in the presence of the great Napoleon, proved a complete failure as a military weapon. We next find that there is no simplicity whatever about it. It is complicated, and should there be the slightest injury to the sere, the weapon would be utterly useless. The needle-gun differs in external appearance from every other fire-arm.*

---

* In 1827, the Russian Government had submitted to it a needle-gun, by John Nicholas Dreyse. It was a muzzle-loader, filled with a needle propelled by an ordinary hammer. The charge did not contain any gunpowder, but consisted of a bullet and fulminate, fixed in what must must be considered the all-important carrier wad. The breech was, as far as practicable, closed by a copper disk, having a hole in the center, allowing the needle to pass, and which disk had to be renewed after every sixty rounds. The Russian Government did not adopt this gun. Dreyse's experiments, however, became known to Frederick William II., King of Prussia, who invited him there to conduct a series of experiments, and, to assist him, furnished him liberally with money, and arranged that he should have skillful officers and engineers to consult with. From 1829 to 1836, these experiments were continued, until, in the latter year, the present needle-gun was perfected; and, in 1841, the Prussian Gov-

From the engraving, it will be seen that it is a rifle without a hammer, and with a small iron knob directly in the rear of the breech and in front of the barrel. " This knob is a portion of the breech, which can either be turned in the cylindrical breech-receiver or be made to slide longitudinally. The breech being opened, the cartridge is inserted, when it (the breech) is again closed, and ready for firing. The needle is attached to the needle-bolt, which slides with the lock, and this latter slides within the breech. There is an air-chamber in the rear of and in communication with the cartridge-chamber of the barrel, around the front part of the needle-bolt. The main-spring, by which the needle is shot forward, is of spiral form, and coiled around the needle-bolt in the rear of the collar. This collar forms a catch for the sere, and thus keeps the bolt drawn back when the hammer is cocked. In the same piece with the sere is the sere-spring, at the end of which is the trigger. To load and fire this gun, the following motions are required : First, pulling back the knob to withdraw the needle from the breech ; second, opening the breech ; third, inserting the cartridge ; fourth, closing the breech ; fifth, turning the knob, so as to bring it in front of the shoulder ; sixth, firing the piece. It must be remembered

---

ernment had served them out to the extent of sixty thousand to the army.

that these are only the motions connected with the machinery of the gun ; if we include the 'lowering' of the piece, handling of the cartridge, raising of the piece, aiming, etc., we have not less than thirteen to fifteen motions.   But it is of the piece itself that we write, and its defects may be stated as follows : First, the presence of the handle on the side of the barrel, which must, to some extent, destroy the accuracy of the aim ; second, the necessity of pulling back the knob before loading, and the danger of a premature discharge in consequence thereof.   (It is stated that the needle-bolt can be drawn back by a handle attached to the lock-spring independently ; but this only further complicates the gun, and renders it more objectionable.)   Third, the extreme nicety of its mechanical construction, by which the slightest irregularity will render it useless ; fourth, its inability to fire with sufficient rapidity ; fifth, the tendency of the needle to break."

Nothing more is known than that the passage of the needle through the powder creates a friction, which sets fire to the fulminate as soon as the needle reaches it.   There are certainly some commendable points about the needle-gun, but the opinion (outside of Prussia) is universally entertained, that it is one of the most inferior breech-loaders at present before the public.   Its merits are simply these :

"First, the construction of the cartridge; and, second, the *Zundspiegel*, or igniting material. In the first the use of copper is rendered unnecesary, the cartridge being encased in paper. The powder is placed first, then follows a compressed paper sabot, which cleans the bore of the gun, and in which is fitted the bullet. The fulminate is placed in front of the gunpowder, and between it and the sabot. When the gun is fired, the needle first pierces the gunpowder, but does not fire it until it enters the fulminate, when the explosion instantly takes place. And this brings us to the Zundspiegel, which, translated, means igniting-glass. This is a secret known only to the inventor, and whether the power of ignition lies in the needle alone, or by contact with the fulminate, can not be told. By this we mean that it is not stated whether the fulminate could be ignited by other means than by the needle. From all that can be ascertained, it is evident that no other ammunition than that expressly made for the gun can be used, so that the only conclusion to arrive at is, that the fulminate possesses some secret power by means of which ignition takes place the instant the needle is brought into contact with it. The mere passage of a needle through the fulminate of one of our metallic cartridges would fail to explode it, a sharp blow from a solid front being required."

Of its inferiority to other breech-loaders, and the improbability of its answering the purpose for which it was designed, Hans Busk thus writes :

" Of the Prussian Zündnadelgewehr, or needle-gun, I need say but little. After innumerable trials, it has been found to possess in its present form many palpable defects, and, although in skillful hands it is undoubtedly an effective weapon, it is not well adapted for general military purposes. The works require to be continually cleaned after use ; besides which, there are various other objections, which it is not necessary to specify, as this form of arm is no longer here in any favor. The ammunition requisite for this musket, too, is necessarily of a dangerous character, for as each cartridge contains the detonating material, interposed between the powder and the bullet, it is obvious that a projectile of almost any kind passing through a cartouch-box, or any ammunition-wagon, would infallibly cause such cartridges to explode with disastrous effects. One of those who, of late years, has written a good deal on these matters, without apparently possessing much practical knowledge, observes with regard to those weapons, that ' the only point to be determined in practice is, whether they fulfill their theoretical indications. Now, the testimony on this subject may be shortly stated as this : In England, authorities say that, if made, they would not answer ; in Prussia, however, being made and largely employed, they are found to answer.' "

This, however, is not quite consistent with fact. True it is, that these needle-guns were once made and largely employed in Prussia, sixty thousand having been issued in four or five years ; but all experienced military men are now satisfied that they did not fulfill the expectations originally entertained respecting them, and no country but Germany has been guilty of the "folly of adopting them." This folly (as it is called) of adopting the needle-gun was the means of enabling the Prussians to inflict a disastrous defeat on the Austrian army, at Sadowa. The arm was found to answer so well, that Prussia, with the experience of the war before her, has refused to change it, and no less than one million one hundred thousand have been ordered since the war. This does not look as if it had failed to fulfill the expectations originally formed of it. So it is, every new invention meets with the same opposition. As stated in the beginning of the book, the introduction of fire-arms at all was vehemently opposed, and so it has always been, and ever will be.

THE CHASSEPÔT BREECH-LOADER.

The example of the Prussian army in the campaign last summer in Bohemia, having shown that the possession of a breech-loading rifle musket is quite indispensable to every military power, the French government lost not a day in making inquiries and experiments to determine the best kind of weapon for the use of its troops. The special commission appointed by the minister of war on the 11th of July, and presided over by General d'Audemarre and General Bourbaki, instituted a series of trials of different kinds of

breech-loaders at the camp of Châlons, with a view
to compare their "practical qualities, the solidity
and safety of their mechanism, and their capacity of
easy handling and of rapid loading and firing."
These were the only points to be considered; they
did not apply any test of precision or accuracy of
fire, the latter being a matter of subordinate importance in the operations of a line of infantry in the
field.   The commissioners unanimously decided in favor of the immediate adoption, with one or two slight
modifications, of a breech-loading needle-gun and
cartridge, invented by M. Alphonse Antoine Chassepôt, the head viewer of the Central Depôt at Paris,
who has since been rewarded with the title of Cheva-
lier of the Legion of Honor.   A decree of the Emperor
Napoleon, on August 30, ordained that this weapon
should be supplied to all the French troops.   I shall
now proceed to give some explanation of the illustration.

"Fig. 1, in the engraving, is an external view of the Chassepôt rifle, which is one meter twenty-nine centimeters in length
(about four feet three inches), and weighs a trifle above four kil-
logrammes, or less than nine pounds. Its caliber is eleven milli-
meters, or four hundred thirty-three thousandths inch; and it is
rifled with four spiral grooves, turning from left to right, and
going once round in the space of fifty-five centimeters, or twenty-
one and one-half inches.

"Fig. 2 is the central longitudinal vertical section, showing
the position of the parts after firing; that is to say, with the

breech closed and locked, and the hammer and needle forward.
Fig. 3 represents a central longitudinal section of cartridge.

" The barrel is screwed into a breech-receiver, *a*, in the upper
part of which is a longitudinal opening, and in the right-hand
side of this longitudinal opening there is a shorter lateral opening to allow of the working of the breech-bolt, *g*. It is through
this lateral opening that the cartridge is inserted. The breech-
bolt, *g*, resembles a door-bolt, except that it is bored centrally
throughout, and it has a lateral projection, *h*, on the right side,
to enter the aforesaid lateral opening in the breech-receiver.
The knob or handle, *i*, by which it is turned and drawn back,
elevated to an upright position, as it is when the gun is at half
cock. When the knob is thus turned up, the bolt can be drawn
back to open the chamber of the barrel for loading. After loading, the bolt is moved forward, and by turning the handle
to the right, the projection, *h*, is brought into the lateral opening of the breech-receiver, and the bolt is thus locked.

" Into the front end of the hollow bolt, *g*, there is loosely fitted
a sheath, *j*, which serves as a guide to the needle by which the
fulminate priming is exploded and the charge fired.

" In the explanation of the different parts and their working,
we must first attend to the means by which the hinder end of
the chamber is closed up after putting in the cartridge. Unless
this were secured, a breech-loading gun would not be able to
shoot at all, since the explosion of the powder, instead of driving the ball forward through the barrel, would merely send a
jet of flame backward into the soldier's face. In the ordinary
muzzle-loading gun, the hinder end of the tube is hermetically
closed, the whole being one solid piece of iron, with only the
very tiny orifice beneath the nipple on which the percussion-
cap is to be placed, and through which the fire from the
percussion-cap is to enter the chamber and ignite the powder.

" This closing of the hinder end of the chamber, therefore,
in the rear of the cartridge when inserted, is obtained in the
Chassepôt rifle by the instantaneous compression, in the very
act of firing, of a small disc or plug of vulcanized India-rubber,
a, which is situated just in front of the sliding bolt, and has

THE CHASSEPOT BREECH-LOADER.

Fig. 1.

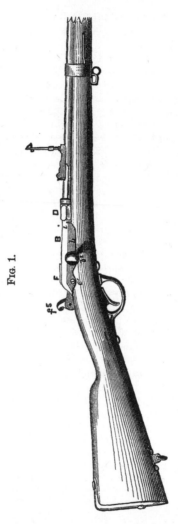

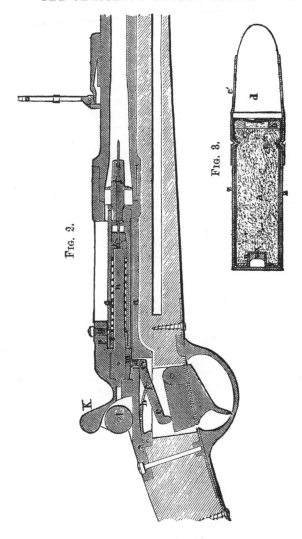

FIG. 2.

FIG. 3.

a metal cap between itself and the cartridge. The diameter
of this India-rubber plug is naturally rather less than the internal diameter of the chamber; but as it is partly elastic
(that is, composed of three layers, the middle layer being
elastic, the outer layers not), so, when the powder of the cartridge is ignited, the force of its explosion causes a pressure of
the metal cup on the India-rubber plug, which, being squeezed
thereby, expands and tightly fills up the whole width of the
chamber, allowing none of the gas from the explosion of the
powder to escape in the rear. When the rifle is discharged, the
elastic plug returns to its former shape, and easily passes into or
out of the chamber, following the movements of the sliding
bolt, by which, pushing it backward or forward, the hinder end
of the chamber is opened or shut.

" The cartridge used in this arm, shown in fig. 3, has a cylindrical case, z, of paper, which contains the powder, provided at
its ends with pasteboard discs, y and b'. The fulminate, v, is
contained in a small flanged copper can, n, x, which has two
holes in it through which the fulminate, when ignited, passes
to the powder, a. The cap passes through a hole in the disc, y,
and is inclosed within the paper case, z. The ball, d, has a
paper case, c', open at the rear, which fits over the top of the
powder case, z, and is tied thereto, or otherwise secured in a
suitable manner.

" The entire handling of the Chassepôt rifle, including the
operations of cocking, loading, and firing, is performed by five
simple movements, as follows :

"1st movement. To cock—The rifle being held in the soldier's left hand, with the butt-end resting against his left side,
he puts his fore-finger in front of the guard (see fig. 1), and, seiz-
ing the top of the slide, f 5, with his thumb, draws it backward.

" 2d movement. To open the rifle—He turns the handle, b
2, from right to left, and draws the bolt backward.

" 3d movement. To load—He takes the cartridge with his
right hand, and puts it into the chamber by the aperture in the
right side of the breech-piece.

" 4th movement. To close the rifle—He pushes the bolt forward, and turns the handle from left to right.

" 5th movement.   To fire—He pulls the trigger.

" The report of the French military commission states that
the rifle can be loaded and fired twelve times in a minute, and
that the soldier can keep on firing at this rate four minutes
consecutively.   The mechanism is very easily managed, and
it requires but little instruction to make the men familiar with
its use.   The cartridge is entirely consumed, so that nothing
remains in the barrel after firing ; and the discharge of one
hundred fifty rounds, without cleaning, scarcely leaves a speck
of rust."

As regards the rapidity of fire, which appears now-
a-days to be the principal desideratum, a man with a
lot of loose cartridges beside him can fire the Chassepôt musket twelve times in a minute ; but that rate
the most skillful and robust soldier can not keep up
beyond thirty or forty rounds : past that the fire
perceptibly slackens.   The same thing occurs with
the Prussian needle-gun after the twenty-fifth round.
The cause is purely physical ; i.e., the fatigue of the
man, whose left arm has often to support, unaided,
the whole weight of the weapon.   If, instead of having loose cartridges by the soldier's side, he has to
take them out of his pouch, the rate of firing declines
to six rounds per minute, but an average of eight
could be obtained if they were kept in a loose bag at
his side.

The accuracy of the weapon has been ascertained
by making the men fire at targets two meters high by
two in breadth, at a range of five hundred meters,

using a rest for the rifle. At that range, a great many men, firing one hundred rounds, hit the target every time. The point-blank range of the Chassepôt musket is fixed at five hundred meters, the extreme range exceeds one thousand meters ; and the weapon needs no cleaning for two hundred and fifty rounds ; over twelve hundred rounds have been fired out of the same gun without its sustaining any injury. The Chassepôt musket may therefore sustain very advantageously a competition with the needle-gun. Its superiority arises chiefly from the more perfect closing of the breech, which is complete, while it is very defective in the *Zündnadelgewehr*. All the gases developed by the ignition of the charges are utilized to propel the bullet, which adds to its range and penetrating power, while the perfect combustion of the powder naturally obviates the necessity of frequent cleaning, which the Prussian weapon can not do without. It is greatly to be regretted that this weapon does not seem likely to answer as a military arm, as it was found that, after a number of charges had been fired rapidly out of it, it became so hot as to be absolutely dangerous. The haste with which this arm was adopted precluded any proper trial so that its defects could be brought out. It is understood that five hundred thousand have been manufactured. Unless some means be obtained of obviating this de-

fect, Napoleon will be obliged to try some other arm.
If he invites a competition of rifle-makers, to take
place before him, with the understanding that the
successful competitor will receive the order for sup-
plying the French army, some of our best rifles will
be presented, and the Chassepôt will stand but a poor
comparison with the Remington, Spencer, Peabody,
Berdan, or others of our superior arms.

THE SNIDER-ENFIELD RIFLE.

Before proceeding to describe the Enfield rifle as
converted on Snider's plan, and which has been adopted as the national arm for the British troops, it may
be proper to give some description of the Enfield
rifle, which I shall proceed to do in the words of
Hans Busk, in "The Rifle, and how to Use it."

"In many respects, it is a beautiful weapon, especially if con-
trasted with its predecessor. Some time will probably elapse
ere a better military implement of destruction will be perfected,
or at any rate one better adapted for the use of the 'line.'

"The rifling is effected by three grooves, cut slightly deeper
at the breech than at the muzzle, and making one complete
revolution in seventy-eight inches. The barrel is three feet three
inches long; diameter, five hundred seventy-seven thousandths;
weight, four pounds two ounces; total weight of arm, with
bayonet, nine pounds three ounces; length, six feet one inch;
without the bayonet, four feet seven inches. The regulation
charge of powder is two and a half drachms (F. G.), the weight
of the bullet five hundred thirty grains; of sixty rounds of

ammunition, five pounds three ounces eleven drachms.   Total
weight, with bayonet-scabbard, fourteen pounds eleven ounces
three drachms.

"This rifle-musket can, it is said, be turned out at Enfield
at an expense of about three pounds four shillings sterling (sixteen dollars).   When supplied by contract, it costs somewhat
more.

"An ordinary marksman can make good practice with it at
eight hundred yards, but in the skilled hands of a more experienced shot, still greater range is attainable.

"The manufacture of this arm is proceeding at Enfield at the
rate of between seventeen hundred and two thousand a week,
but the demand as yet far exceeds the supply.

"The raw material for the barrels first makes its appearance
at the factory in the form of slabs, about half an inch thick and
twelve inches long, by four broad.   In forging these, care has
been taken in the manufacture to make the short square fibers
of the iron cross and recross at right angles.   These pieces of
metal are first heated and bent into short tubes, somewhat resembling rough draining-tiles.   In this state they are again
heated, and, while white-hot, passed between iron rollers, which
weld the joining down the middle, and, at the same time,
lengthen each tube about three inches.   They are again heated,
and again passed between rollers of a smaller gauge, which
lengthens them still further ; and this process is repeated
altogether twelve times in two hours, when the barrel at last
assumes the form of a rod about four feet long, having a bore
down the center a quarter of an inch in diameter.   The muzzles
are then cut off, the 'butts' made up, and the process of welding
on the nipple-lump (to sustain the nipple) commences.   This is
a difficult operation, and requires considerable quickness, care,
and skill.   To insure rapidity of striking while the metal is at
a bright-red heat, the breech, with the cone-seat attached, is held
in a steel die under a small hammer worked by steam, striking
four hundred blows a minute, and under which the metals are
united in the closest possible manner.

"The forging being thus completed, the barrels pass from

the smithy to the boring shops, where the operation of boring (exclusive of rifling) is repeated five times; the barrels being arranged horizontally, and the first-sized borer being drawn upward from breech to muzzle, not forced down, as the bend of the boring-rod would in that case render it difficult to attain absolute accuracy. The second boring is effected with rapidity, the third slowly, when the barrel is finished to within three thousandths of an inch of its proper diameter. The outside is then ground down to its service size. The next process is to straighten the barrel after the worm for the breech-piece has been tapped. This straightening is one of the roughest portions of the whole process. From the very soft nature of the iron used, and the want of substance of the metal itself, a slight blow is enough either to bend the barrel, or else so to dent it as effec-tually to destroy all precision in shooting. Thus, in the various stages just detailed, notwithstanding the greatest care, the bar-rel is almost always found to require subsequent correction. This is accomplished by hand; a skilled workman looking through the tube, and tapping it with a light hammer wherever it appears to him to need such adjustment.

" Yet rude and unsatisfactory though this operation appears, it is found to give satisfactory results, even when the accuracy attained is tested to the thousandth of an inch.

" Altogether the barrel undergoes sixty-six distinct operations, and after having been bored out for the fourth time, its strength is tested by a proof-charge of one ounce of powder and one ball. Very few fail under this ordeal; the majority, indeed, will bear, uninjured, the explosion of two and a half ounces of powder, and the discharge of eleven, or even of as many as thirteen balls. . . . . . The next important step is the rifling. In this particular arm the grooves are comparatively broad and shallow, with a pitch of half a turn in the length of the barrel. The depth of the rifling is five hundredths at the muzzle, and thirteen hundredths of an inch at the breech; the width of each groove being three-sixteenths of an inch. Each groove is cut separately, the bit being drawn from the muzzle to the breech.

" After rifling, the barrel is again proved with half an ounce
14

of powder and a single ball. It is then sighted, trimmed off, milled, leveled, browned, gauged, and at last finished to such a degree of accuracy that the steel gauge of five hundred seventy-seven thousandths of an inch passes freely through, while that of five hundred eighty thousandths will barely enter the muzzle.

"The regulation projectile, formed by compression of very pure lead, is a modification of the Minie ; smooth at the sides, and having a boxwood plug instead of an iron cup fitted into a cavity at its base."

This projectile did not bring out the best qualities of the rifle, and doubtless would soon have been cast aside for the Pritchett.

I may sum up the principal points to be noted in this arm in the language of Lieut.-Colonel Dixon, the Superintendent of the Small-arms Manufactory, at Enfield :

"That the grooves are limited to three.

"No greater spiral allowed than is necessary to keep the bullets in the grooves.

"The most perfect facility of loading.

"The expansion into the grooves, to ensure the necessary rotation, is effected at the instant of the inflammation of the charge of powder, in consequence of the "upsetting" of the lead, assisted possibly by the wooden plug which closes the orifice, at the base of the bullet, but which, no doubt, prevents any collapsing of the sides of the bullet when leaving the barrel,—a circumstance which would otherwise happen, and thus disfigure its shape, and act prejudicially in other respects. The advantages on the side of the plug are, besides the above, the less-frequent fouling of the barrel ; in fact, the grooves are cleaned out and lubricated after every shot.

"The caliber of the arm, five hundred seventy-seven thousandths, allowing of a bullet of sufficient weight to do all that is required of it, but not so heavy as to prevent sixty rounds being carried easily by the soldier.

"The shooting of this arm as a line-infantry weapon is most superior; and when carefully made throughout, corresponds to every requirement of the best-instructed infantry soldier.

"At long ranges—that is to say, up to one thousand yards— the arm makes very good practice, and thus becomes qualified for a rifle arm for special corps."

This, then, is the weapon that the British army being armed with, that government, stirred up by the wonderful results of the Prussian needle-gun, determined to convert into a breech-loader. They invited the scientific of all nations to present plans for this purpose; a great number were sent in, but, on being tested, all failed except the system proposed by Jacob Snider, an American, which, with some slight modifications, was adopted; thus affording another triumph for American mechanics over those of the world. A large sum of money was accorded to Snider, but, owing to delays and litigations, he never enjoyed it, having died before the money was wholly paid.

Fig. 1 is a perspective view of the gun, with the greater part of the barrel omitted to facilitate representation; and fig. 2 is a top view of the breech-loading construction. Both views show the breech-block thrown open for loading.

The method of conversion is very simple. About two inches of the upper half of the barrel are cut

SNIDER-ENFIELD BREECH-LOADER.

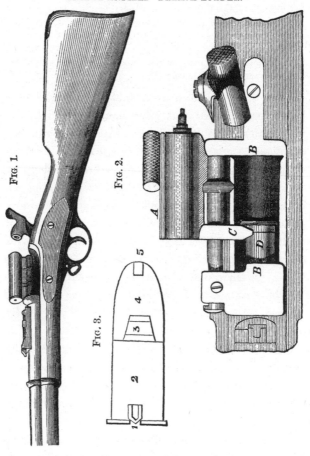

Fig. 1.

Fig. 2.

Fig. 3.

away at the breech to form a breech-receiver, B, into which is fitted the solid breech-block, A, which swings sideways in a hinge attaching it to one side of the barrel. So far as above described, the breech somewhat resembles that of some of the older breechloaders in this country; but it has, in addition to the swinging movement sideways, a longitudinal backward movement, for the purpose of drawing out the exploded cartridge shells from the chamber of the barrel by means of an attached spur, C. Fig. 2 shows the breech-block, A, thus drawn back, and shows the shell, D, as partly drawn out. The spur C, does not eject the shell, like the shell-extractor of most of the newer American breech-loaders, but the gun being canted as the breech-block is drawn back, the shell drops easily out. The firing is effected by the hammer striking upon a sliding pin passing through the center of the breech-block, the blow being transmitted by the front end of the pin to the fulminate priming, which is in the center of the base of the cartridge.

Fig. 3 is section of cartridge. 1. The percussion-cap; 2. Powder; 3 is a piece of clay inserted in hollow of ball to cause explosion; 4. Ball; 5. Piece of wood inserted in conical end of ball to steady flight.

From the engraving and the text, the reader will be able to form a very good idea of the nature and appearance of this powerful weapon. In general design the Snider looks not unlike a Springfield rifle, as converted at the Springfield Armory for the American Government, with this important difference, that, instead of opening upward on a hinge, the steel plug with the needle which explodes the cartridge opens sideways like the lid of a box.

The cost of converting the Enfield rifle is estimated at about twelve shillings per arm, and the expense of the ammunition will be one-third greater than with the muzzle-loader. On the other hand, the shooting of the converted rifle is at least one-third better than before—due, perhaps, in part to a slight alteration Mr. Snider has made in the existing Enfield bullet. With the original Enfield muzzle-loader, the mean radial deviation at five hundred yards' range was eighteen and six tenths inches; at the same range, the deviation with the Snider-Enfield was twelve inches.

The mode of closing the breech may be briefly described as follows :

"A cylindrical steel block, fitting into a shoe, opens sideways on a hinge in front of the hammer, the block having a certain longitudinal play upon the hinge. This shoe or frame is but slightly larger than the breech end of an ordinary rifle-barrel, and contains a spring for retaining the block, which can, however, be opened with the greatest ease. No part of the apparatus could be so damaged by ordinary rough usage as to become inefficient, and the steel block, even when open, presents the smallest possible mark to the enemy's fire."

" The cartridge is of very thin sheet-brass, rolled up into a cylinder, so that there is a considerable overlap. This sheet-brass cylinder has a stout metal base with a rim, which base fits into the breech end of the barrel proper. In the center of the metal base is a fixed percussion cap, fired by means of a piston passing through the otherwise solid steel block, the piston being urged forward by the hammer. On inserting the cartridge in the open end of the barrel, the block is closed down into the shoe, the hammer pulled back to full cock, and the piece fired at once. With the improved-pattern Snider there have been no misfires.

" In the act of opening the block, a projection upon its fore end catches in the rim of the metal base of the cartridge, and by sliding the block back on its hinge, the old cartridge is removed, and it falls to the ground by a mere twist of the rifle with the left hand. A spring urges the block forward into its place again in the improved pattern, but at first this had to be done by hand. The time now consumed in removing the old cartridge is quite inappreciable.

" The overlapped cylinder of thin sheet-brass is expanded by the discharge of the powder so as accurately to fit the barrel, effectually preventing the escape of gas. This has been amply proved by experiment. If, before introducing the cartridge, we cut the sheet-brass sides by repeated blows against the sharp edge of a table,—in fact, if we destroy its shape as much as possible without breaking completely through the brass,—it still comes out, after the discharge, a most perfect cylinder.

" During the recent experiments carried on at Woolwich, it was found that a well-trained man, taking accurate aim, fired with the Enfield muzzle-loader ten rounds in four minutes forty-six seconds ; with the Snider-Enfield, ten rounds in one minute forty-four seconds. Without taking aim, but simply raising the piece to the shoulder, he fired with ease fifteen rounds per minute. We may compare this result with the six rounds per minute said to have been fired under similar conditions by the needle-rifle."

The first performance of these guns, on being

issued, hardly met the expectations that were formed
of them, besides which, some slight accidents took
place from the escape of gas at the breech, and forth-
with a cry was raised, that the gun was a failure.
Nothing could be further from the truth.   The cause
is easily explained.   The breech action of this gun
is not adapted to withstand even a very slight escape ;
and any failure on the part of the cartridge tends to
throw the breech violently open, and to cause a
dangerous backward explosion.   The first cartridge
adopted for the arm had the original Pottet base, a
thin cup of brass, into which the body of the cartridge
was wedged.   When these bases were made absolutely
perfect, as in those cartridges with which the first experiments were made, the security against explosion
was all that need be desired ; but the slightest crack
or flaw in the brass, by weakening the base, rendered
it less capable of sustaining the severe strain thrown
upon it at the moment of firing.   When the cartridges
had to be made by millions, perfect and invariable
freedom from flaws could not be guaranteed ; and it
was found necessary to adopt a stronger base, and so
to provide a large margin for imperfections of manufacture.   The cartridges of this second pattern have
proved thoroughly satisfactory, and no failure or
tendency to explosion has been noticed in the large
numbers which have since been made.

With regard to the reports of the want of accuracy of the Snider, the following account of the proceedings in the House of Lords, will show upon what a slight basis reports damaging to the arm are built :

HOUSE OF LORDS March 7th, 1867.

*   *   *   *   *   *   *

The Earl of Longford said, reports had been current much to the disadvantage of the Snider system of converting rifles, the fact being that, although they had been tested and experimented upon in every possible way, only some small defects had developed themselves in the cartridges and in the mechanism of the arm.   The first cartridge tried was not found satisfactory. A second was then tried, and though not found satisfactory, it was, at all events, serviceable, and a third had been adopted, which, there was every reason to believe, would be perfectly satisfactory.   The small defects which had developed themselves in the mechanism of the arm, were such as could be easily rem. edied without making any change in the original plan of the arm.   He held in his hand a letter from Sir James Yorke Scarlett, who is commanding at Aldershott, and whose attention had been directed to the exaggerated reports which the noble lord had referred to.   It was as follows :

" Aldershott, Feb. 26, 1867. *   *   * I forward a letter from Captain Thompson, District Instructor of Musketry, under whom the practice so erroneously described took place. . .   Though I believe a still simpler plan will be produced, I consider the present pattern Snider rifle an admirable weapon, and perfectly efficient, when well made and well handled."

The enclosure from Captain Thompson was dated February 25, 1867, and was in the following terms :

" Having noticed an article respecting the recent trial of Snider rifles and ammunition at Aldershott, which is likely to lead the public to form erroneous opinions as to their general efficiency, I think it right to inform you that the trial which took place here, instead of proving not very favorable to the new arm and ammunition, may be considered the reverse. Out of eight thousand rounds fired, only twenty cartridges burst, none of which in any way injured the breech arrangement, and only three missed fire. In very few cases were the old cartridge cases found difficult to withdraw, and those frequently from the awkwardness of the men who were firing for the first time with an entirely new weapon. As regards accuracy at five hundred and seven hundred yards, notwithstanding an apparently inferiority of the Snider to the Enfield at the longer ranges, I think that the very little practice which was made with the Snider rifle at the longer range, should not be received as a test of accuracy, as the *sighting of the rifle is altered in consequence of the reduction of the weight of the bullet;* and the accuracy of the Snider may probably not be found inferior to that of the Enfield rifle, when the soldiers become accustomed to its use, which, up to the present time, they have had no opportunity of becoming."

Sir. J. Yorke Scarlett added: "My only regret is, that the correspondents who furnish information on military matters to the press, do not first make themselves acquainted with the sub jects on which they write."

He trusted that that explanation would be satisfactory to the noble earl; and he might add, that the government would not have proceeded with the conversion if they had lost confidence in the arm.

From this it will be perceived that the British troops are provided with an arm vastly superior to any now in use in Europe. Whether it is superior to the Peabody, Berdan, and Remington, remains to be seen. They all possess great merit; but I am inclined to believe that, for all purposes of warfare, and to stand the rough usage to which they must necessarily be exposed, that the Snider-Enfield and Berdan converted, are the two best arms yet produced, the Snider-Enfield being the very best. This is but an individual opinion, and by no means tends to disparage the great value of the other breech-loaders.

Since the above was written, the result of the great annual match at Wimbledon has come to hand, which quite bears me out in the above statement. The shooting was of a most extraordinary character, and I can not do better than record it in the language of the report.

"In the military breech-loading competition some extraordinary scores were made yesterday, so remarkable indeed, that at first sight they appear almost incredible. A volunteer named Andrews, belonging to a Kent corps, and firing with a Snider-Enfield breech-loader at the five hundred yards' range, succeeded in firing off no less than fifty shots in the prescribed five minutes—that is to say, exactly ten a minute The shots moreover, instead of being fired off wildly, were delivered with steady aim. In the fifty shots, he made forty-six hits, of which ten were bull's-eyes, twenty-one centers, and fifteen outers, equivalent in all to a score of one hundred thirty-three. At the very same range, not four hours previously, a competitor had been cheered for making ninety-seven, which was then by far the highest score. The astonishing success which had thus been obtained with the government weapon became known very speedily all over the camp, and the Council were actually pressed to confer upon Sergeant Andrews some special mark of recognition. His score, however, was eclipsed by the very last shots fired at the two hundred yards' stage of the same competition. In the space of three minutes allowed at this range, a volunteer named Oswald fired thirty-eight shots, or at the rate of thirteen a minute, of which thirty-seven were hits. His score consisted of six bull's-eyes, twenty centers, and eleven outers; total, one hundred six.

The value of such firing may not be well understood by many of my readers, who are unacquainted with the system of marking followed in England. It will be better appreciated when I inform them that, out of the eighty-eight shots fired in eight minutes, at five hundred and two hundred yards, eighty-three would have each "knocked over" a man in an advancing column, four abreast, sixteen would have each killed a man standing alone, fifty-seven of them would have put a cavalry picket *hors de combat*. From this it will be seen what a tremendous weapon the Snider-Enfield is. As a military weapon, it is unquestionably the *very best* ever produced.

PRINCE'S AND LINDNER'S BREECH-LOADERS

The first-named of these breech-loading rifles was experimented with at Brussels, in 1856, and favorably reported on. Its recoil was found to be less than that of any other gun in Belgium, with a charge of seventy grains of powder and four hundred seventy grains of lead; the length of the ball being one and eighteen hundredths inches, length of the cone double that of the cylinder, and the diameter fifty-nine hundredths inch. At a distance of from sixteen hundred and forty to nineteen hundred and eighty-six yards, it was claimed by the inventor that the bullets would carry with sufficient force to inflict a dangerous and often mortal wound. The gun was, however, never adopted, because of its being too complicated for the use of any others than experts in the use of fire-arms. The Lindner gun is merely the conversion of a muzzle-loader into a breech-loader, and it contains so many objectionable features that it can never be adopted as a military arm. The conversion is as follows : The breech-piece of the muzzle-loader is cut away, and the barrel lengthened over the small of the stock. In this lengthening piece is a bolt, which, when moved backward, opens the breech, and when moved forward closes it. At the near end of the bolt is a handle, which moves it longitudinally, or turns it, as the case may be. The bolt is threaded internally, and a portion externally, so as to enable it to work freely backward and forward. On the front end of the bolt is a loose conical piece, from which projects a pin, forming a claw for extracting the sabot of the cartridge. On the front end of the bolt is a screw-pin, which enters a slot provided for the purpose, and thus prevents it from coming out of the lengthening piece of the barrel. To open the breech the bolt is turned to one side for the purpose of freeing the threads, and then drawn back the required distance.

By reversing the movement, the conical piece is tightly screwed up and the breech thoroughly closed. The lock is of the old pattern, and the cartridges are encased in paper, a cap being placed upon the nipple of the gun to discharge it. Altogether the Lindner "converted" rifle is even inferior to the needle-gun, by reason of the length of time required to load and fire a charge.

THE CORNISH BREECH-LOADER.

This is a new arm, and is entirely unknown on this side of the Atlantic; indeed, I have not even seen a description of it published in any of our papers, and I am indebted to a recent number of the *London Times* for the following particulars respecting it:

"This new weapon is a gun invented by Mr. Kenneth Cornish, and the claim made in his behalf is, that, while retaining all that is good of the system common to the guns of Snider, Strong, and others, it avoids the faults which tend to render particular weapons unsuitable to the rough uses of war. The invention can certainly boast of having simplified the mechanism of the breech in a wonderful manner; in fact, at first sight, it is difficult to believe that a breech so simple can be altogether safe in its action. Imagine a child's cross-bow, minus the arc and string; and that is the shape of the stock and barrel of the rifle. A bullet put in at the muzzle would run down the barrel and out in a straight line along the groove upon the stock; for what in the cross-bow is the place for introducing the arrow is in this rifle the place for dropping or pushing in the cartridge. Across the barrel, at a point somewhat higher up than where this joins the stock, is the breech-piece, not a solid hinged block, as in the Snider rifle, but a species of flap, set on edge, and in shape and action not unlike the knife of a guillotine. This is simply lifted up or pressed down as occasion may require; and when raised, by pulling it open somewhat further than it would go of its own accord, the extraction, worked by a sere-spring, is set in motion and draws; or, if the motion communicated be quick and sudden, throws out the copper-based cartridge from the barrel. It is part of Mr. Cornish's theory that cartridges made of metal and on the central-fire principle, are more effectual in rendering military weapons gas-proof than any ingenious construction of the breech itself, since the fittings, however accurate originally, must be disarranged as the weapon heats. And hence he contends that, using cartridges with a metallic base, the mechanism of the breech may be much simplified and cheapened, since the breech has only to support the rear of the cartridge case,—which is, in fact, an inner barrel,—during the explosion, and not to keep in a subtle and imprisoned gas. The needle works through the breech-piece, and hence is short and not liable to get out of order. A critical examination of the closing apparatus would probably suggest that in this respect strength is capable of being added with advantage. A spring, not one that interfered with the efficiency of the gun, for it was fired many times afterward, but still a small spring, gave way under rough usage on Saturday. And a breech-loader, meant to be handled by the rank and file of the army, ought to be as free as possible from the risk of such accidents. The design, however, is quite novel, and, of course, susceptible of modification and improvement. It unquestionably has on its side the great recommendations of cheapness and simplicity, and they are precisely recommendations of the kind which tell in the long run. It is alleged that the cost of the gun when new will not exceed that of an ordinary Enfield, and that the process of conversion is cheaper by some shillings, and capable of being effected faster than by any other patent."

CARLE BREECH-LOADER.

The Russian Government are arming their troops with rifles on this principle, which I understand to be a modification of the needle-gun; but not having seen it noticed anywhere, I am unable to give any description of it. The same may be said of the

THE WERNDL BREECH-LOADER,

Adopted by the Austrian Government, and which is claimed to be the "best breech-loader" yet invented. I have never seen any account of it, and the only allusion to it is contained in the letter of the Vienna correspondent of the London *Times*, who says—

"The Austrians are arming their troops as rapidly as possible with a new breech-loader. It is the invention of Herr Werndl. It is simple in construction, will fire twenty-four rounds a minute, and will penetrate a four-inch deal at twelve hundred yards. It is very light, and costs only about forty-five shillings. But the most remarkable thing about it is its capability of sustaining the roughest usage. The correspondent says: 'After the usual tests of dipping the lock in water, smearing it with dirt and sand, etc., and then firing, H. Werndl took the gun, and, out of the window on the first floor from which we had been practicing, flung it repeatedly over the lane on a piece of hard and stony ground beyond. It was brought up and again fired over and over again, having suffered no damage beyond a few bruises from pebbles on the stock. The fact is, that the barrel and backpiece being of one piece of steel, and supported moreover by a very strong stock, there is nothing to break.' H. Werndl asks nothing for his patent, but offers to make two hundred thousand rifles a year. He has refused all foreign contracts."

Modest Werndl! to be satisfied with the profits on the manufacture of two hundred thousand rifles a year!

PRINCE'S BREECH-LOADER

In this gun the barrel slips forward about three inches, disclosing a steel cone, provided on either side with inclined planes, forming a segment of a screw, and locking tightly into slots at the breech end of the barrel. The cartridge is dropped into the open space at the extremity of the cone, the lever is depressed, pulled backward, and then pushed into its place. The barrel and cone are thus tightly locked together, and until they are in this position the gun can not be fired ; thus combining safety and strength in a great degree. This arm seems a very good one, and has been fired with great precision up to the longest ranges. Sixteen successive shots were put into a small sheet of note-paper at one hundred yards, and twelve following into a sheet of foolscap at two hundred yards; the average of the twenty-eight shots being but two and five-eighths inches. The cartridge in use with this gun, and which can be used equally well with a muzzle-loader, is very ingenious. It is formed of two thicknesses of peculiarly-prepared paper, through which the flash of the cap passes with certainty, consuming the paper during the explosion, leaving no residue whatever behind.

TERRY'S BREECH-LOADER.

Though somewhat resembling Prince's, is in principle entirely different. In Prince's the whole of the barrel moves forward : in Terry's it is fixed, and the admission of the cartridge is effected through an opening at the base of the breech. Above the lock, and flush with the barrel, is a lever which, being raised and drawn with a half turn to the rear, gives immediate access to the receptacle for the charge. A thick felt wad, saturated with grease, is fixed to the bottom of the cartridge, for the purpose of lubricating the barrel after each discharge. The wad, before the ignition of the powder, rests against the end of a small cylinder, which projects into the barrel, and thus serves to break the recoil. A breech-loading carbine on this principle was tried on board her Majesty's ship "Excellent," in 1858, under the the supervision of Captain Hewlett. Eighteen hundred rounds were fired without cleaning, with "unprecedented accuracy at all ranges, and without any recoil. The rifle missed fire but twice in the eighteen hundred rounds, and whether discharged by officer or man, eighty-six per cent. were hits." I do not know what objections to it were found to be sufficiently valid to prevent its adoption.

WESTLEY RICHARDS' BREECH-LOADER.

This eminent gun-maker has also invented a breech-loader, which has given a great deal of satisfaction in England, and has been partially adopted as a military weapon, the cavalry being supplied with weapons of this description. The bore is four hundred fifty thousandths inch, and of an octagonal form, completing one turn in twenty inches; length of barrel, thirty-six inches; weight of projectile, five hundred thirty grains; charge of powder, eighty-five grains. The military weapon differs a little from this. At Wimbledon this gun was tested before General Hay, and performed admirably. Out of forty shots at four hundred yards, the hits gave an average of seven and a half inches; at six hundred yards, nine inches; at eight hundred yards, about fifteen inches. The gun was fired from a rest of the most accurate construction, but the day was stormy and unfavorable. By the insertion of a bolt, which is provided for the purpose, this gun may be used as a muzzle-loader.

There are still a number of breech-loaders possessing merit, such as Green's, Snider-by-Aston, Henry, Montstorm, etc., etc., that might be described; but the compass of this volume will not admit of it. Among the latest inventions is "The Breechless Gun." I have not seen it, nor any description except that furnished by the *London Builder*, which says—

"A startling invention in gunnery has been announced by Mr. Harding, who makes not merely a breech-loader, but a gun without any solid breech! He takes a tube open at both ends, and this forms his gun, which is loaded and discharged with deadly effect. The plan is simply this: that a piece of wadding is rammed in at one end of the tube, then another piece, leaving a space, and, of course, some air between them, closely compressed; then the powder is placed in, and then a ball on the powder. The breech is practically formed by the air contained between the first and second pieces of wadding. Others are inquiring if gunpowder itself should be got rid of altogether midst all these changes. Captain Dixon says yes, and sends us one of his gun-cloth charges, a piece of rolled tape, so to speak, in a paper case, open at one end. The patentee claims for the gun-cloth charges, freedom from all risk of accidental explosion, 'except when confined in a gun-barrel or bombshell. They are non-explosive; they burn, but do not explode; if lighted and held in the hand they are harmless; they may be dropped down a red-hot barrel without fear of danger. A hundred may be lighted at once, and the result will not be more explosive or dangerous than setting fire to a handful of shavings, neither would the firing of a whole magazine be attended with more danger than the burning of so much wood, cotton, or paper.' The recoil is scarcely perceptible; the report is only one-half; smoke there is none; the combustion is perfect; and no residue is left to foul the barrel; and, withal, these charges are superior to gunpowder as a propelling force—

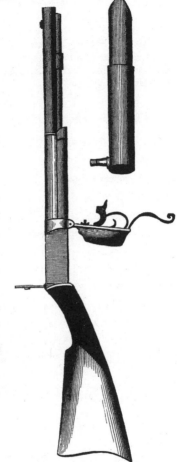

BOOTH'S BREECH-LOADER AND CARTRIDGE.

Length of barrel, twenty-eight inches; size of bore, twenty-eight hundredths.
Spiral, one in twenty inches: weight, nine pounds.

at least so says the inventor. Gun-cotton was, as formerly made and used, an uncontrollable, unmanageable, capricious force, besides being liable to ignite at a low heat, and fire by spontaneous combustion. Gun-cloth, this patentee says, is a strong but docile servant; weight for weight many times stronger than powder, and capable of being used with entire safety in existing fire-arms. Well, we shall see."

BOOTH'S BREECH-LOADER.

Mr. Booth, of Ottawa, whom I previously mentioned, when speaking of "crack shots," has also introduced a breech-loader, intended for sporting purposes and target practice, and which has been found to answer very well. The breech opens underneath, and the cartridge, which is long, and contains a small firing-pin, is inserted, and the "trap" being closed, it is ready for action.

With this gun I have seen excellent firing made; indeed, the best I have ever seen done by a breech-loader. I am informed by a gentleman of this city that, at seven hundred yards, ten consecutive shots were fired into a target only fifteen inches square.

PAPE'S "CHAMPION" BREECH-LOADER.

The last gun that I shall introduce to the reader is that which I consider the simplest and best of all breech-loaders, for purely sporting purposes. Mr. Pape, of Newcastle-on-Tyne, the best gun-maker in the world, having devoted a good deal of time and attention to the subject of breech-loaders, has produced that which is known as "Pape's Combined Snap and Lever Action."

FIG. 1.—GUN OPEN FOR LOADING.

A.—Between and below the barrels a bar of steel, which fits into the false breech, preventing any shaking to right or left, and when crossed by the two wedges a perfect dove-tail in steel is formed.

B. and C.—Slots in the steel center-bar, which give the bearing surface for upper and under wedge.

D.—Lever.

FIG. 2.—ACTION.

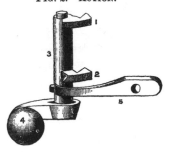

No. 1. — Upper wedge. No. 2.—Under ditto. No. 3.—Center shaft. No. 4. —Thumb-piece or lever, by pressing which the wedges are moved out of their slots in the steel center base; the gun then opens. No. 5.—The action-spring which gives the rotary motion to the center shaft. The breakage of the main-spring does not throw the action out of order, for it can be worked as readily with the lever 4 above.

This action, for sound mechanical principles, is superior to any yet invented, the gun being self-locking by the closing of the barrels, which are securely bound by two powerful bites at the extreme end, attached to an upright shaft turning in a circle from right to left by slight pressure, thereby throwing the breech open. It is simple and pleasant to work while rapidity, with strength, security, and binding power is perfectly combined. The objectionable side-levers, or large under-levers, are replaced by a simple thumb-piece under the right lock. No danger of this action wearing loose. It possesses the great advantage of a self-continuous leverage pressure upon the barrels; any defect from wear upon the bites being self-adjusted by the action of the lever. This self-locking action, where leverage power is combined with snap-bolts, procuring perfect solidity and powerful binding power at the extreme breech end, insures the most regular and powerful shooting. The demand in England for guns on this principle (both shot and rifle) has been so great, that few have been sent to the United States. For any sportsman who wants a super-eminent double or single barreled rifle, and can afford to gratify his taste, I could recommend one of Pape's guns. They are made at all prices from eight pounds sterling (about fifty-six dollars currency) to sixty-five pounds sterling (equal to four hundred fifty dollars currency) ; and though the price may appear high, yet for finish, material, workmanship, and good shooting qualities, they have no equal. The cartridge for this gun is made of strong paper, the same as a shot cartridge for an ordinary breech-loader, with brass or copper ends, having a brass lining running up the inside for two-thirds the length of the case ; this gives a very strong back end to the cartridges, prevents them splitting, which causes an extra escape of gas, and leaves them in good condition to be recapped and used again. No better form of cartridge can be u ed than this. It can be used as pin or central fire. Mr. Pape has not yet produced a military breech-loader, but purposes devoting some attention to the subject. He is of opinion that his principle will suit as well for military as sporting purposes.

Having given a very full account of the different breech-loading fire-arms now before the public, both in this country and in Europe, I will conclude this chapter with a few remarks thereon, and a comparison of the merits of breech-loading and repeating rifles. The great success of the needle-gun, in the recent war between Prussia and Austria, has stimulated the other European governments to obtain some kind of breech-loading weapon for use in their armies. England has adopted the Snider, France the Chassepôt, Austria the Werndl, and so forth, of which I have given descriptions in the preceding pages; and though each possesses merits, to American inventors is due the credit of producing breech-loading fire-arms which, for simplicity of construction, accuracy, and rapidity of discharge, are vastly superior to all others. For though in the Snider, the English possess one of the best military arms now in use, the inventor was an American. Although Prussia may claim the credit, not of the invention, but of having reduced it to some practical form, to the United States belongs the honor of having converted an uncertain and complicated contrivance into a reliable and effective weapon.

There are two kinds of American breech-loaders, single-loading and repeating; that is, either loading every shot, or having a magazine, where from seven to fifteen can be stored, and which can be discharged in a few seconds without having to incur the delay of reloading. I have no hesitation in declaring that the single breech-loader is very superior to the repeater as at present made, notwithstanding that there is a strong prejudice in favor of the repeater. It is unquestionable that the Berdan, Remington, Snider-Enfield, Peabody, and Ballard are the best single breech-loaders yet brought forward. Experiments have shown that a man armed with the Berdan can fire no less than sixteen shots in a minute, without any more danger or fatigue than would result from using the ordinary muzzle-loading rifle.   Again has America proved her supremacy in the inventive arts; and, by placing in the hands of her soldiers weapons equal, if not superior, to those of other nations, she adds materially to the respect which is now evinced by other countries for her resources as a military power. With respect to the relative merits of single breech-loaders and repeaters, it seems clear that while the Spencer rifle proved its superiority over the muzzle-loader during the recent war, it did not satisfy our leading ordnance officers that it was the most effective of *military arms*.   Looking upon it merely as a mechanical contrivance, its power must be admitted ; but taking a practical view of its merits and defects, we are compelled to conclude that the single-loading breech-loader, though not a superior arm, is better adapted to warfare.   In the first place, the mechanical portion of a repeater is too complicated ; the danger of injury is too great, and the waste of ammunition too excessive, to admit of its being placed in the hands of a private soldier.   Soldiers are proverbially careless, and during the war, many Spencer rifles were picked up in the battle-fields with cartridges in the magazine the reverse position to what they should have occupied. Of course it would have been utterly impossible to fire the gun, as soon as a cartridge thus inserted had entered the breech-piece. It would never have been able to enter the barrel, and the result must have been to break or otherwise injure the internal machinery. The mistake here mentioned arose either from the carelessness of the soldier, or from his hurry when filling the magazine. But, in addition to this, with the knowledge that his gun contains seven loads, each of which can be fired without reloading, until every cartridge is exhausted, the soldier indulges in a reckless waste of ammunition, without doing any material damage to his enemy.* The same objection that applies to the Spencer is applicable, and with double force, to the Henry or Winchester guns. Repeating rifles of the last-named pattern are entirely too complicated for the use of an army. In the hands of experts, they may do tolerably well, but nine out of ten soldiers are

---

* Since writing this, I have seen a Spencer, with what is known as the "Stabler check," which converts it, at will, into a single breech-loader. This is a very ingenious contrivance, and adds greatly to the value of the gun, not only by combining the advantages of single-loader and repeater, but by disposing of the principal objection urged against the Spencer. By means of this check, the gun can be used as an ordinary breech-loader, keeping the charges in the magazine in reserve for an emergency.

not experts in the use of fire-arms, nor do years of active service render them such. In addition to requiring rapidity of fire, strength and durability are necessary; neither of which the Henry or Winchester gun possesses; they are delicate, complicated weapons, and therefore they would be utterly useless to an army. The Spencer is not open to the same objection, the mechanism being strong and serviceable. Experiments made with the Spencer, Berdan, Peabody, and Ballard show the following results :

Spencer.—One hundred shots in eight minutes and a half, being an average of a little less than twelve shots per minute.

Peabody.—One hundred shots in seven minutes, or fourteen and two hundredths per minute.

Ballard.—One hundred shots in six minutes and a half, or about fifteen per minute

Berdan.—One hundred shots in six minutes, or sixteen and four hundredths per minute.

Thus showing that the Spencer could not be discharged so rapidly as any one of these first-class single-loaders ; the time consumed in filling the magazine partially neutralizing its merits as a repeater. Advocates of repeaters have asserted that prejudice alone prevented the adoption of that kind of arm ; but this is not borne out by facts. Search-

ing investigations and tests, similar to the one referred to above, have conclusively established the
fact, that for military purposes the single loader is the
best.   For special service, and in hands of experienced shots, the Spencer possesses great advantages
over the others, and as a sporting arm answers admirably.   But even admitting that the repeater can
be fired as often or oftener than the single-loader,
wherein is the advantage?   The firing of so many
shots in such a short space of time would most likely
have an injurious effect upon the soldier, and would
most assuredly " demoralize " him ; for it would be
simply impossible for him to take any aim, the fasci-
nation of being able to discharge a given number of
shots in such a short space of time being too much
for him.   No such thing can happen with the single-
loader ; for the time necessarily consumed in loading,
etc., enables him to collect his thoughts and take
aim.   With the single-loader, an average of eight
shots can be obtained with ease, and surely this is
sufficiently destructive.   And as it unites simplicity
with great strength,—qualities in which some of the
repeaters are deficient,—it seems natural to conclude
that it should be preferred to the repeater.   I append the Report of the Board that sat in Washington
last year, and a few remarks thereon.

REPORT OF THE BOARD.

The Board begs leave to submit the following report:

The experiments of the board lead it clearly to the following conclusions:

First.—That the forty-five hundredths inch caliber ball has given the best result as to accuracy, penetration, and range.

Second.—That all rifle muskets and single-loading carbines used in the military service should, if practicable, be fitted for the same cartridge.

Third.—That the charge for muskets should be from sixty-five to seventy grains of powder, and from four hundred eighty to five hundred grains of lead.

Fourth.—That the Board recommends the plan of alteration submitted by H. Berdan. This gives the stable breech-pin, secures the piece against premature discharge, and involves only a slight change of our present pattern of arms. The bore of our present barrel (as has been proved by experiments before the Board) can be reduced to the desired caliber by reaming out the grooves and inserting a tube.

Fifth.—The Board has carefully examined the various patterns of new breech-loading arms presented to it, but finds itself unable to recommend any one of them for adoption for future construction by the Government. While fully impressed with the great mechanical ingenuity displayed in many of the plans, no one offers advantages for service superior to the altered musket recommended; and therefore the Board considers that, in view of the large number of excellent muzzle-loading muskets now in store, and the slight changes of machinery necessary to make new arms on that plan, should more arms be deemed necessary, there can be no justification for an entire change of model, and the great expense consequent thereon, until some further improvement shall be devised, producing more decided advantages than any of the arms yet presented.

Sixth.—The Board is not decided in the opinion whether it would be best to have only magazine carbines in the cavalry service. From past experience the Board would be unwilling to dispense entirely with magazine arms, and as these arms can be used ordinarily as single-loaders (retaining a number of charges in the magazine for extraordinary occasions, free from danger of ignition in the ordinary use of the gun), the only objections to their exclusive use are the additional expense of this arm over the simple single-loader, and the greater inconvenience of the use of a lever-gun compared with some patterns of the hinge breech-gun which have been presented to the Board.

In consideration of the above, and also of the manifest advantages of having single-loading carbines (if needed) and muskets made upon the same pattern, except in length of barrel, the Board recommends that, until a suitable plan for new muskets can be obtained, offering decided advantages over the proposed plan now recommended for altered muskets, no single-loading carbine should be constructed for the army.

The experience of the late war, as well as all experiments by this Board, prove that the Spencer magazine carbine is the best service-gun of this kind yet offered. Our experiments detected a defect in the arrangement for the extractor, which has been corrected by the manufacturers, upon the suggestion of the Board, producing, in the opinion of the manufacturers themselves, a decided improvement in the arm, and one that will lessen much the liability to become disabled in the service. It is believed, however, from models and from experiments of the Board, that the magazine arm is capable of further improvement; and the Board would therefore recommend some delay in adopting definitely a pattern "for future construction of carbines for cavalry service." Should new carbines be previously needed, it is recommended that the Spencer carbine, with the modified extractor, be used.

Seventh.—The Board is of opinion that for facility of handling, lightness, accuracy of fire, it will be of advantage to reduce the length of barrel, when practicable, to not less than thirty-three inches, retaining the present length of bayonet; and also that with the adoption of the metallic cartridge, the present cartridge-box should be modified.

WINFIELD S. HANCOCK,
Major-General U. S. Vols., President of the Board.

The Chief of Ordnance, General Dyer, dissents from the conclusion of the Board, with respect to the best caliber. He considers that the disadvantages arising from the great length of the cartridge more than counterbalance any advantage it possessed in range and penetration. He highly approves of Remington's, Berdan's, and one or two other systems for the conversion of the Springfield musket; and recommends that no plan be adopted until thoroughly tested in the hands of troops; and in order to make a comparison between them and original breechloaders, he further recommends that the following be issued in equal quantities to the same troops, for comparison; viz., Remington, Peabody, Sharp, and Laidley.

General Grant concurs in the recommendations of the Chief of Ordnance, except the proposition to place new patent arms in the hands of the troops for trial. He says—

"There being such a large number of arms on hand, capable of economical alteration, it seems unnecessary at present to experiment with new arms, many improvements in which will no doubt be made by the time they will be actually required.

"The superiority of the forty-five hundredths caliber in accuracy, range, and penetration, seems to have been placed beyond a doubt, but a uniformity of caliber being so desirable, and there being such a large number of arms of caliber fifty hundredths on hand, it may be advisable to adopt this caliber."

From all this, it appears that our own Government

16

have as much difficulty in settling questions between the various breech-loaders as the British War Department had.   A good deal of blame has been cast upon their military boards, for taking such a length of time to decide the question ; and now we find the American Government, who certainly are not addicted to red-tapeism and over-caution, deciding "to wait for something to turn up" in the way of an improved weapon, before they go any further than the conversion of the weapons now on hand, as a temporary expedient.   The conclusion may be considered fully established, that the best possible form of small arms is not recognized as in existence, by those who have made this subject their study, and that the converted Enfield or Berdan Springfield, is equal, if not superior, to any other weapon now in use.   When a repeater or magazine arm shall have been invented, which will be free from the liability to derangement,— which is the great objection to all now in use,—and possess range and penetrative power, combined with accuracy, equal or superior to the Enfield or Berdan, then, and not till then, will the question be answered, as to the best weapon possible.   I have devoted a great deal of space to the consideration of breech-loading guns, as I considered that the importance of the subject demanded it.   I shall now proceed to consider the best kind of rifle to be used for target and sporting purposes.

CHAPTER IV.

THE RIFLE, HOW TO CHOOSE AND HOW TO USE IT.

IN the last chapter, I have entered into very full details of all the guns principally in use, whether muzzle or breech-loading ; and it will be a matter of very little difficulty for the beginner to select a good weapon from among them. In case he should not have the confidence to do so, or should feel confused amidst such a variety, I will offer a few suggestions that may aid him in his selection.

In the first place, it is to be considered for what purpose he wants the gun, whether simply for target practice, or for sporting purposes, or for both combined. I do not propose to deal with the subject of a military arm, leaving that question to be settled by the Ordnance Department.

With respect to a target-gun, it will be for him to to consult his exchequer, whether he will have a finely finished Whitworth or Rigby rifle, costing him from one hundred seventy-five to three hundred dollars in gold, and equal to any gun in the

world for firing at long range, with open sights, or
whether he will adopt the more patriotic course of
patronizing some American maker, of whom there are
scores scattered over the length and breadth of the
country, who, if they have not a world-wide reputation, are nevertheless capable of turning out a gun
that will shoot with the greatest nicety, and that too
at a moderate price. As but very few are likely to
purchase foreign guns, I will confine myself to the
consideration of the proper kind of rifles for target
shooting ; these vary according to the taste of the
purchaser, or the caprice of the maker. The "American Target Rifle" may be considered almost in the
light of ordnance, weighing, as it does, from eighteen
to forty-five pounds, or even heavier, and always being fired from a dead rest, generally with telescope
sights and a hair trigger. Any performance with
such a gun can not, in my estimation, be counted
shooting ; it is certainly a test of the gun, but I claim
that it is not a test of the *man*, and, moreover, this
kind of shooting is most injurious, as it completely
"demoralizes" a man for shooting in the manly style
of *off-hand*. Cleveland coincides with me in this, for
he says : "Having thus proved your gun" (by means
of the rest), "if you hope ever to deserve the name of
rifleman, do not be tempted to make any further use of
a rest, but confine yourself strictly to *off-hand prac-*

tice. I speak feelingly on this point, from having suffered such a loss of power as I fear I shall never be able to regain. In my sporting days I never used a rest, and yet I never had a doubt of securing my game at any reasonable range ; but for the last two years I have been mainly engaged in experimenting with different kinds of guns, for which purpose I have always used a dead rest, and now I feel literally lost when I undertake off-hand shooting, and can feel no confidence of placing my shots in the target with any tolerable accuracy." Unquestionably there is a great deal to be learned from this style of shooting, that is very valuable to know, and which probably could not be learned in any other manner, such as the effect of the wind, of different quantities and qualities of powder, weight of ball, etc. ; but the idea of setting a great ponderous machine, fitted with a telescopic sight and hair-trigger, in a solid frame-work of wood, with a screw for depressing or raising the sight, and then, with eye fixed upon the streamers of cotton placed at short distances to indicate the force and direction of the wind, when a favorable moment arises, touching the trigger and calling it rifle shooting, is far different from my notions. Such kind of shooting will never make marksmen. To be a marksman, in the universal acceptation of the term, requires certain qualifications that are not possessed by all, but any one may improve by adopting certain rules, and rigidly adhering to them, but not by such manner of shooting as spoken of above. Such work would never qualify our marksmen to take part in the great national rifle contest at Wimbledon, in England; at the *Tir National*, at Brussels, or in Switzerland; at all these the system of artificial rests is discouraged.

As corroborative of my views of this subject, it may be well to give an extract from a letter written by the well-known "crack shot," Mr. Peck, of Albion, N. Y.

"You may have seen in the newspapers some account of the contest in rifle-shooting at our State Association, in which it was stated that I had the second prize. It was a very unequal contest, and you may wonder why I entered, when I explain. There were eight or ten entries, but only three guns made strings. The 'Maynard' contended with two muzzle-loaders, each weighing about thirty pounds. They fired from a rest or bench, upon which was a heavy cast-iron plate with a groove, and adjustable set-screws for leveling and holding their rifles. I held mine in my hands, and fired from the shoulder. All the competitors who proposed to shoot with their *hands* rather than by machinery, except myself, withdrew. I went in to show the judges and officers how unjust, under their rules, the contest would be, and to show what a breech-loader could do. Five trial shots only were allowed. I beat the Utica gun and its owner—being used by him only. I beat the Rochester gun in the hands of its maker, but another man took it at the end of his string, and beat me an average of one inch in each of ten shots at three hundred yards. Practically, he had fifteen trial shots, for the sights were moved and adjusted during the firing of the first eight shots of the first string. The judges called mine *shooting*, and commended it highly, while they ridiculed the other as 'artillery practice'—not deserving a prize in a contest with practical guns, but under the rules they must give it to the shortest string.

LINUS JONES PECK.

Albion, N.Y., June, 1867.

Very remarkable practice has been made with this kind of gun at the target, and it has, in very exceptional cases, done service in the field ; but it must be apparent to the most superficial observer, that its weight, and the delicacy of the telescopic sighting apparatus, would entirely unfit it for any ordinary purpose. It may, as a matter of interest, be used by a few to ascertain how close a number of bullets can be placed ; the only deviation of any account, it seems to me possible, must be caused by a flaw of wind. I have never used this gun, and will therefore avail myself of the experience of Chapman and Cleveland, in addition to some details I have previously given in speaking of its performance. At page 53 of his book, the latter records some practice made by Mr. Merrill; at forty rods, ten shots are placed in a target of about half the size of a playing-card. The gun weighed forty-two pounds, and took for a charge about a third of an ounce of powder, and a ball weighing five hundred and seventy-seven grains. Chapman, at page 99, gives some interesting details of shooting done with this kind of gun, and records that, in 1846, he won a fat ox at a shooting match, making a five-shot string at thirty-six rods (one hundred ninety-eight yards), that measured only five and three-quarters inches. This rifle, with the telescopic sights, was made for him by James, of Utica, whom he confidently recommends as a first-class workman; and, from what I have heard of his performance, I should style a first-class shot, with the rifle now now spoken of. But again to use Cleveland's language in corroboration of my views : " As I have just been setting forth the merits and powers of the heavy target rifle with telescope sights, I do not like to leave the subject without expressing my conviction, that the grand object of rifle-practice—that of training men to the ready and skillful use of the weapon *in the field*—is *in no wise promoted* by the use of such unwieldy instruments, requiring a dead rest, or such external equipments as must always be abandoned in active service.   .   .   .   .   .   But the object of rifle practice being to fit men to make a ready and skillful use of the weapon in the field, no guns should be used in target-practice which are not available for such purpose, and no rest should be allowed." As I cordially indorse these views, I shall not take any further notice of the " American Target Rifle," but pass on to a consideration of those kinds of guns with which he may be expected to make such practice as will enable him to emulate the feat of Lieutenant Godfrey, who, during the Crimean war, silenced a Russian battery at over six hundred yards with his rifle, an ordinary Enfield ; or to stop an antlered buck dashing at full speed through the woods in October. The beginner, having settled the question with himself as between muzzle and breech-loader, should apply to some gun-maker, who has a character established for good work, and order a gun made *to fit* him. This idea of fitting may sound curious ; but I can assure the uninitiated that it is as necessary to have the gun fitted to him as his clothes, if he hopes to make good work. The length and set of the stock is a most necessary consideration, as also the weight of the barrel. On this latter point, as well as the size of the bore, opinions are greatly divided, and it is a most unusual thing to find two sportsmen or rifle-makers agree. Of course, in considering this question, it must be remembered that the service for which it is required is the main point. If for sporting purposes solely, the same considerations will not prevail. Any gun that will throw a good-sized ball, strong and accurate for a couple of hundred yards or so, is likely to answer most of the demands that the sportsman or hunter will make upon it. But if, on the other hand, the learner is anxious to distinguish himself at target-practice, he will do well to remember that the gun that will perform well at forty rods may not possibly meet his expectations at eighty, owing to the difference in the length of barrel, size of caliber, etc., etc. It may, however, be considered as established, that from twenty-eight to thirty-three inches length, with a three-eighths inch bore, is the most suitable size for a barrel. With regard to the spiral, I favor one turn in twenty-four inches, though some prefer one turn in twenty inches, as Whitworth's rifling is on that principle. With regard to what is known as "the gaining" twist, opinions vary very materially; one first-class shot telling you that the good shooting he does is attributable to his rifle having the gaining twist; another, that no good results can be expected from it. Chapman, who is admitted to be a good authority, says that no good firing can be expected from a rifle that has not a "gaining" twist, and he devotes a good deal of space, in his valuable and useful work, to prove this. He states that "I should not dwell so long upon this point, did I not know that an erroneous opinion is entertained by some respectable mechanics. It is not generally known, by rifle-makers and others, that an increasing twist is a true geometrical line, formed by the application of an arc of a large circle to the surface of the cylinder; and the radius of this circle must of necessity be longer for a slow, and shorter for a quick gain." Stabler, whose name is well known throughout the

States as a crack shot, is against the "gaining twist."
He winds up his views on the subject as follows : "I
have found no advantage of the 'gain' over the
'even' twist ; and my experience and observation
so far, is against the former." Whitworth, in his experiments, found that an "even" twist was the best,
and he experimented to a larger extent than perhaps
any other man. Who is now to decide when "doc-
tors disagree"? Good shooting is made by both,
and every man must choose his own style. I prefer
the "even" twist. A rifle weighing from eight to ten
pounds, with plenty of metal at the breech, carrying
a half-ounce ball, with from twenty-eight to thirty-
three inch barrels, by a respectable maker, will be
found a workmanlike tool, and, either in the forest
or at the target, is likely, *if well held*, to give a good
account of itself. Seth Green, the best shot in New
York State, and an ardent sportsman, prefers a rifle
made by Billinghurst, of Rochester, on Miller's patent.
It is a seven-shooter, having a cylinder similar to
Colt's, patch ball, round or long, and pill-lock. In
loading, the powder is put in the cylinder, and the
ball patched and pushed down the barrel to the
cylinder, turning the barrel every time a ball is put
down, until the cylinder is loaded ; then drop a pill
in the prime-hole, and tallow it over, and you are all
right for seven shots. With this kind of rifle, Green

has shot for many years, and always found it answer well; in his own words, "When you are in the woods, with one of the above guns, you feel that you are monarch of all you survey, and do not fear any thing that wears hair." A very excellent kind of rifle for sporting purposes is thus described by Frank Forrester: "I should choose, for my own use, a double-barrel to carry a conical ball of precisely one ounce weight, the round bullet being proportionably lighter, of from twenty-eight to thirty-inch barrel; the shorter length, if to be used principally, or much on horseback, with a weight not to exceed ten pounds. It should have a plain fowling-piece stock, for quick shooting, and rather an open V-shaped back-sight to facilitate rapidity of taking aim, though it might be furnished also with a telescope back-sight, and thread-and-ball end-sight, for target practice and rest-firing." I can readily understand such a rifle to be first-class for hunting purposes, but I much question its suitability for target practice, from the difficulty of placing the axes of the barrels exactly parallel with each other, so that each barrel would shoot equally well with the same sighting at all ranges. The adoption of separate sights for each barrel would obviate this, but at the price of the loss of all elegance of appearance. Such a gun seems to be greatly in vogue with African hunters. Cumming used one, by Dickson, of Edinburgh, for a long time; and when it burst, he felt " cut to the heart; it was my main-stay; and as I thought of the many services it had performed for me in the hour of need, I mourned over it as David mourned for Absalom." Such a weapon is not, I think, likely to become very popular in this country. When a man abandons the single barrel, he will take to the breech-loader or repeater; and indeed as far as my experience goes, a breech-loader is the only thing likely now-a-days to be used, more particularly in the plains in pursuit of buffalo, elk., etc. In writing thus, I know that my views are diametrically opposed to those of Frank Forrester, who says, at page 116 of his "Complete Manual for Young Sportsmen," "No breech-loading rifle has probably ever been made, with which the best and most rapid marksman could fire two shots, loading for the second, at one animal running at speed away from him, or across him, unless it were once in a thousand times, on a perfect open and level plain, at a very large object. . . . . In point of rapidity of firing, therefore, for sporting purposes, no breech-loading rifle can ever equal, much less surpass, a finely made, accurately sighted, double-barreled hunting rifle." In my experience,—and I do not pretend to be either the best or the most rapid of marksmen,—I have found the reverse of this. Last fall, when out deer-hunting, I fired at a buck, and only slightly wounded him, my aim being disconcerted by jumping on a large pine tree; I immediately reloaded and brought him down. I had scarcely time to put in a fresh cartridge before another deer came bounding down the run-way, and I dropped her in her tracks. Where would the double-barreled rifle be about that time? Why, the charges of powder would scarcely be measured out in the time I took to slip in a cartridge and knock over the hind. The rifle I used was one of Frank Wesson's.

Stabler, in a letter to Cleveland, gives his opinion on this subject in the following words: "I took my rifle with me on my recent trip to the Alleghany mountains, and having pretty much got through my business, I took an afternoon hunt. A light snow had fallen, and I soon came upon the tracks of a couple of deer, which I followed for a mile or two, coming on them within fifty or sixty yards; they standing three or four feet off each other. I dropped the first in his tracks, and before the second had moved twenty-five yards, I had reloaded and knocked him down also. So much for the Maynard rifle."

For sporting purposes solely, I do not think that any man, desiring to be considered a sportsman, would any longer carry the single-barrel muzzle-loading rifle. Repeaters or breech-loaders will prevail; and the only question to be decided is, which one out of the many good ones offered will he select?

I do not wish to advocate any rifle in particular, and will therefore leave the selection of the gun to his own judgment ; and he will be difficult to please, if, among all those mentioned, he can not find one to suit his taste. I consider the Ballard, Spencer, Wesson, Remington, and Ball as the best. I will reproduce here the remarks of Frank Forrester on the choosing of a rifle. "The mode of selecting a rifle to suit the shooter is identical with that of choosing a shot-gun. The way to ascertain its operation is for the buyer to have it tried in his own presence at arm's length and at rest, at long and short ranges, with the wind, against the wind, and across the wind,—which last, if it be blowing any thing like a respectable breeze, is the hardest test of all,—by some one in whose shooting, if he be not confident of his own, he may have perfect reliance. If it execute quickly, surely, and forcibly, he may be sure that he has got what he requires. But, by all means, let him insist on trying it, or seeing it tried, in the open. No testing in a gallery of fifteen or thirty paces is worth sixpence, as a real proof of the weapon or the shooter ; and none but a tyro would dream of purchasing on such a childish assay."

Having now, I trust, given such directions as will enable the beginner to make his selection, I will offer a few suggestions with respect to the manner of taking care of it. It must be laid down as a golden

rule, never to put away a rifle in a dirty state ; no
matter how tired you may be, always see that your
piece is properly cleaned. This, in a breech-loader,
is a very slight matter, as most of them are now provided with a kind of brush-wiper, which, by simply
passing it through the barrel, cleanses it of all im-
purities ; but with a muzzle-loader, a great deal more
pains is required. Some first-class shots say that no
water is to be used, but with a number of pieces of
oiled rag, thoroughly cleanse the barrel from all
fouling, and having lightly oiled it inside and out,
rub carefully with a flannel cloth, and put away in a
dry place. Chapman recommends pouring a table-
spoonful of good bear's or lamp oil into the barrel,
having previously stopped the vent and cone, and
allowing it to remain until again required ; but I do
not see that any thing is gained by this, and prefer
to do up the job at once. Almost any animal oil is
good, such as sperm, carefully clarified neat's-foot,
etc. ; only avoid using vegetable oils, as they are
liable to get gummy. In England there is greatly in
vogue a preparation known as " Wishart's Com-
pound," for cleaning the rifle, which has been found
very efficacious. I believe it to be prepared from
coal-oil. I do not consider that these methods properly clean the rifle ; for I am confident that some
portion of the fouling will remain in the grooves,
and be forced down into the breech. I think it

better to clean the rifle well with cold water, after which use a small quantity of hot water, the hotter the better, as it dries quickly, the barrel becoming heated from it ; force it well through the nipple, and then carefully dry your barrel with successive rags, or, if you can obtain it, good dry tow, then use very slightly oiled rags ; and having stopped up the muzzle to exclude air, place it in a dry corner, care being taken to look at it from time to time, and occasionally wipe it out for fear that rust might gather. Forrester thinks loon-oil, "the sovereignest thing in the world to prevent rust," and I do not doubt it ; but as it is not easily obtained, we must be content with what is recommended above. With respect to the lock, I would counsel the beginner to leave it alone ; if it requires any easing, oiling, or regulating, let him go to the nearest gunsmith, and he will set it right for him in a few minutes ; to old sportsmen, of course, I do not presume to offer any advice, as they are fully as competent, in most cases, to adjust their locks as a gunsmith. And now, having chosen our gun, and received instructions how to take care of it, I propose in the next chapter to offer a few directions as to the manner of using it.

17

CHAPTER V.

THE RIFLE, AND HOW TO USE IT.

IT may be proper, before proceeding to the target, to offer a few remarks on sights, bullets, powder, etc. Respecting the sighting of a rifle, I find Cleveland's remarks so completely explain the subject, that I can not do better than quote him. The telescope sight is only applicable to the heavy target rifle, and therefore useless to sportsmen. The " globe" and "peep" sights consist of a small metallic disk, pierced with a very minute aperture, and fixed upon the stock of the gun by a screw or slide, by which it may be raised or lowered, and a bead or globe upon the point of a slender steel wire on the barrel, just over the muzzle, protected by a cylinder of steel in which it is inclosed. The bead is sighted through the pin-hole of the back sight, and, being brought in line with the target, affords a very perfect means of directing the shot. But even this is too delicate an arrangement for field service, and is rarely used, except for target shooting, though commonly furnished with the equipments of a thoroughly furnished rifle, to be made use of when required.

The most common arrangement consists of a bead or " knife-edge," of bright metal, fixed in the top of the barrel just over the muzzle, and called the " fore-sight," and an " after-sight " or guide-sight, near the breech, which is constructed with a notch like the letter V, through which the fore-sight must be aligned with the target. If these sights are properly arranged, so as to be in the same vertical plane with the axis of the barrel, the line of sight drawn through them should coincide precisely with that of the flight of the bullet, except so far as the latter is affected by external influences. It is rare, however, that the sights are arranged with perfect accuracy as they come from the gun-maker's shop; but the error may be detected by a few experiments, and rectified by moving the fore-sight a little to one side or the other, as it is commonly fixed upon a plate which is moveable in a slot cut across the barrel.

The after-sight being so arranged that it may be raised or lowered, the proper degree of elevation of the line of fire for any distance, within the range of the piece, may be given, and the line of sight still directed exactly at the target. In order, however, to render this power practically useful, it is necessary that the degrees of elevation for different distances be ascertained by actual trial, and marked upon the slide or screw of the sight, and also that the shooter should acquire the power of estimating distance by the eye, so that he may be able to tell by a glance at the object at which he wishes to shoot, the degree of elevation required. And the longer the range the more important it becomes to estimate exactly the distance; because, at the end of a long flight, the bullet is falling more rapidly, and describing a much shorter curve, than at the end of the shorter one, and consequently the probability is much greater either that it will fall short or overshoot its mark, than when it is moving more nearly in a horizontal direction. From this it will be understood that for *fine* shooting, " peep and globe " sights are necessary; but for ordinary sporting purposes, where "snap" shots are common, a sight must be used by which aim can be taken *instantaneously*. A very large number and variety of sights are in use in England and on the Continent, and a long chapter might be written upon them, but I do not purpose dilating at greater length upon this subject. The sights above noted are quite sufficient, if used to advantage, to enable the learner to attain to such a degree of excellence as will enable him to experiment for himself. In Captain Heaton's " Notes on Rifle Shooting " will be found some very interesting particulars respecting sights and sighting.

One point must not be omitted,—avoid all brightness of metal about the sights, or it will be found impossible to make good shooting from the glare caused by the sun shining on bright or polished metal. The fore-sight, if open, should be of a dead black, and let the back-sight at the V be smoked, or in some way blackened, to avoid the reflection. In using a muzzle-loader, great care must be taken in the preparation of the bullets, if good shooting is to be expected ; the purest lead must be used and the greatest nicety observed in casting them. Use a large ladle, and do not make the lead too hot ; the bullet-mould can not be too clean, in my judgment, though some writers advocate smoking it; and it is desirable that it should be heated before commencing, or otherwise lay aside a couple of the first cast ; by this means the mould is in good order, and the bullets will drop readily from it. When a number have been cast, they should be passed through a steel gauge of the precise intended diameter. They should then be trimmed off, oiled, and put together and worked in a bag, after which they are to be " swedged," and laid aside for use.

Among the many ingenious inventions connected with breech-loading fire-arms, I must not omit to mention PECK'S PATENT PATCHED BULLET, which is thus described by the inventor :

"No rifle-barrel can be made perfectly true in its inside caliber; and it is the universal practice among riflemen, where close shooting is required, to patch the bullet, in order to insure a smooth, even fit, and perfect lubrication between the bullet and bore of the rifle. The ease with which this is accomplished with the old muzzle-loader, and the want of any device for doing the same for the breech-loader, have caused the old rifle to retain its place among riflemen for sharp shooting. With the use of the invention herewith illustrated the breech-loader will, in addition to its other advantages, possess all the accuracy of the muzzle-loader. Fig. 1 represents the bullet cast as it comes from the mould and ready to receive the patch—which patch

FIG. 1.   FIG. 2.   FIG. 3.

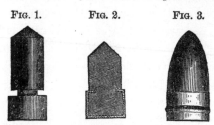

may be of cloth, parchment, paper, or other material. The patch is by means of a die brought over the end and the edges turned into the groove around the casting, where it is secured by pressing down upon it the the upper portion of the casting, leaving it as shown in fig. 2, which is then placed in another die which gives it any form required for muzzle or breech-loader, as in fig. 3, which is designed for use in the metallic cartridge of the breech-loading rifle."

Having no experience of the merits of this invention, I can not pass any opinion on it, though it appears as if it might be serviceable.

The next item, and a most important one it is, to be considered is the powder. Never use any but the *very* best; it is the poorest economy, and causes great vexation to use common powder. All writers and "crack shots" urge this point. Captain Lacy, in his work the "Modern Shooter," says, "It is the very life-blood of shooting; for if indifferent, the very best guns are comparatively of but little use." If good at first, and afterward kept perfectly dry, as it ought always to be, it will retain its virtues unimpaired for a considerable time; but if it once gets damp, and particularly if it remains so for any time, the grains have a tendency to dissolution or decomposition, which no after-drying can ever so fully recover as to restore the powder to its pristine strength. It ought to be kept wholly excluded from atmospheric influence, as the saltpetre, especially if not of the purest kind (and it is often impregnated with marine salt, which vastly increases its tendency to absorb moisture), readily imbibes damp; and powder will preserve its strength,—to say nothing of greater safety from accidental explosion,—better for two years in tin than for one in wood. It is unnecessary for us to inquire who invented gunpowder, whether it was known (as is claimed by some writers) to the Chinese as far back as two thousand years ago, whether it was used at the seige of Mecca in the year A. D. 690, is of very little consequence. It was not manufactured in England until 1346, and was necessarily of very rude

make. It is composed of sulphur, saltpetre, and
charcoal in the following proportions : twelve,
seventy-four, fourteen ; very little variation from
these proportions being made by any nation. The
very best powder that I know of is Curtis & Harvey's
No. 5 or 6 ; next to that the Roslin Mills. Some of
the American powder is very good, particularly the
" Orange," manufactured by Smith & Rand, of New
York, and which is unquestionably the best that I
have met with of American manufacture. At the test
of arms in Washington in 1866, cartridges made with
this powder gave far superior results as to penetration, range, and cleanliness, than those made from any
other American powder. Another proof of its superiority is the fact that at the State trial of arms, at
Albany, May 18, 1867, it was one of the conditions
that " the powder to be use is the Orange Rifle
Powder, Fg." It possesses all the necessary qualifications, such as uniformity in appearance of the
grains, which are crisp and sharp to the touch, and
not easily reduced to dust by pressure between the
fingers, nor dusty in handling. I have full confidence in recommending this powder to gentlemen
desirous of obtaining a good article of native production. It is claimed that powder that is very
slow of combustion is best suited to the purpose
of target firing ; and Chapman recommends that

made by the Boston Company, for Mr. Wesson, on account of its " *mildness and moderate strength*, because the English and some other noted powders are too good and strong for the target rifle." A quality of powder is made in England and America, expressly for rifle-shooting, and known as " Rifle Powder," so that no difficulty will be found in selecting the right kind. Fire a number of shots with different kinds, carefully noting the results, and that kind that gives the *closest* and *most uniform* shooting, is best suited to the gun.

I had purposed making some remarks on the adaptability of gun-cotton as a fulminate, but fear to do so, owing to the transition state the manufacture of it is in. Numerous experiments are being made to utilize it, and, doubtless, ere long we shall see some satisfactory solution of the problem. Billinghurst uses it with his small pistol, and some extraordinary shooting has been made with it. It is also proposed to enclose it in a waterproof casing of India-rubber.

Having now, I believe, laid down such principles and given such directions as will enable the young beginner, I trust, to understand the principles of rifle-shooting, and having chosen his arm, I propose now to offer him a few remarks how to go to work, to make a practical use of what he has already learned.

CHAPTER VI.

PRACTICAL APPLICATION OF THE FOREGOING RULES.

WE will now suppose that the beginner, having chosen his rifle, prepared his ammunition and feeling in " good case," chooses a fine clear day to try in practice what he has learned in theory. We will begin by offering a few remarks on the important subject of loading. As I do not imagine that he will undertake to have any dealings with the "Target Rifle" and telescope sight, until he has become somewhat perfected in his art, I will not take it into account, referring him to Chapman's excellent treatise for full information on that subject. but deal with an ordinary eight or ten pound muzzle-loading rifle. The greatest care and nicety are required in loading, as a few grains too much or too little powder will alter the range of the bullet, and it, on its part, if not placed accurately in the barrel, will come out at an irregular angle, and, instead of going straight to the mark, will be turned sideways. This is corrected, or, properly speaking, avoided, by the use of a " starter," an implement that can be seen at any gunsmith's, and which will be better understood by being so seen, than it could be by any written description about it; suffice it to say, that the one most in use is made of brass, and has a socket to fit over the muzzle, with a starter working up and down in it. But to proceed with our subject. In the first place, it will be necessary for him to choose some place where there is no danger of accidents ; for the flight of a rifle ball is so great, and the liability to accident so serious, that the greatest care must be exercised. I have known a man seriously injured at nine hundred yards distance, and who stood over one hundred and fifty yards to the left of the firing point. Indeed, instances innumerable could be quoted of the *eccentricity* of a rifle ball ; if it should happen to strike a stone, stump, or any projection, it will go off at an angle, and, may be, do an injury long after the firer thought that it had become inert. Cleveland has some excellent remarks on this subject, which I reproduce for the benefit of the beginner, as they can not be too strongly impressed upon his mind. The remorse that would ever attend a right-minded man, if by carelessness he had been the means of depriving a fellow-creature of life or limb, would be very great, and the way to guard against it, is by paying due regard to these remarks. "A rifle bullet is easily fatal at a mile's distance, and no man should ever send one out of his barrel without considering the possibilities of its range. Yet many men, who know this fact, are constantly regardless of it, shooting not only at targets without regard to the course of their bullets beyond, but at any bird in a tree which offers a fair shot, though the elevation required must necessarily send the bullet to such a distance that it is impossible for them to know what may be in the range. It is true, the chances are that no mischief will ensue, and most men seem to be willing to trust to chance rather than common sense, perhaps owing to the fact that they have not enough of the latter commodity to make a perceptible difference of effect. But this is precisely the kind of carelessness from which an accident occasionally results, which is sounded as a warning through the newspapers, while nobody hears of the thousand narrow escapes which indicate the frequency of such carelessness. I was surveying not long since in a field within ten miles of Boston, when a bullet cut the sod within a foot of where I was standing, shot from such a distance that I had no time to go in search of the worthy to whom I was indebted for the attention.

"The danger from 'ricochets,' or glancing shots, is one also of which no one can have a realizing appreciation who has not witnessed their eccentricities. I have known bullets which the shooter supposed to be safely lodged in the hillside against which he had placed his target, to glance out at a widely divergent angle from his line of fire, and be heard cutting through tree tops a quarter of a mile off. In fact, unless shot into an embankment, which is very nearly perpendicular, they will rarely fail to glance out, and their further course is one which can not possibly be foretold. Neither is this danger confined to the case where the bullet strikes upon hard or stony ground. They will ricochet from a soft peat meadow, even when shot downward at a very considerable angle; and I have known a bullet shot into a stream from a high bank to rebound and lodge in a tree at least fifty feet above its surface on the other side."

Having arrived on his chosen ground, let him put up his target and measure off the range, placing a stake at every fifty yards; be careful to measure the ground accurately, as a few feet make a difference. The target I would recommend would be six by two feet, or about the size of a full-grown man. A good plan is to have a frame of iron with strong canvas laced on to it, and stout paper pasted over it ; divide this into sections of six inches, with an eight-inch bull's-eye in the center ; this will do very well for a beginning. Of course, when a certain degree of accuracy has been obtained, much finer work will be necessary, and he will be expecting to put a "succession of bullets into a hole the size of a dime," as I have heard some worthies boast of doing, but never saw accomplished. Being now prepared, he can proceed to load his gun, which is to be done in the following manner : Take hold of the barrel near the muzzle, turn it round so that the lock is outward ; then pour out of your flask the proper charge, which the maker of the gun has furnished you with, being particularly careful to see that you have the charger full each time, for it is necessary to have every thing uniform to do uniform shooting. Some marksmen weigh their charges, but I do not think this necessary, as when holding the flask reversed, two or three sharp raps will generally answer the purpose of filling the charger. Pour it gently down the barrel, being particularly careful to hold it upright, so as to avoid any particles sticking to the sides, and thereby losing a certain portion of the power ; place a " patch," which has been previously prepared from the finest linen, oiled, or as some recommend, greased with spermaceti ointment, and cut out with a punch twice the size of the butt of the bullet ; on the muzzle, the greased side downward ; now place the ball perfectly straight and true in the muzzle, and with the "starter" press it down two or three inches, using the ramrod to force it home. And here let me offer a word of warning, avoid the common error of "ramming" home the bullet, for two reasons; firstly, because the bullet being jammed on the powder, meals and grinds it, thereby depriving it of a portion of strength; and secondly, because injury is done to the face of the ball, which is thereby prevented from following a perfectly true and accurate flight. Nothing is more common than to see men, after driving the ball home with some violence, make the ramrod rebound in the barrel, to assure themselves that it is "home." Nothing can be worse than this; a moderate pressure, to satisfy yourself that the bullet is home, is quite sufficient. It is a good plan to mark on the ramrod how far into the barrel it should be, and then it can be seen at a glance if the ball is down. Place a cap on the nipple, and you are ready for action. The position in which you should be for "off-hand" shooting, and it is for such shooting I propose giving directions, is one that admits of a good deal of discussion. There is great difference of opinion on the subject, some good shots contending that they never could see any difference in their shooting, whether they were in one position or the other; while others maintain that it is absolutely necessary to good shooting that certain fixed rules should be adhered to. There are three recognized methods of firing, viz., the British or Hythe position, the Swiss, and the American. In the former the rifleman stands perfectly erect, head slightly bent forward, feet at right angles to each other, the left advanced about twelve inches, the right arm raised well up, the left hand advanced so as to take a firm yet easy grip of the rifle, the butt of which is to be pressed firmly against the right shoulder, the right hand grasping firmly the small of the stock. Captain Heaton describes the second as follows : "Next we have the Swiss standing position, in which no particular manner of placing the feet is required. The whole body is kept perfectly rigid, the chest expanded as much as possible, against which the left elbow is allowed to rest, the rifle being held with the left hand, as near the trigger-guard as possible. The Swiss rifles have a kind of handle for this purpose. The upper part of the body is thrown back. Before firing, you may notice the Swiss marksman taking a long, deep inspiration, which he holds until the bullet has left his rifle, when he gives a loud grunt of satisfaction if the shot has pleased him."

In the latter the legs are kept wide apart, body slightly bent backward, the left shoulder a little back, with the left hand he grasps the rifle well out, bringing the arm nearly under the barrel, so as to form a support, the right arm is thrown out square, similar to the style adopted in the Hythe position. The butt of the rifle is not pressed against the shoulder, but in the hollow between the biceps muscle and the shoulder. Cleveland prefers this method to the Hythe, but I do not. I think that by pressing the butt close into the shoulder one is less likely to feel the recoil or "kick," and in addition, it (the Hythe) is less constrained than either of the others. But good firing can be made in all these positions, so I will leave the learner to choose that one which seems to suit him best, and now to reduce all this theory and instruction to practice. Every thing being in readiness, we will suppose him about to fire his first shot. The rifle is brought up carefully to the shoulder, the eye being steadily fixed upon the object to be fired at, gradually raise the barrel until the sights and the object are in a direct line, and the instant that this is obtained, *press* the trigger, keeping the eye steadily fixed upon the mark, and the rifle in position for a second or two after delivering your fire. Just before the muzzle sight is made to cut the center of the bull's-eye, the breath should be held ; and in pressing the trigger, the forearm alone should act, the arm and wrist being stationary ; no movement of the body should take place until you see the result of the shot. I am in favor of a tolerably quick aim. I do not see what is to be gained by

18

pausing or dwelling; the finger should obey the
brain. On this point Frank Forrester says: "Though
it is necessary to get a sure aim before firing, it is not
necessary to dwell on it before doing so. Every second between the having taken true sight and the
giving fire is a second lost, or worse than lost; for
the longer the rifle is held to the face, the greater the
tension of the muscles and nerves, and the likelier are
both to shake and give way. The first true sight is
always, with all fire-arms, the *best* sight, and a quick
shot has as much or more the advantage over a slow
shot, with the rifle as with any other weapon." The
finger should be held well down toward the point of
the trigger, and a slight pressure commenced from
the moment the aim is begun. I may here mention
that the pull of the trigger is a very important consideration; it should not be so slight as to go off almost involuntary, nor so hard as to require force, but
so, that by a gentle pressure, commenced at the moment of taking aim, the slightest extra *squeeze* will
cause the hammer to fall at the very instant the aim
is perfected. I consider a pull of from two to three
pounds about the proper thing. The method of
ascertaining the pull of the trigger will be shown by
any gunsmith. If you should not be satisfied with
your *first* aim, do not *hold on* endeavoring to better it;
drop the rifle and rest the eye for a few moments.

It is better to take a few seconds extra than to jeopardize the success of your shot ; for, once you tap the trigger, it is too late then for reflection. I must not omit to caution the beginner against canting the rifle in his hand. This we are all liable to do ; even the grip of it in the left hand tends to this, and it is necessary that the greatest pains be taken to see that the sights are perfectly upright, as the slightest deviation from a vertical position will cause the bullet to incline to the right or left, according to the inclination of the foresight. A very common practice prevails, among some riflemen, of wiping out after every shot. I do not think that this is at all necessary in ordinary target practice, though it may be advisable to do so with the heavy target rifle, where large charges of a low grade of powder are used. But, on the other hand, do not continue to fire with a rifle after it has become foul. No accuracy can be obtained after the barrel is dirty. In target practice, the effect of the wind, sun, atmosphere, etc., must all be taken into account ; and though I do not believe that I shall be able to lay down such rules as will enable the learner to overcome all the adverse effects of these various elements, still I think that, by carefully attending to the few simple directions I shall give, when he is about to practice, his chance of making good work will be materially increased. I will first deal with the

wind, as there is nothing so difficult as to acquire a
knowledge of the force of it, and to know what allowance to make, if from front, right, left or rear.
Crack shots in England use various instruments, such
as anemometers, etc., and adopt various devices for
ascertaining the force of, and registering the pressure
of the wind and its direction ; but as the learner is
not supposed to carry an instrument maker's shop in
his pocket, I will not take up his time by describing any of them. It is well to bear in mind that a
wind from the rear elevates the ball, while a wind
from the front depresses it, but in a greater degree.
The effect of a side wind is two-fold, it not only
causes the bullet to deflect from its course, but likewise depresses it, so that with the wind from side or
front, a slight elevation will be required, while from
the rear, a slight depression from the elevation is
necessary. Captain Heaton believes it to be necessary to make more allowance for the wind blowing
from the left than from the right, as in the former
case, the wind and the "drift" are acting in concert
with each other, whereas in the latter case, they are
struggling one against the other, and the drift partly
overcomes the influence of the wind. The spiral of
the barrel being from left to right, causes the ball to
have a tendency to incline to the right, this is what is
known as "drift," and which at long ranges is very

great. To counteract the effect of the wind, wind-gauges have been invented, and are used by many shots, but are not I think generally approved of, at least Heaton, who, on this subject, may certainly be said to be a judge, quotes Mr. Fellowes approvingly, when he says of wind-gauges, "No sportsman, I need hardly say, ever makes use of such contrivances ; he knows that one of the great principles of shooting consists in having faith to aim, on certain occasions, away from the object, either in consequence of the motion of such object, or the deflecting influence of the wind, or of the gravitation on the bullet. Now, there is unquestionably a strong natural tendency to project a missile on all occasions directly at the mark.

" Inexperienced shots, and indeed many in whom the use of fire-arms might have been expected to dispel the illusion, are very apt at the moment of firing to cheat themselves with the idea, that a direct shot must strike correctly, although common sense shows the occasional fallacy of the supposition ; the act is involuntary. A knowledge, then, of the amount of allowance, quickness in the application of this knowledge, and faith in the result, are qualifications on which success materially depends, and long experience alone can master."

It is a common fault to make too little allowance

for the wind, indeed, many riflemen can not ever make up their minds to lose sight of the bull's eye, and so frequently miss the target when they were confident of a good shot; however, it will be found that the amount of allowance to be made, etc., etc., can only be gained by experience. It is not possible, within the compass of a volume like this, to lay down the rules and give the calculations necessary to arrive at a perfect understanding of this subject.

The influence of the atmosphere upon the bullet is dependent upon the quantity of moisture it contains; the greater the quantity the *lower* will be the elevation. It is generally noticed that better shooting is made in damp weather than in dry; this arises from the fouling becoming moist, instead of being hard and gritty. A dull grey light is most favorable to rifle practice. Great heat has also an effect on the aim. It no doubt has often been noticed that the air seems to dance on one of these very hot days. This will cause you to aim above the target, it being apparently raised; this is caused by refraction, and to correct this you will require *less* elevation. The effect of the sun is very diverse, and a careful series of experiments by Captain Heaton has led him to form the following conclusions: that if shooting on a dull day, the sun suddenly appears and lights up your sights, still leaving the target dull, *more elevation* will be required ; that is to say, if you continue to shoot with the same elevation that you had before the sun appeared, your shot will fall *low*. If shooting under similar circumstances, the sun appears and lights up the *target*, you require *less* elevation. If shooting on a clear, bright day, with the sun shining *on the target*, you will require *more* elevation than when he is hidden behind a cloud; and *less* elevation will be required when the sun is hidden, if you were previously shooting with his rays shining on your *sights*. He therefore suggests the following rules for shooting at five hundred yards, allowance for other ranges to be made accordingly :

" When shooting on a dull day, if the sun appears and lights up the *target*, aim two feet *lower* ; if it appears in front, and lights up the *sights*, and *not* the *target*, aim two feet *higher*.

" When shooting on a bright day, with the sun in front, if it disappears, aim two feet *lower ;* if the sun be at your back, or on one side, so as to light up the *target*, and it disappears, aim two feet *higher*."

Having now, I believe, touched upon all points necessary for the instruction of the beginner, I will conclude this chapter by a few general remarks, and offer a little advice that may aid him in carrying out the principles previously laid down. I have not made any mention of a rest, as I am opposed to rest firing;

but it may be advantageously used for the purpose of sighting a rifle, indeed you cannot properly sight your weapon without it; and I will therefore describe one suitable for the purpose. Have a bench made about three and a half feet long and ten inches wide, with four stout legs standing out at a considerable angle. The height should be about level with the breast, when sitting down. At one end place a stout piece of wood about five or six inches high, cross-wise, with notches cut in it to lay the barrel in, and well covered with cloth, or something soft; this should be securely fastened to the bench; the end of the bench nearest the shooter may be hollowed out a little for the breast to fit in, and now you have the rest. If any one wishes to go into rest-firing, and de-sires to know how to make a superior one, I advise him to consult Chapman at page 70. A rough-and-ready rest may be made of three moderately stout stakes, tied together near the top, and then twisted out at right angles; place your coat or any con-venient thing to rest the rifle on in the crotch, and you will find that you can manage very well. Or a rest may be extemporized out of a ramrod and a couple of walking-sticks. A very excellent practice will be found in judging distances, as, without the power of estimating distances, he will find, be he ever so good a shot at a target at a set and known distance, that

that skill may not avail him when called upon to exercise it in the battle-field or the forest. By a knowledge of judging distances, he will be enabled to render his skill available at critical times. An error of a few yards in distance will cause the best-directed bullet, either to bury itself in the ground at the foot, or to pass clear over the head, of the foe. From this it will be apparent that, unless the rifleman possesses this knowledge, he will be of very little use on the field, where, during the vicissitudes of battle, the distance at which he encounters his foe is ever changing. I could not, within any limited space, give such directions as would enable any one to master this subject, but he can learn a great deal by himself, by making a practice, when out walking, of taking points and estimating the distance to them, and then, accurately measuring them, he will find that he makes

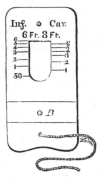

rapid progress in this way; he will likewise find a "stadium" a great aid to him. This consists of a small brass instrument with a cord, of which I give a rough outline. It should be about three inches high and an inch and a half wide. It is provided with a sliding-bar, B, and is made to enclose the figure, whose distance it is required to measure. The end of the cord is held in the left hand close to the eye, and the right arm is extended at full length, holding the stadium upright. As the distances are graduated with great accuracy, very satisfactory results are attainable by its use. If the learner is desirous of perfecting himself in this branch of the subject, I would advise him to get Hans Busk's "The Rifle and How to Use It," and therein he will find the necessary directions to enable him to do so. Should the learner not have many opportunities of practising, do not let him imagine that he will not be able to become a good shot. At the musketry school of Hythe, it is held that the less previous practice a man has had with fire-arms, the better is the prospect of making him a marksman, as he has no bad habits to unlearn. The system adopted there is the result of innumerable trials, and having carefully ascertained the best way for performing every thing requisite to become a marksman, they have proved, that by a "rigid adherence to them, far more than average proficiency in shooting is attainable, without the expenditure of a single ball-cartridge." This may seem incredible ; but it is nevertheless true. It is done by constant attention to a course of aiming and position drill. Let the learner practice for a few minutes, morning and evening, or whenever convenient, at a mimic target, carefully following the directions laid down, and he will be surprised at the result. A very excellent practice is that of snapping caps ; let him carefully aim and go through all the motions as though the gun were loaded. He can further improve himself in the evenings, in his own room, by placing a candle a few feet from the muzzle, and taking aim at the wick. He will find that if the aim has been true, that the explosion of the cap will extinguish the candle. There is no greater fallacy in the world than to believe that a man can only become a good marksman by a liberal consumption of powder and lead.

In the present unsettled condition of our country, only partially recovering from the late fratricidal struggle, and looking to the position of affairs in Mexico, and the "war-cloud" which now hangs lowering over Europe, it is impossible to predict what may be the course of events. Under such circumstances, it behooves every loyal man and true that he should become familiar with the use of fire-arms, in order to qualify himself to assist his country in time of need. Volunteers, expert in the use of the rifle, have on many occasions played a prominent part in warfare. In this country we can point with pride to the part they took in the struggle with England, that resulted in achieving our independence. It was to a body, chiefly consisting of rifle volunteers, that Burgoyne and his entire army, composed of the finest troops in the world, surrendered at Saratoga in 1777. The indomitable prowess of volunteers again prevailed in 1781, when Lord Cornwallis and another English army were compelled to lay down their arms. The deeds of valor performed by the German student volunteers, in 1813–15, are too well known to need recital here. Again, the whole might of Russia, with half a million of troops at her back, in a long and sanguinary war, extending over thirty years, hardly accomplished a success worth recording against the hardy volunteers of Circassia. Nor must we forget the gallant deeds performed in Mexico under Scott and Taylor. I cordially endorse the following sentiments, extracted from a writer in "Frazer's Magazine," and as well as part of the above, quoted from Hans Busk : "What is wanted for home protection, is your patriotic home guerilla force, lining hedges, popping from pits and tree-tops, galloping from point to point, and blazing away at foragers, skirmishers, and outposts, and so thinning off the foe marvellously, and making him, to his bitter astonishment, 'small by degrees and beautifully less!' . . . But for real loss to an invading army, post me five hundred quick-sighted and quick-footed amateur riflemen, in their own well-known woods, and see how they'd pick off all the lieutenants, and colonels, and artillerymen half a mile away." This matter is well understood in England, and every effort is made to induce a proficiency in the use of the rifle; and the wonderful advance in the numbers and excellence of the rifle-shots of Great Britain is a constant source of congratulation to that country. I have not space to give details of the shooting average of thousands and tens of thousands of the young men of England; but it displays wonderful results. By the training of our youth to the use of the rifle, we would not be found again in as unprepared a state as we were when the late stupendous rebellion burst upon us. Nor would we see such records as those of the battle of Bull Run, where many thousands of rifles were picked up after the battle, improperly loaded, and where, by a careful computation, for every man killed, *his own weight in lead was expended.* If by my writing, and by precept, I am able to help to better such a state of things, I shall feel amply repaid.

CHAPTER VII.

BISON.

Far where the glittering, snowy thrones
Of the Rocky Mountains uplift their cones,
In grassy meadows and valleys around,
One endless pasture of flowery ground,
The tawny herds of the buffalo rove,
Or browse at will in the shady grove;
There hunter's rifle and Indian spear
Spread wasteful slaughter and frantic fear.

ISAAC McLELLAN.

THE American Bison (*Bos Bison*, Linn.) is an animal of vast size and strength, and of a most savage nature. He has a long shaggy mane, which forms a kind of beard under his chin; his eyes are fierce, his forehead broad, and his horns extremely strong. They are common to almost the whole of the uninhabited parts of North America, from Hudson's Bay even to the frontiers of Mexico. The more southerly their situation the larger is their size and the greater their numbers. Modern American travelers, particularly Lewis and Clarke, and Dr. James, bear frequent testimony to the almost incredible numbers in which they assemble on the banks of the

Missouri.   "Such was the multitude of these animals," says the former gentleman, "that, although the river, including an island over which they passed, was a mile in width, the herd stretched, as thick as they could swim, completely from one side to the other."   And again ; " If it be not impossible to calculate the moving multitude which darkened the whole plains; we are convinced that twenty thousand would be no exaggerated number."   Dr. James writes, that, "in the middle of the day, countless thousands of them were seen coming in from every quarter of the stagnant pools ; their paths," as he informs us elsewhere, "being as frequent and almost as conspicuous as the roads in the most populous parts of the United States."

The American male bison, when at its full size, is said to weigh two thousand pounds, though twelve or fourteen hundred weight is considered a good growth in the fur countries.   Dr. Richardson gives eight feet and a half as its length, exclusive of the tail, which is twenty inches, and upward of six feet as its height at the fore quarters.   The head is very large, and carried low; the eyes are small, black, and piercing; the horns are short, small, sharp, set far apart, for the forehead is very broad, and directed outward and backward, so as to be nearly erect, with a slight curve toward the outward pointing tips.   The hump is not

a mere lump of fatty secretion, like that of the zebu,
but consists exclusively of a deposit of fat, which
varies much in quantity, of the strong muscles attached to the highly developed spinous processes of
the last cervical and first dorsal vertebræ, forming fit
machinery for the support and movement of the
enormous head.   The chest is broad, and the legs are
strong ; the hind parts are narrow, and have a comparatively weak appearance.   The tail is clothed with
short fur-like hair, with a long, straight, coarse, black-
ish-brown tuft at the end.   In winter the whole body
is covered with long shaggy hair, which in summer falls
off, leaving the blackish wrinkled skin exposed, except
on the forehead, hump, fore quarters, under jaw, and
throat, where the hair is very long and shaggy, and
mixed with much wool.   Catesby observes, that on
the forehead of a bull the hair is a foot long, thick,
frizzled, and of a dusky black color ; that the length
of this hair hanging over their eyes, impedes their
flight, and is frequently the cause of their destruction;
but that this obstruction of sight is in some measure
counterbalanced by their good noses, which are no
small safeguard to them.   A bull (says he) in summer
with his body bare, and his head muffled with long hair,
makes a very formidable appearance.   In summer the
general color of the hair is between dark umber and
liver-brown, and lustrous.   The tips of the hair, as

it lengthens in winter, are paler, and before it is shed in summer, much of it becomes of a pale, dull, yellowish brown. In the female, the head is smaller, and the hair on the fore parts is not so long as in the male.

It will be observed that I have always used the word Bison, which is the correct term, though the animal is generally, yet incorrectly, termed buffalo in this country. The buffalo is an entirely different animal, and a native of the East; but as the name is, as above stated, familiarly used by all in speaking of the bison, I will adopt it in the following directions for hunting them, for which I am indebted to the courtesy of a western gentleman of high standing and wide-spread popularity. This kind of hunting is of a most exciting character, and not unaccompanied with danger, and a proficiency in it can only be attained by those inured and accustomed to a life on the great plains of the Far West. It is an existence peculiar to itself, and not only requires the experience and training of years, but a natural adaptability. Buffalo shooting is quite a simple affair; but their pursuit, as followed by the Indians, hunters, and trappers, involves all the requirements of a thorough prairie life. It is not, however, my purpose to enter upon the details and requirements of a life on the prairies, but to offer such advice and information as would enable a party of amateurs to fit themselves out for a dash upon the prairies, which is, in almost every respect, different from the requirements of the hunter and trapper, who turn their backs upon civilization for months together, and make their home upon the boundless prairie.

The buffaloes are fast disappearing before the "star of empire," and are now only to be found in the far off and unfrequented portions of the great plains of the far West. Their habits are eminently gregarious, and they move together in numberless small bands, so that hundreds of miles may be traversed in the buffalo range, before striking a fresh trail ; but once upon them, the herds extend for miles, dotting the whole surface of the country farther than the eye can reach, and moving gradually in an uniform course. The Indians and trappers, who pursue them for food and profit, follow them up, camping within a short distance of their range. The robes are only valuable in the winter, when they are full-furred. It is but seldom that straggling bands or single buffaloes are found far from the consolidated band, and then only after having been incessantly hunted by different parties ; under such circumstances, they spread out over a great extent of country, to re-unite when undisturbed. They are exceedingly timid, and scent danger from afar, and when alarmed, scramble rapidly away in an ambling kind of gait. The hunter approaches from the windward upon the feeding band, and as soon as they take the alarm, dashes upon them, and, having selected a fat cow, ranges alongside, and taking aim, immediately behind the shoulder, fires at the distance of but a few feet; the buffalo, feeling the death-stroke, swerves to gore its foe, but the horse, accustomed to the chase, anticipating this movement, swerves suddenly and widely at the report, still dashing on and keeping up with the band, until the hunter has reloaded, and, selecting another victim, the same thing is repeated. He continues the chase until warned by the distance he has gone and the number that he has slain, that it is time to return to camp. The robes, humps, and other choice portions of the slain animals make no inconsiderable load, and he returns laden with the spoils of the chase, and round the camp-fire, after feasting luxuriously, the hunters kill o'er again their game. The horse best suited for this kind of hunting is one of a good strain, reared by the whites ; but it is absolutely indispenable that he should have a prairie education, as the life he is required to lead, and the service he is called upon to perform, are entirely different to those he has been accustomed to. It will require long and difficult training to accustom and perfect him in approaching and pursuing them, as the very sight of the great shaggy brutes is calculated to strike him with terror; but if surrounded by millions of them thundering over the plains, making the earth vibrate, he would become completely panic-stricken. The horses used by the Indians and trappers are those of the plains, the wild horse; and though much inferior in speed and endurance to what is called by them an " American horse," or one raised by the whites, yet he would be the most serviceable and reliable for amateurs, unless by great good fortune a real good " buffalo-runner " could be obtained. This is a very difficult matter, as good horses are highly prized, and their owners are very unwilling to part with them. The saddle most in use is the Mexican tree, with a blanket strapped over it. As to arms and equipments, the best and easiest weapon for shooting buffalo, on horseback, is a large-bore holster pistol, the range is never more than a few feet, and a pistol can be readily and effectively used with either hand. Of rifles, the best in the world is a double-barreled Purdy; but as the cost will prevent its use by any but the wealthiest, I would recommend a thoroughly well-made, substantial rifle, of from forty to sixty to the pound. The hunter or sportsman cannot be too careful in his selection of a weapon for use upon the plains (or indeed any where else), for upon that he alone depends for every thing. A rifle, of the caliber above noted, requires the transport of but small weight of ammunition. A great desideratum for prairie life is to render your "pack" as light as possible. The best rig is a flannel shirt, hunting-shirt of buckskin, pants and moccasins of the same material, and a soft cap,—no change is needed, for when they wear they can be patched,—a good blanket, knife, and ammunition, your rifle and your horse, and you may start for a month on the prairies, with the pleasing episode of occasionally encountering bands of Indians prowling about, bent upon their favorite amusement of scalp-hunting.

Such is the substance of the advice of that accomplished gentleman and ardent sportsman, Charles P. Cassilly, Esq., of Cincinnati, and those who know him—and who in the western country does not— will admit that he is qualified to give advice on so momentous a question, as he has been "thar." I can not but believe, with all due deference to so good an authority, that one of the many good breech-loaders at present before the public would be a most serviceable weapon for buffalo-hunting ; and though both the Ballard and Wesson are well suited for the purpose, yet I think that the Improved Spencer, with Stabler's check, would be found to answer every requirement ; and would be such a tip-top article to have on hand, in case of encountering any of those "pesky" red warriors, who are just now making the great plains such an uncomfortable camping-ground. This, however, is a point that will be decided by each man according to his own taste and judgment.

CHAPTER VIII.

MOOSE.

When the winter snow lies heavy and deep,
In rounded hillock and drifted heap,
When the shaggy moose and the caribou,
With clattering hoofs scarce wallow through,
Then forth to the howling wilderness
The hardy trappers and hunters press:
Their limbs are of iron, and strung to toil,
And the snows are crimsoned with their spoil.
                                    ISAAC McLELLAN.

THE North American Elk, or Moose, is principally found in the Eastern States and Canada, though a few are still to be met with in the northern parts of the State of New York. Its habitat extends to the frozen regions of Hudson's Bay. But I do not propose to write of it as a naturalist, but as a sportsman, and I shall therefore confine myself to the region wherein it is generally hunted. Maine, New Brunswick, and the country north of Quebec, between the Saguenay and Ottawa rivers, is the best sporting range.

The moose is the largest of the *Cervidæ*; a full-grown male stands from seventeen to eighteen hands high, and weighs from one thousand to twelve hundred pounds. In appearance they are very ungainly, owing to the big head, short neck, and disproportionately long fore-legs, which characterize them. The summer coat is of a light ash color, excepting on the legs and belly, where it is of a lighter hue; the hair is long and exceedingly brittle : in winter, the coat assumes a much darker hue, becoming almost black in an old bull, a bristly mane of a few inches in length, and a tuft of coarse hair under the throat, sum up their distinguishing characteristics. The cow is smaller than the bull, and is of a redder color; she has but one at a birth at first, but subsequently very generally two. It is stated by some writers, that the young remain with the mother until the following year, which is a most unusual circumstance. The growth of the horns is a very slow process, growing only about an inch the first year, and so gradually until the full growth is attained. In very large animals they sometimes measure six feet from tip to tip. They are generally shed very early in the spring, yet so rapid is the growth, that they are again fully developed by early summer. The young males do not shed theirs until late in the spring, and are consequently later in reproducing them. Major King states that the horns of an old moose will weigh from fifty to sixty pounds.

Moose-hunting begins in October, and lasts until

late in the spring. By the game-laws of Canada, it is not lawful to kill after the 1st of February; but in Maine it is carried on until much later. It is greatly to be desired that sportsmen in the two countries would endeavor to have a stringent game-law passed to prevent the wholesale destruction that has of late been going on among them. Various methods are adopted at different seasons to hunt the moose, but the most common are calling, stalking, and hunting them in winter on snow-shoes. For a description of the former method I am indebted to Major King's "Sportsman and Naturalist in Canada."

"Calling, which is practiced generally in September and October, as soon as the bellow of the bull begins to be heard at night, is thus managed: On a calm, light night, the hunter, accompanied by an Indian or Canadian, skilled not only in wood-craft, but in the imitation of the call or bellow of the cow-moose, repairs to the forest or swamp in which the animals are known to be feeding. The instrument by which the call is produced is a cone or trumpet of birch-bark, about a foot and a half in length. With this the native mounts a high tree, in order to enable the sound to travel further.

"After the startling sound of the call has echoed away through the dusky forest, the ordinary deathlike silence again ensues, till the answer of the bull is faintly heard in the distance, for the range to which the call reaches on a still night is almost incredible. When necessary to guide or encourage the advance of the approaching moose, the call is repeated; but he generally makes straight to the point with wonderful accuracy, even from a distance of a mile or more. Listening for the first response to the call, and still more anxiously for the slightest indication of an approaching animal, is a period of some excitement ; but the moment the formidable beast is heard actually advancing nearer and nearer, crashing heavily through the obstructing branches in his onward course, now emitting a dull hollow grunt, now striking his antlers sharply against the trunks of the trees, every nerve is strung to the highest pitch, till the mighty tenant of the forest stands before the concealed hunter, who hardly dares to draw his breath as he steadies his hand for the fatal shot.

Sometimes an animal on approaching comes to a stand, apparently seized with vague doubts, and the caller lures him on again with a suppressed grunting sound, the imitation of which at close quarters is the most difficult part of the accomplishment. If the sounds are clumsily executed, the disappointed animal, though he would not hesitate, if confronted, to attack any one rash enough to meet him, takes alarm at an invisible danger, and beats a rapid retreat, at the very moment when the anxious watcher was about to realize the reward of his toil and patience. When this unfortunately happens, the sport is over for the night, and there is nothing to be done but light a fire and smoke, or lie down and sleep till a little before daylight, which is a very favorable hour for calling, and by that time the alarm has generally subsided, or other moose have fed up within call."

Should it happen, as is sometimes the case, that two bulls chance to meet, a terrific combat immediately ensues; they will rush at each other with tremendous force, roaring and bellowing in a most furious manner. Their antlers occasionally becoming locked, and thus both perish.

The greatest caution is necessary when hunting the moose in the foregoing manner, as he is very wary, and invariably comes up wind, often making considerable of a *detour* to do so, and therefore not easily led into ambush.

The moose is also hunted by being driven to the hunter by Indians, in the same manner as red-deer are hunted with hounds. The hunter posts himself on a likely stand or "run," and patiently awaits the coming of the gigantic game. The Indians, having ascertained the covert where the moose is concealed, get round it, and advancing through, drive him up toward the sportsman.

When moving through the forest, they carry their heads thrown back, with their noses pointed high in the air. It is astonishing with what speed they will go through the densest wood, avoiding striking their vast horns against the trees all the while. Their gait is a kind of slouching trot, though I believe they are capable of a gallop if hard pressed.

Still-hunting is also practised in the pursuit of the moose, and great care and skill are here necessary to ensure success; for the moose is very wary and keen of scent, the sense of hearing being also very acute. When the hunter arrives in the neighborhood where he expects to find moose, he exercises great caution in his movements through the forest, as the snapping of a dry twig may send a herd scampering off in hot haste, and he may have to travel weary leagues ere he again sees the game. I do not purpose speaking at length on this part of the subject, as I feel sure that no one will set out to hunt moose in this manner, unless he has an Indian guide, who will be eyes and ears and all things necessary to him, or he has already taken his degrees in wood-craft; and to whom any instructions I could offer would be but a repetition of that which he perhaps knows better than myself. The proximity of moose is known by a faint smell of musk that taints the air, and this should put the hunter doubly on the alert. In the fall their color so closely assimilates to surrounding objects, that not unfrequently the first knowledge that the hunter has of the near presence of a moose, is the flapping of his great coarse ears.

On the Upper Ottawa, the lumbermen and Indians "shine" the moose, in a manner similar to that practised in the Southern States in the pursuit of the common deer; only that instead of a fire in a cresset, they ordinarily use a small bull's-eye lantern. I have heard of Indians in this manner approaching a moose so close that they could lay their hand upon him. But, as I said before, he is pursued in season and out of season, and all kinds of means are adopted to secure the prey. I will not further dwell upon those methods, but come at once to that in general use in Eastern Canada and the Lower Provinces, and which tests a man's endurance and mettle to the very utmost; no standing quietly on a runway, no easy "drive," but downright hard work, that sweetens the reward all the more, when the noble fellow has been made to bite, not the dust, but the frozen snow.

Having been furnished with every requisite for camping in the bush, and well provided with snow-shoes, we will suppose our hunters arrived at the farthest point practicable for winter vehicles. Here the *impedimenta* are packed on tabogans, or light boards turned up at the end, to serve as hand-sleds, and drawn by the Indians.   Every thing being in readiness, they set forth on their tramp into the trackless wilds of the northern forest, the dusky guide needing no path, his unerring instinct serving to guide him in the right direction.   Having arrived at a likely place a camp is made, a snug and sheltered spot being selected ; the snow is dug or scooped out, and a lot of "sapin" branches being gathered and placed on the ground, the buffalo robes are spread over them, and the bivouac is complete.   A blazing fire adds cheerfulness to the scene, and enables the hunters to boil their pot and fry their fat pork.   On turning in for the night, all hands lay with their feet to the fire, and pack together as closely as possible, as it may be well imagined that it is no easy matter to keep up the caloric exposed to the rigors of a Canadian winter, the thermometer often marking as low as forty degrees below zero.

The Indian guide having found "sign," all is in commotion ; camp is broken up, and the excited hunters, donning their snow-shoes, and looking carefully to their priming, are ready for the fray, and eagerly set forth in pursuit of their noble quarry.   Having come upon the tracks, great care is taken to keep to leeward of them, and every nerve is strained to overtake the fleeing moose, but this is not a matter of easy accomplishment; for though the laboring creature sinks knee-deep at every stride, cruelly lacerating itself against the hard crust, it is able to go at such speed, that ofttimes hours, and even days, of tremendous effort are necessary to come up with the chase. When sighted by the hunters, renewed exertions are put forth to secure the prize, but this is met by the hunted deer by desperate efforts to escape, and again the pursuers are left in the rear ; but on and on they press with a will that knows no defeat, and soon again they close with the now exhausted yet furious animal, who, seeing escape hopeless, turns at bay, and with heaving flanks and distended nostrils, presents a grand yet terrible sight, and woe is he that possesses not a cool head and steady hand to send the leaden messenger on its deadly errand. The noble beast being dispatched, the Indians immediately set about flensing him, and selecting the choice bits for the hunters, who meanwhile are making preparations for a " snack," which will be eaten with a zest, such as the choicest viands prepared in Delmonico's best style would fail to induce; and while enjoying that greatest solace of a hunter, a good smoke, arrangements are made for a homeward tramp, or if the chase has lasted till late in the afternoon, as is often the case, they arrange a bivouac, and prepare to pass the night as best they can. The choice parts are the tongue, palate, *mouffle*, and marrow-bones, though the flesh, when in good condition, is excellent, resembling beef somewhat, though much coarser in grain. The fat is quite soft, differing in this respect from all of the *Cervidæ*, that portion of it known as the *depouillé*, being the layer covering the chine, is greatly esteemed. I should have mentioned that the *mouffle* is the upper lip, which is of extraordinary length and prehensile power, enabling the animal to obtain its favorite food of young twigs, and the small and tender shoots of trees, at great height.

It will be apparent from the description that the pursuit of the moose requires a rare combination of skill and endurance, and to be successful, requires such a trial of these, that none but the most robust need hope to endure. The hunters in this pursuit use snow-shoes, the form and construction of which, I presume, are perfectly familiar to my readers, and so I need not give any description of them, but state that they are very trying at first, and unless the tyro practises somewhat before setting out on a hunt, he will be laid up completely, the strain on the muscles being so severe.

Some parties prefer a double-barreled rifle for moose-hunting, but I should counsel a good breech-loader. I would like to see it fifty-four caliber, as it takes a heavy ball to administer the *coup de grace* to an old bull, and, if wounded, he is apt to be an ugly customer. But *chacun à son gout,* each one to his taste, and so long as a man has a good gun and dry powder, he will do well enough. A breech-loader has a vast advantage in the cold weather, as the cartridge is easily inserted, while with the muzzle-loader, it takes some time to load, more particularly with the thermometer thirty or forty degrees below zero; and then the misery of fumbling, with half-benumbed fingers ; the cap.

20

CHAPTER IX.

CARIBOU.

*   *   *   *   *   *

Mounted on snow-shoes, with their food,
   And blankets on light sledges pack'd,
The hunters of the wild stag cross
   The snow's immeasurable tract.
*   *   *   *   *   *

Until the browsing "yard" is found;
*   *   *   *   *

Then comes the conflict—rifles flash,
   And all is wild, tumultuous fright;
The wounded, bellowing, madly dash
   Thro' the dense wood in headlong flight!
While many a forest monarch lies
   Bleeding and struggling till he dies,
Encrimsoning with spouting gore
   The forest's white, unspotted floor.

                         Isaac McLellan.

THIS animal (*Cervus Tarandus var. Caribou*) which only inhabits high northern latitudes, has been frequently confounded with the reindeer (*Cervus Groenlandicus*) by writers. This arises from the fact of its being of the same family, and that no perfect skeleton exists in any European collection.

The tract of country over which the caribou is found, reaches from the southern shores of Hudson's Bay to the frontiers of Maine, extending in a westerly direction to Lake Superior's northernmost shore. They are found of a larger size the farther northward they are discovered ; indeed, there are two kinds known to sportsmen, the upland and the lowland, the former of which greatly exceeds the other in size. As to size, the North American Caribou is much larger than the reindeer, a full-grown male standing from three feet six inches to four feet in height, six feet in length, and weighing from four to five hundred pounds, when in good condition. The horns of the caribou present a very peculiar appearance. They are well described by Major King, at page 79. Partly palmated and partly cylindrical, the caribou antlers are of singular and fantastic form, and though of great expanse—apparently but ill adapted for a forest life—are so slight, that their weight seldom exceeds nine pounds. The stem of the horn is considerably curved, the concave side being to the front, and the extremities of the palmated brow-antlers project nearly fifteen inches over the face. Sometimes only one of these brow-antlers occurs on one or other of the horns, though they are more frequently present on both, especially in the case of the older males; and it is doubtless their peculiarity of form which has led to the belief that they are intended by nature for the purpose of removing the snows of winter in search of food. The fact, however, that the male animal sheds his horns about the commencement of that season, demolishes the theory in his case ; and it is well known that he uses for this purpose his fore-feet and muzzle only, the skin of the latter being exceedingly hard and tough.

The female is furnished with antlers as well as the male, and it is a curious fact, that while he sheds his at the commencement of winter, she, in common with the rest of the *Cervidæ*, retains her until the spring.

There is a great difference between the horns of animals at different stages of growth, the younger ones having them in the shape of plain, slender, and very slightly curved stems, bearing equally slender cylindrical brow-antlers, or rather tines, with no appearance of any tendency to palmate.

The appearance of the caribou is not at all elegant; his short and thick legs, large head, and want of general symmetry, making him very dissimilar from most of the beautiful and elegant family to which he belongs.

The hair is rough and short, of a tawny or reddish-brown color, inclining to grey in winter ; the throat and belly being white. This animal is much troubled in summer by a kind of "tick," which causes it a great deal of annoyance, and sometimes are so numerous as to render the skin quite unserviceable. He is far more gregarious than the moose, being generally found in herds of five to ten, in the vast and solitary wilds north of Quebec, and about the head waters of the Ristigouché, in New Brunswick, these being the localities where he is principally hunted. His favorite food, the *Cladonia rangiferna*, a kind of lichen, being very plentiful, he is found in considerable abundance in these parts of the country, though he may also be met with in the districts of Argenteuil and Ottawa, where, according to D'Urban, the gneiss rocks are covered with its peculiar food. It also browses upon leaves, bark, buds, and young twigs

It is hunted by being stalked, after the manner of the red-deer of the Highlands ; its immense speed setting any other method at defiance, unless when there happens to be a light crust, just capable of sustaining the hunter on his snow-shoes, but letting the hunted animal through at every step, cutting his legs, and so crippling him as to put the hunter more on an equality with him ; but even when thus crippled, it is no easy job to run down a strong, well-conditioned bull, though the females being generally fatter than the males, and not being in a condition to run, are much easier run down.

The greatest care and circumspection are necessary in the pursuit of the caribou ; for, though not so wary and suspicious as the moose, he is ever on the

alert. The hunters generally provide themselves
with Indian guides, and, by strictly following their
directions, are generally successful. The caribou,
when closely pressed, will turn and stand at bay,
and then he is an animal not to be despised. They
do not "yard" like the moose, but depending upon
their swiftness, and from the conformation of their
feet, being better able to travel on the snow, they
usually roam through the forest in herds, of sometimes a dozen or more. The flesh is tender and well-
flavored, and by most people esteemed superior to
that of the moose.

I have dwelt so fully on the method of hunting
the moose, that I think it unnecessary to say any
thing on the subject in this connection, as the method
to be pursued in this case is the same as is adopted
when hunting the larger animal.

CHAPTER X.

DEER.

Where the forests primeval—a golden domain—
In sylvan solitudes hold their reign,
The dun-deer, in bosky thicket and wood,
Scour the wild passes or stem the flood,
Crop the sweet grass, or seek retreat
In tangled copse from the sultry heat,
And these the keen-eyed hunters attack
With deadly rifle and yelping pack.

ISAAC McLELLAN.

IT seems almost unnecessary to give any detailed
description of the common deer of America
(*Cervus Virginianus*), as it must be well known to
nearly every dweller in this country, and must be an
old acquaintance with all sportsmen, yet, for the information of the tyro, I will venture on a few remarks
respecting its appearance and habits. It is light and
graceful in form, being one of the most elegant of
animals. The horns, which are very beautiful, are bent
backward from the base, and then curved outward
and forward, having from three to seven tines ; the
one nearest the skull springs from the fore part of the
horn, while the remainder start from the upper edge

of it ; they are smooth and light, seldom weighing, in
a good specimen, more than six pounds. They are
shed in January and February, and almost immediately begin to re-appear, so that they are fully
grown by the end of August. A full-grown buck
stands about four feet high ; their color changes with
the season. In summer the coat is of a yellowish
red, being lighter on the sides and legs ; as winter
draws on a change takes place, the hair turning to a
kind of roan or grayish color; the under parts always
remaining white. I have seen some that were of a
very dark iron-gray. The hair grows much thicker
in winter than in summer. The hind generally has
one fawn at a birth, though two are by no means unusual. During the first summer, they are beautifully
spotted ; these spots, however, gradually disappear
as they grow older. This animal is scattered all over
the country, from the sunny South to the frigid regions of the North ; it is very plentiful in some parts
of New York State, and in portions of the Upper Ottawa the country teems with them. It feeds early in
the morning and again late in the evening, generally
resorting during summer to some shady nook to pass
the intermediate time ; it may also often be seen in
lakes quite up to its neck, whither it has resorted for
the double purpose of cooling itself and escaping the
attacks of the flies. They will remain around clear-

ances, and constantly make inroads upon the settler's turnips and potatoes, for which they not unfrequently pay with their lives; for the backwoodsman, or his hardy son, having seen "sign," posts himself in some suitable locality, and when the noble buck or timid hind comes all unsuspiciously to enjoy its favorite food, he "pots" it over with his old rusty smoothbore. Various modes are adopted in hunting them, such as watching at "salt licks," shining, still-hunting, driving, etc. The first of these is such a cowardly, unsportsmanlike style of obtaining meat, that I shall pass it by. The second method I have very little experience of, though I believe that in some parts of the States, more particularly in the South, it is practised to a considerable extent. It is thus described: "A blazing light of birch-bark and 'fat pine' is kindled in an iron cresset, fixed in the bows of a canoe, precisely as in salmon-spearing; the rifleman sits amidships, covered by green boughs, and the steersman, similarly concealed, gently paddles the little skiff along the dark-wooded shores of the lake or river, at the hour when the deer, after the heat of the day, repair to the cool waters. As the strange light glides noiselessly toward them, they stand transfixed, and apparently fascinated by the glare, until its reflection in their glittering eyeballs discovers their position to the concealed marksman, who, at close

quarters, fires between the two with deadly effect."
This is the manner adopted in Canada, or where there
may be water. Of course, it is somewhat different in
following them into the forest: one carries the fire,
and another, with his rifle cocked, is ready to "blaze
away" when he sees the shining orbs in front of him.
I now come to the two remaining methods, stalking
or "still-hunting," and driving with hounds. Each
of these has its strong advocates ; he who practises
the one generally denounces the other. For my part,
I believe that both are legitimate and really sports-
manlike ; the former doubtless calls for more skill
and patience than the latter ; but, on the other hand,
the sport of driving is more exhilarating. The melo-
dious refrain of the dogs as they dash along in full
pursuit of the quarry, on a fine crisp day in glorious
October, is the finest music it is possible to imagine.
But to get our deer by stalking. The extreme wari-
ness of the deer is such, that it requires the utmost
circumspection to advance toward them. When they
are approached, it must always be done upwind, to
prevent the animal effluvia of the sportsman being
received by the quick-scenting powers of the deer.
A circuit of very considerable extent, in some cases
even of miles, must be traversed to enable the hunter
to approach the game undetected ; and it not unfrequently happens that all the toil and labor are lost by

the sudden snapping of a twig, or something else apparently as trivial. Having approached the game within a certain distance, the hunter has not unfrequently to crawl carefully on all-fours, or insinuate himself, like a snake, through the brushwood to effect his purpose. No sound must be heard, the stillness of death must reign around, for the work of death is at hand. Approaching thus cautiously, and having been especially careful to gain the wind of the deer, he comes within shot, when carefully drawing up, he takes aim, and touching the trigger, the bullet speeds on its deadly errand. If the aim has been well taken, the stricken deer gives a convulsive leap and dashes off with furious speed. The hunter at once knows whether he is mortally wounded or not, by the way the tail is carried ; *if down*, it is a sure sign that he is done for, and he may find him within a few yards in the agonies of death. So great, however, is the tenacity of life in the deer, that they have been known to run long distances after being mortally wounded. They are easily traced by the blood on the fallen leaves and snow, and a smart chase brings the hunter up to his game. The throat is immediately cut, and the animal being "gralloched," is hung upon the nearest tree, or at once "toted" into camp. Dogs are oftentimes used when thus hunting the deer, as it is well known that they will stand for a deer, if they get

a chance, just as they would for birds. Frank Forrester does not believe in the fact, that more than one
man in every ten thousand ever goes out "of set purpose" to beat for deer with setters.

Well, I gather quite a different idea from what my
friend Seth Green writes, and what he says is worthy
of attention, as he is a mighty Nimrod. I infer that
it is not at all uncommon, in New York State, for
sportsmen to go out for deer with dogs, he often does
it himself; he says : "For still-hunting, I have used
a pointer ; he was broke to stay with me ; he was
learned to stand a deer the same as he would a bird.
I have killed a *great many* deer when old "Sport" or
"Othello " was on a dead point. I never use but one
dog at a time ; he was learned to go about six feet
ahead of me, that is all the breaking he needs."
From this it will be seen that it is not at all unusual
to hunt deer in this manner ; and though I have no
experience of it, yet I must say that I have no fancy
for it.

I now come to that most exciting sport, "driving,"
or runway shooting. My manner of doing this is very
different from that described by Major King, who
says, at page 93 of the "Sportsman and Naturalist in
Canada :" "The dogs and drivers enter the forest at
a distant point, and the intervening tract is hunted
with loud halloos and the barking and yelping of the

motley pack. These dogs, however, are not taught to keep together on one deer, but are allowed, or rather encouraged, to chase different animals, a part of the pack following the original or first viewed one, while the rest in twos or threes are hunting others." I must acknowledge that I read this with a great deal of surprise, as it was so different from every thing I have seen or previously heard of. The idea of going through the woods hallooing, accompanied by the "barking and yelping of a motley pack," is a thing unknown to me or my brother sportsmen. I think the gallant major must have believed himself at a German battue, or beating up the jungle for a royal Bengal tiger.

I will describe one of our hunts, as I believe that a short narrative of one will be the most suitable method of conveying the information I desire to. I will suppose all preliminaries arranged, and the parties about leaving camp. Breakfast having been dispatched, a short consultation is held as to the most suitable localities for the day's hunt ; this agreed upon, the various stands are allotted, and away we all go, eager for "blood." Alick, that noble forester, after allowing us ten minutes' law, starts for the woods with the hounds in leashes. He has not gone far before Patch, the little villain, cocks both nose and tail, indicating that he sniffs something more than com-

mon. He is immediately cast off, and at once begins
to seek, beating back and forward with short, quick
yelps; ere long he comes upon the track, or, mayhap,
the very spot from which the deer has just sprung,
and, with a long deep-toned note, dashes off in pursuit, giving tongue from time to time, by which the
anxious hunters are warned of the whereabouts of the
game ; for at the first sound of the dogs giving
tongue, every gun is cocked, and the utmost caution
is observed. As they cast their eyes in every direction, each one hopes that the chance will be his, and
in turn they are encouraged by the turnings and
windings of the deer, which strives by all means to
throw off the dog ; but this can not be, and in his endeavors to escape, he dashes down the runway, where
"friend Pittman" (who is known throughout the
whole district wherein he lives as an ardent sportsman and whole-souled fellow) is standing, finger on
trigger, his eagle eye taking in the whole scene. He
is tuned up to the highest pitch by the sweet music
of the hound giving tongue, and with beating heart
yet steady nerves, he waits the moment when the
antlered buck in all his pride shall dash by. Louder
swells the refrain, as Patch closes with the chase, and
the next instant his anxious eyes are gladdened by
seeing the noble game. In a moment he levels his
"Westley Richards," and with sight taken almost by

faith, so well does he know the weapon, he touches the trigger, the report wakens the echoes of the woods, the stricken deer plunges madly along, and with drooping tail—an unerring indication that he is mortally wounded—disappears from view. Hastily reloading, he follows the gory track, and finding him, mayhap a few yards off, either stone dead or struggling in the last agonies, he draws his *coteau du chasse*, and speedily bleeds him, and then wakes the echoes by the "death halloo," which brings in from all points the rest of us, to find him sitting on the dead deer, enjoying to the full the soothing influence of the Virginian weed. Such, in a few words, is our method of hunting; and I submit that more enjoyment and real sport is afforded by it than is found in solitary stalking through the woods. I have not given any directions for posting the party on the stands, or for laying on the dogs, as this kind of sport will never be undertaken unless one or more experienced hunters are in the party.

I cannot do better than quote Frank Forrester's advice to the beginner, which is, "If placed at a stand, to hold himself perfectly silent, perfectly motionless, perfectly observant and attentive, neither to smoke cigars nor go to sleep ; neither to fire his gun at any thing but the deer, nor to let the deer go past without firing at him. In a word, let him keep his mouth shut, his eyes open, and his head clear, trust in Providence, and be patient."

The best kind of gun for this shooting is assuredly a breech-loader; if a rifle be used, or what answers well, a good double-barreled gun throwing a heavy ball, aim so as to hit at the point of the shoulder, and if you should be a little behind, you will put such a hole into a chap as will soon stop his gallop.

Deer are also occasionally "coursed" with hounds; some gentlemen having the large rough hound, which when put on, run with such amazing swiftness, as very soon enables them to pull down the stoutest buck; but I see no sport in such work, so merely mention it *en passant.*

CHAPTER XI.

THE HOUND.

Soon the sagacious brute, his curling tail
Flourish'd in air, low bending, plies around
His busy nose, the steaming vapor snuffs
Inquisitive, nor leaves one turf untried
Till, conscious of the recent stains, his heart
Beats quick ; his snuffing nose, his active tail,
Attests his joy ; then, with deep-opening mouth,
That makes the welkin tremble, he proclaims
The game.
                                   SOMERVILLE.

I AM induced to add a few remarks on the hound used in hunting the deer, his rearing and breaking, as they may be of interest.

Two kinds of hounds are used in pursuit of the deer ; one runs by sight, the other by scent. With the first I have nothing to do ; for though greatly used in Scotland and highly esteemed, the manner of hunting in this country is so different from that practised there, they are very little used. I shall therefore confine my remarks to the animal in general use in America. I believe that the hound most in use is the English foxhound, though by various crossings he

21

may have lost somewhat of the characteristics by which he is so strongly marked. "It is generally admitted," says Blaine, "that the 'Talbot' (*Canis sagax*, Linn.) is the original stock from which all the varieties of the scent-hunting hounds are derived. His own descent is, however, not so certain, although we venture to hold out the probability that he is only a modified and lessened type of the bloodhound of early times." Few genuine specimens of the talbot now remain : we ourselves remember to have seen two only. These dogs were remarkable for their great size and strength, the depth of the chest and the length of the ears "that swept the morning dew." The head of the hound should be neither short nor thick, but it should with proper length have sufficient breadth of nose, and an open but not greatly elevated forehead; graced with open nostrils, and a pair of ears fine in substance and of a good length. The neck likewise should present both length and fineness. The shoulders, like those of the race-horse, ought to incline obliquely toward the back, and, without being coarse, they should be muscular. The fore-arm is particularly required to be strong, and of such length as to extend the knee low down in the limb, exactly after the fashion and on the principles of the formation of the race-horse. When the fore-legs are either crooked, or there is too much length from the knee to the ground, before, and from the hock to the ground, behind, great speed is not to be expected of that hound. The haunches or gaskins, as the huntsman calls them, should be expansive as well as firm to the the feet; and the hock is required to be broad as well as low placed. Reject a flat-sided hound as you would a flat-sided racer, both of them being soon winded. The feet also must be well balled, well clawed, and well knit up, *i. e.*, the toes must be firm and resisting against any trifling attempt to straighten them ; a loose-clawed dog soon gets foot-sore. The fore quarters of a hound can hardly be too deep, nor his carcass too much trussed up, provided his back be straight and his loins sufficiently broad ; without which advantages he can be neither speedy nor lasting. It is not necessary that his croup should be as square as that of the pointer, which would confine his strides ; but it must not be let down with the rotundity of the Newfoundland dog, or cart-horse. The stern should be slightly curved upward, and its under surface be fringed with a moderate line of hair. Somerville describes a perfect hound as follows :

. . . "See there, with countenance blithe,
And with a courtly grin, the fawning hound
Salutes thee cow'ring; his wide op'ning nose
Upwards he curls, and his large sloe-black eyes
Meet in soft blandishments, and humble joy ;
His glossy skin, or yellow pied, or blue,
In lights or shades by nature's pencil drawn,

Reflects the various tints : his ears and legs
Fleckt here and there in gay enamel'd pride,
Rival the speckled pard ; his rush-grown tail
O'er his broad back bends in an ample arch ;
On shoulders clean, upright and firm he stands ,
His round cat-foot, straight hams, and wide-spread thighs,
And his low, drooping chest, confess his speed,
His strength, his wind, or on the steepy hill,
Or far-extended plain ; in every part,
So well proportion'd, that the nicer skill
Of Phidias himself can't blame thy choice
Of such compose thy pack."

The color of the hound is with some a great object;
but I agreé with Mr. Beckford, who observes that "a
good dog, like a good horse, can not be of a bad
color." Venus, one of the best hounds I ever saw,
and the property of a sporting friend, is white, pied
with black, and yellow or tan eye-patches. For appearance, style, and working, she seems to be the
perfection of a hound ; she never commits a fault,
and once laid on knows no "give up." I have a
young dog out of her by Patch (mentioned elsewhere), and if he only resembles her as much in
quality as he does in appearance, I shall be thoroughly
satisfied.

Frank Forrester says : "The American foxhound,
as used wherever deer-hunting on horseback or by
driving is practised, is in fact actually the hound,
unaltered and identical, of Beckford and Somerville.
I am of opinion, moreover, that he is the best adapted

hound for this country, where so much of the hunting
is in difficult, intricate, entangled woodlands, marshy
brakes, and deep forests, where perfection of scent is
the most desirable of qualities, and where great speed
is not attainable, owing to the nature of the ground;
and not desirable, owing to the extreme difficulty of
following the hunt, which must be kept in hearing
rather than in sight by the sportsman."

From twenty-two to twenty-four inches is about the
proper height for a hound; and, when choosing him,
endeavor to have him come as near Beckford's description of what a hound should be as possible. The following passage in that author is the one alluded to :
"Let his legs be straight as arrows, his feet round
and not too large ; his shoulders back ; his breast
rather wide than narrow ; his chest deep ; his back
broad ; his head small ; his neck thin ; his tail thick
and bushy—if he carry it well, so much the better ;
. . . a small head, however, as relative to *beauty*
only; for as to *goodness*, I believe large-headed hounds
are in nowise inferior."

With regard to the breeding of the hound, I will
only say, that having hit upon a good strain, stick to
it. As a general rule, in the reproductive system of
all animals, "like will produce like." Mr. Beckford
says, "Consider the size, shape, color, constitution,
and natural disposition of the dog you breed from, as

well as the fineness of his nose, his stoutness, and method of hunting. On no account breed from one that is not stout, that is, not tender-nosed, or that is a skirter." Great care must be taken in rearing the young dogs, as all fine-bred dogs are peculiarly liable to disease. Let them be fed as soon as they will take nourishment, and give them plenty of air and exercise. For fuller particulars, I would counsel the inquirer to consult "Dinks on the Dog," a very popular treatise, and the most perfect and comprehensive work in existence for the dog-fancier and dog-lover.

The breaking of the young hound consists mainly in teaching him to adhere to the scent and follow the track of the game, to hunt close without loitering too much, to avoid skirting and overrunning the scent. The best way to do this is to couple the young dog with an old and tried one, that will act as a mentor to him. "Stoop the young hound to his proper game, and that only, is a maxim that ought not to be departed from, but under very particular circumstances. The blood which he first tastes of his own killing is that which he will, in all probability ever after prefer." This is the advice of one of the best writers on field-sports (Blaine, "Rural Sports," p. 478). A judicious course of rewards and punishments should be adopted ; and whatever is done toward training the hound should be done with temper and firmness.

CHAPTER XII.

TURKEY SHOOTING.

THE wild Turkey of North America (*Meleagris gallo-pavo*) is one of the finest birds pursued by the sportsman; and when in prime order, as they are in the fall, are well worthy of the attention of the hunter.

They are found in all parts of the States, though of course the advancing tide of civilization drives them further and further into the unfrequented wilds.

The length of the male bird is nearly four feet; its head and neck are covered with purplish-red excrescences, on a naked blue skin, thickly overspread with bristles, and a tuft of horsetail-like hairs hangs from the breast similar to that seen in the domestic bird, but larger and longer. The game-looking head is smaller than that of the latter, and the general hue of the plumage is a beautiful golden copper, with purple and green reflections, mottled and banded with a deep soft black. The lower part of the back is an iridescent brown, and the tail, which is of a darker hue, has a broad black band at a short distance from the extremity, with an outer border of dark yellowish brown. About sixteen pounds is an average weight, when in good condition, though they have been shot weighing double as much ; they vary greatly in this respect, according to the season, and to the abundance or scarcity of food obtainable. In the summer months they are poor and lean, and much infested with vermin, but improve rapidly when the beech-mast comes in, and are in their highest perfection late in autumn. The flesh is darker in color than the domestic bird, and has a more gamelike flavor.

The female bird is much smaller than the male, and far less showy in plumage. The legs are red in both sexes. Their breeding season is from the beginning of March to the end of April, according to the latitude. The hen lays from ten to fifteen eggs at a time, scratching a hollow in the ground for the purpose, and filling it with dead leaves.

The wild turkey subsists principally on nuts, beech-masts, acorns, wild strawberries, grapes, and dewberries ; corn, when it can be got, and grasshoppers and other insects, whenever they chance to come in its way. Though properly speaking not migratory, these birds range very widely in search of food, and the common impulse to desert an exhausted country for fresh ground, causes them to wander, as well as to assemble together in the flocks which are commonly met with in the month of October ; but they invariably return to certain localities in which they may be said to be resident.

As a sport, the pursuit of the wild turkey ranks high in the estimation of the sportsman. The proper season for hunting them is late in the autumn, when, after a summer diet of strawberries and wild fruit, they have had a six-weeks or two months' run among the acorns and masts. It is then a splendid bird in every respect, and so wild and difficult of approach as to require no inconsiderable skill in stalking. A bird with these qualities, excelling also in point of size, beauty of plumage, and culinary qualities, may well rank among game birds of the highest order.

Various means are adopted to bring this noble bird to bag, the principal of which are stalking, calling, and hunting with small dogs. As the latter method is only followed when using a shot-gun, I shall pass it over and speak of the others. "Calling" is practised in a similar manner to that pursued in following the moose. The sportsman having provided himself with a pipe, proceeds to the woods, and ensconcing himself in a suitable spot, proceeds to imitate the crying of the hen during the breeding season, which has the effect of bringing the cock-bird within range. A good good deal of skill and patience are necessary to effect the desired object.

But the most legitimate and exciting way is by "stalking;" for it requires both skill and caution to come within range. The old birds, even while feeding, are ever on the alert, and having a quick ear and keen eye, combined with great watchfulness, are enabled to quickly detect the presence of danger, and it therefore requires all the caution and address of the practised stalker to steal in upon them. The chief difficulty is the absence of sufficient trail to indicate their proximity, whence it happens that one may either never find a flock at all, or may come on it unawares, and frighten the birds away before there is a chance of a shot.

A rifle carrying a very small ball is best adapted to this sport, and should be light and handy.

I have had very little experience in hunting the wild turkey, and am indebted for a great portion of the above to Major King's "Sportsman and Naturalist in Canada."

In the foregoing pages, I have endeavored to give such plain and simple directions as may prove of use to the beginner; but the impossibility of teaching him to do all these things is well described by Frank Forrester, when he says, at page 351, of his "Manual for Young Sportsmen:"

"Of all those grander wild sports of the extreme North and West, the moose and caribou hunting of the British provincial forests, and of the hyperborean regions of Maine; the elk, buffalo, and antelope hunting of the western plains and prairies; the bear-hunting of Arkansas and the Southwest; nay, even the deer and turkey-hunting of the regions wherein those animals are still to be found, survivors of the innumerable multitudes which formerly roamed unmolested from ocean to ocean; there are no rules positive which can be laid down, no instructions which can be of much use to the young sportsman. Where the rifle is the implement, beyond the mere directions how to take aim, load, and fire to the best advantage, nothing can be taught.

"Of all things wholly unteachable by writing or oral instruction, unless upon the spot, with practice and example to illustrate precept, the most impracticable is wood-craft.

"How to follow or find the trail of an animal, itself not discernible to the sharpest unpractised eyes, in the seemingly untrodden grass, or on the leaf-strewn surface of the pathless soil of the wilderness, can not be taught by words written or spoken. How to judge by the foot-prints, half seen, of bear or deer, as a woodman will do at a glance, whether the animal which left the sign was young or old, fat or lean, going to or returning from his lair, how long he has gone by, and whether it avails to follow him or not, can only be learned by long experience, attentive observation, and a course of pupilage on the ground, under thorough and competent teachers.

"In the same way it is evident that one can not give directions how one shall steal up, unseen and unheard, within rifle-shot of a herd of deer, a gang of elk, or a watchful moose or caribou. This may be told, and this is about all, that you must invariably advance on all wild animals which it is desirable to stalk, *up wind*. If you attempt to go down wind on them, their unerring scent will frustrate your every endeavor, and render it impossible to approach within half a mile, much less within gunshot of the quarry. It is wise also to stalk game so far as it is possible, owing to the state of the wind, with the sun on your back and in their eyes."

And now my work is done, and the reader and I must part; but ere we do, let me commend to his perusal the following remarks on the important influence of this branch of field sports, taken from the writings of an ardent lover of the art: "Shooting is one of the great branches of our field sports, and is keenly relished, and almost universally practiced, throughout every part of the country. Looking at shooting as a mere sporting art, it has many things to recommend it. It can be personally enjoyed. It does not bring a man into a crowd, where reflection is almost impossible, but it leaves him at liberty to think and contemplate, and to measure out his amusements in strict accordance with his circumstances, strength, and inclination. Shooting augments the pedestrian capabilities of man, on the due balance and effective exercise of which so much of his real health of body and mind depends. Its pleasures are gently exciting, without precipitating him into a state of revelry and danger. Its well-regulated enjoyment is connected with all that is manly, energetic, and healthful. It is a wholesome, mental tonic, giving the intellect that gentle, material impulse so requisite for preventing it from sinking into the mopish nervousness and sedentary sensibility which impair a man's power to grapple with, and successfully overcome, the necessary evils and perplexities of human life. 'There is no one,' says Zimmerman, 'who may not, by quietly traversing the mountains with his gun, learn to feel how much the great secrets of nature will influence the heart, when assisted by the powers of the imagination. The sight of an agreeable landscape, the various points of view which the spacious plains afford, the freshness of the breeze, the beauties of the sky, and the appetite which a long ramble procures, will give energy to health, and make every new step seem too short. The privation of every object that can recall the idea of dependence, accompanied by domestic comfort, wholesome exercises, and useful occupations, will add vigor to thought, and inebriate the heart with the most delicious sensations.'

" We hold the sport of shooting to be susceptible of imparting the most lively gratification to all well-constituted minds, and to be a most necessary relaxation from and counterpoise to the wasteful pressure of incessant toil and watchful thought. The social and individual advantages of field sports are beyond calculation.

"A love of field sports generally, and of shooting in particular, takes us from the noise, and filth, and moral degradation incident to large towns. It places us in the midst of the cultivation of the soil—the real foundation of all national wealth and happiness. Every thing connected with the wanderings of the sportsman is calculated to foster the best and noblest feelings of the soul, and to impart to the mind the most lofty and sublime ideas of universal nature.

" To men of genius and contemplative habits, the roaming among the mountain wilds and the green fields, give rise to the most refined intellectual enjoy-

ments.   Such persons may be said to live in a world
of their own, and are the recipients of joys and
sorrows with which the world at large doth not
intermeddle.   How pure, refined, and exquisite are
the delights which fill the mind from gazing on
the mountain pass, the woods, the rocks, and water-
falls!"

APPENDIX.

AS I was obliged, when preparing the foregoing
pages, to omit the mention of a great many
rifles from the utter impossibility (within the compass
of such a work as this) of describing and illustrating
them all ; and as I think that some have been omitted
that should have found a place, I propose to supply the omission, and to add some further information gleaned since the preceding pages were placed in
the printer's hands. The first rifle that I shall direct
attention to is "Allen's" Patent Breech-loading Sporting Rifle. This gun is very neat and workmanlike, and
has gained an excellent reputation wherever it has been
introduced ; it is very popular among hunters, being
well adapted for sporting purposes. The patentees
confine the manufacture to rifles for that purpose, and
it has never been tested as a military gun ; though it
is believed that it would answer well in that shape.
It has a vertically-sliding breech-piece worked by a
trigger-guard lever, which is locked in position by a
spring-latch. It possesses several novel features, but
which it would be no use to describe without a let-
tered vertical section; it is easy to handle, and it is
claimed that it can be loaded and fired very rapidly,
and with great accuracy.

FIG. 1.

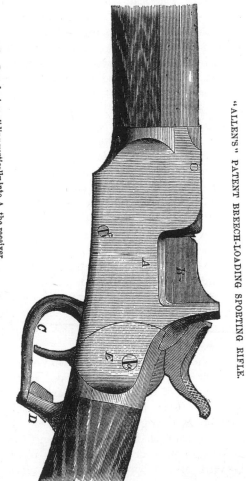

"ALLEN'S" PATENT BREECH-LOADING SPORTING RIFLE.

B.—Breech-piece sliding vertically into A, the receiver.
C.—Trigger-guard and lever for lowering breech-piece ; at the same time extracting cartridge shell.
D.—Spring latch, holding lever in position.
E.—Movable plate, for examination of lock.
a.—Pivot of trigger-guard and lever.

Another American invention is "Roper's Patent Arm," constructed both as a rifle and shot-gun. It is upon the revolving principle, a carrier being substituted for the chambered cylinder. The cartridge shells, which are of steel, and indestructible, are loaded with powder and ball, or shot, and, capped with the ordinary percussion cap, are dropped through an opening in the receiver, covered by a hinge lid. A very full and perfect description of this arm, illustrated by four cuts, was published in that very excellent scientific and mechanical journal, the "American Artisan," of December 5th, 1866. I have never seen this gun, nor was I aware that it was manufactured as a rifle until I saw it described there, though I was acquainted with it as a shot-gun.

Gunn's Patent Breech-loader is one of the latest candidates for popular favor; (patented September 10, 1867.) The breech-block is chambered, and opens and closes in a somewhat similar manner to the Snider; though the manner of locking it when closed is different, and in this and the arrangement and mode of operating the cartridge-shell ejector consists its peculiar features.

The Roberts system of conversion of muzzle-loaders into breech-loaders is pronounced by the New York State Board of Officers "as superior to all others examined;" and, in consequence of this, has been adopted as the principle upon which the State arms are to be converted. In this system the breech-block moves on a pivot or shoulder at its rear end, with its forward end dropping in the receiver below the chamber, to permit the insertion of the cartridge in the latter.

Hammond's Military Breech-loader is another American invention that has attracted attention in England, and has been very favorably commented on. No written description would afford any idea of this gun, so I shall pass it over; as I must also some others, containing certain meritorious properties, as this book is not written as a guide to rifles, but as a guide to riflemen. Great attention is being devoted to the subject in England, and the government are proceeding upon a proper principle. They offer handsome prizes to induce inventors to come forward; the first or highest, one thousand pounds sterling, was offered for the best rifle, forming a combination of all qualities; the second, six hundred pounds, for the best breech mechanism, combined with a sufficiently good degree of accuracy in other particulars; and the third reward, of four hundred pounds, for the best cartridge. A commission of the most eminent experts was appointed for the purpose of ascertaining which arm should be adjudged the best; rules were laid down for conducting the competition, and certain conditions imposed as requisite in military rifles. One hundred and four breech-loaders were sent in; of these, sixty-seven were at once rejected for non-compliance with the conditions laid down; after the first trial, twenty-one more fell out; and a further trial reduced this number to nine, the Remington and Peabody being of the number. Ten rifles of each pattern and one thousand rounds of ammunition were supplied by each competitor, and a series of experiments (which extended from November, 1867, to February, 1868, with slight intermission) were commenced. The points to be considered were accuracy, rapidity, recoil, penetration, trajectory, fouling, and capability of sustaining rough usage. The present Government arm (Snider-Enfield, naval pattern) was made to take part in all the above trials, and it must be very gratifying to the admirers of that gun to know that it endured with the competing arms all the required tests, except that of accuracy, which the regulations fixed by the war-office had set so high that *none* of the competing rifles could reach it. The trials were very satisfactory ; the final result being to leave the Henry first, Burton's (pattern No. 2) second, and the Albini and Braendlin third. None of the rifles came up to the standard fixed by the war-office, and, consequently, the first prize was not awarded, though the second prize was given to the Henry, as it approached the nearest to the required qualifications : it therefore received the prize for the best breech mechanism. The Government will now probably acquire all the desirable points, by compensating the different inventors, and by combining them, produce a composite arm that would be perfection.

The Carter-Edwards rifle seemed at one time to be the coming gun, previous to the trial, when it was one of the rejected ones. Since then, however, the inventors have made some alterations that have overcome the defects then exhibited, and it is now claimed

that it is all that a rifle should be ; though I consider that it has many defects, but I have not space
herein to enumerate them.

Herr Von Dreyse, the inventor of the needle-gun,
before his death (December 9th, 1867), brought forward the grenade rifle, which, in its physical and
moral effects, is expected to eclipse every thing. The
ball, which is hollow, is filled with a charge of two
and a half grammes ; on striking, it explodes with the
greatest certainty, and, dispersing its fragments three
feet in every direction, is reputed to do as much damage as three or four ordinary balls, and create as
much dismay as would a dozen.

I may mention here that the "Henry" rifle referred to above is not the American repeater of that
name, but a gun presented by Mr. Henry, the celebrated gun-maker of Edinburgh. The Daw central
fire cartridge obtained the prize, though it is inferior
to the present (Boxer) Government cartridge, in which
great improvements have been made since its first
introduction. I had intended giving some account of
the various cartridges in use, but find that my space is
too limited. The American cartridges are usually of
the rim fire species, while those of the English are
central fire. It will be seen from the fact that no less
than one hundred and four rifles were entered for the
above competition, how impossible it would have been
to have mentioned all the breech-loading rifles having
good points. I have only drawn attention to those
that have been the most prominent, and it is casting
no discredit on any rifle that I have omitted it.

Just as this sheet is going to press, we learn from *Galignani's Messenger*, May 27, that Marshal Neil, the French Minister of War, has just presented a report to the Emperor on the results obtained from the practice with the Chassepôt rifle. The troops have been armed with this weapon but about a year, and have obtained considerable efficiency in its use. It is claimed that the men can fire 8 to 10 shots per minute, taking aim ; and 14 without shouldering the gun. The range is nearly double that of the old musket, and its precision more than double. The subjoined table shows the average number of hits per cent., and also the great contrast with the old musket:

	Averages obtained.				
	\---*Distance in meters*\---				
	200.	400.	600.	800	1,000.
With the old rifled musket.					
Infantry of the line............	30.8	15.8	8.3	—	—
With the Chassepôt rifle.					
Infantry of the line (instruction recently commenced).........	35.6	26.2	19.7	14.3	8.2
Foot regiments of the Guard (instruction more advanced).....	59.4	37.3	26.0	21.0	16.0
Foot chasseurs of the Guard (complete instruction)............	69.8	46.6	36.1	28.4	24.7

The Minister then points out some defects which have been discovered during the use of the new weapon, but of which none was of a serious nature, and all of which have been in a great measure remedied. The most frequent accident appears to have been the breaking of the needle ; but even that inconvenience was more rare than the fracture of the nipple in the old percussion muskets. Greater attention has now been devoted to the manufacture of that portion of the mechanism, and the number broken is at present inconsiderable.

This is very satisfactory, and far superior to what I believed the Chassepôt capable of.

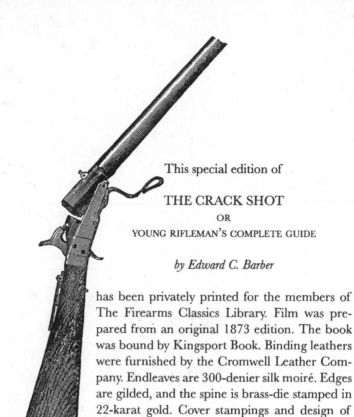

This special edition of

THE CRACK SHOT

OR

YOUNG RIFLEMAN'S COMPLETE GUIDE

by Edward C. Barber

has been privately printed for the members of The Firearms Classics Library. Film was prepared from an original 1873 edition. The book was bound by Kingsport Book. Binding leathers were furnished by the Cromwell Leather Company. Endleaves are 300-denier silk moiré. Edges are gilded, and the spine is brass-die stamped in 22-karat gold. Cover stampings and design of the edition by Selma Ordewer.